THE THIRD HOUSE

The Third House

Lobbyists and Lobbying in the States

SECOND EDITION

ALAN ROSENTHAL
Eagleton Institute of Politics
Rutgers University

CQ PRESS

A Division of Congressional Quarterly Inc.
Washington, D.C.

CQ Press
A Division of Congressional Quarterly Inc.
1414 22nd Street, N.W.
Washington, D.C. 20037
(202) 822-1475; (800) 638-1710
www.cqpress.com

♾ The paper used in this publication meets the minimum requirements of the American National Standard for Information Sciences—Permanence of Paper for Printed Library Materials, ANSI Z39.48-1992.

Printed and bound in the United States of America

05 04 03 02 01   5 4 3 2 1

Typesetting and design by Blue Heron
Cover design by Gary Gore

Library of Congress Cataloging-in-Publication Data
Rosenthal, Alan, 1932–
The third house : lobbyists and lobbying in the states /
Alan Rosenthal.—2nd ed.
p.   cm.
Includes bibliographical references and index.
ISBN 1-56802-438-X (paper)
1. Lobbying—United States.   2. Pressure groups—United States.
3. Parliamentary practice—United States.   I. Title.
JK1118.R676   2001
328.73'078—dc21   2001018425

To Patrick, Kelly, Chas, Dylan, and Tori

Contents

Preface   ix

CHAPTER 1. Introduction   1
The Proliferation of Interests and the Growth of Lobbying   2
How Lobbyists Are Perceived   6
Observing Lobbyists and Lobbying   10
A Preview of the Book   12

CHAPTER 2. The People Who Lobby   15
Who They Are   16
The Business of Lobbying   20
Why People Lobby   25
Qualities and Styles   33

CHAPTER 3. State Government Relations   41
The Culture of the Corporation   42
The Organization of Associations   46
Contracting Out   53

CHAPTER 4. The Interests at Stake   60
Issues Big and Small   60
Keeping Track   63
Fighting It Out   71

CHAPTER 5. The Rules of the Game   79
The Legislative Arena   80
The Capitol Community   91

CHAPTER 6. Building Relationships   108
Natural Development   109
Forging Bonds   111
Trial by Fire   117
How Relationships Pay Off   119
Effects of Term Limits   123

CHAPTER 7. Playing Politics   125
Paying the Freight   125
Engaging in Battle   140
Going for Votes   144

CHAPTER 8. Generating Support   147
Coalition Building   147
Grassroots Mobilization   153
The Media, Public Relations, and Advertising   171

CHAPTER 9. Making the Case   178
The Principles of Direct Lobbying   179
The Elements of Defense and Offense   181
Targets in the Process   186
Education and Information   194
The Art of Compromise   203

CHAPTER 10. Power and Representation   211
The Influence of Lobbyists   211
Clients and Causes   219
Representing Interests   225

Notes   231

Selected Bibliography   245

Index   249

Preface

When asked by friends and colleagues why I was writing this book, I usually explained as follows. I had studied and written about legislators for years, but legislators did not really appreciate my efforts. Then I wrote a book about governors and legislatures. To my dismay, I found that governors are oblivious to mortals who are not themselves governors, so no acknowledgment came from that direction either. It finally occurred to me that if I switched gears and wrote about lobbyists, I could at least expect free food and drink by way of appreciation. Some of my interviews with lobbyists—people who are alleged to be genetically programmed to pick up the tab—were conducted over breakfast, lunch, or dinner. It turned out, however, that I paid more often than they did. So much for my quest for acknowledgment.

Over the years, however, I got some of the acknowledgment I was seeking. People who read the first edition appreciated the book. Experienced lobbyists reported to me that it nicely captured their enterprise. New lobbyists found it helpful. Students thought it was interesting and offered a different perspective on lobbying. CQ Press apparently was satisfied, because Brenda Carter, director of college publications, persuaded me that a revision of *The Third House* would be well worth the effort.

I originally wrote this book to challenge the conventional wisdom about lobbyists and lobbying. That is not to say that lobbyists do not buy legislators meals or entertain them in other ways. They certainly do (much less nowadays than formerly), but there is much more to lobbying than that. Anyone who has spent as long as I have studying and consulting with legislatures would at some point have to become interested in lobbyists. The surprising thing is that it took a while for my interest to emerge. One of my early books, *Legislative Life*, ignored lobbying almost entirely—an enormous oversight. My latest book, *The Decline of Representative Democracy*, does not have the same deficiency.

A few years before writing the first edition of this book, I began to conduct, in collaboration with the State Governmental Affairs Council, a program designed to enhance the professional skills of representatives of member companies and associations. This enterprise involved me in questions of direct lobbying, coalition building, grassroots mobilization, and ethics. It also brought me into contact with many lobbyists. Instead of catching a dread disease, however, I became more and more interested in the subject. Then, in 1990, I was appointed chairman of a New Jersey commission on legislative ethics and campaign finance. The members of the commission (four legislators and five citizens) examined the regulation of lobbying, among other matters, and made several recommendations for legislative action. My involvement with this commission further whetted my appetite.

The lobbying of state legislatures is in need of study. The media have a narrow, and even distorted, perspective on lobbyists and lobbying. The public's comprehension is likewise limited and unduly negative. In contrast, my firsthand observations and experiences have given me an appreciation for both the lobbyists I have met and the institution of lobbying. I have become one of the not-too-many people outside the field who believe lobbying to be an honorable profession. But then I also believe politics to be an honorable profession.

My original account of lobbyists and lobbying in the states was based largely on interviews with about one hundred lobbyists in California, Colorado, Florida, Minnesota, New Jersey, and Texas, as well as a few in Maryland and Washington, D.C. Those interviews remain of value in this new edition, although I have cast a wider net this time and drawn on lobbying in other states as well. Lobbying life is described mainly from the point of view of lobbyists themselves. This vantage point is essential, I believe, for conveying a feel for the enterprise and for understanding what lobbying entails. But it is also important that we make judgments. Thus I have endeavored to step back, acquire distance, and analyze the practices and effects of lobbying and its role in representative democracy.

In writing this book (and also in its revision), I owe special thanks to individuals in several different communities. The first is the community of political scientists, in which I claim membership. Political scientists have by no means been idle in this area. They have produced a substantial body of knowledge on lobbyists and on the interest groups lobbyists represent. Their writings have been extremely useful to me, and their findings are reflected throughout this work. I am grateful to these colleagues and hope that this book contributes to the discipline. Several political scientists were of special help in my writing of the first edition. Allan Cigler of the University of Kansas and Clive Thomas of the University of Alaska read the manuscript and made a number of comments. Malcolm Jewell, Ronald Hrebenar, and an anonymous reviewer offered their critiques of my proposal.

Another community to which I owe a debt of gratitude is the state capitol community, consisting of legislators, legislative staff, lobbyists, and journalists from across the nation. These are the people with whom I have worked and about whom and for whom I have been writing. They have provided material for my book and are primarily responsible for my education—or miseducation—over these past years. I hope that I have helped in their education as well.

Without support from two other communities—the Eagleton Institute of Politics, Rutgers University, and the state of New Jersey, which has paid my salary—I would not have been able to devote myself to state legislatures as I have. I do not take for granted all the privileges we academics have. Academics are a fortunate lot. The late Don Herzberg, my predecessor as director of Eagleton, afforded me my initial opportunity, recruiting me just when the state legislative modernization movement was getting under way. Since then, Rutgers University has enabled me and the rest of us at the institute to take advantage of many opportunities to engage in public service and basic and applied research. I owe special and personal thanks to the institute's faculty and administrative and secretarial staff, and in particular to Chris Lenart, Joanne Pfeiffer, and Erin Toomey.

The publisher has also been helpful. I want to thank CQ Press, which I regard as the foremost publisher of books dealing with politics and government in the states. I trust that the present book in its revised form will advance that enterprise. It is always a pleasure to work with CQ's fine editorial staff.

Finally, I want to thank the most important and ultimately the most supportive community of all—family and friends. My children, who have taken on their own distinctive shapes, are a continuing delight and even an inspiration. I appreciate them and I like them—John, Lisa, Kai, and Tony. Also their spouses—Lisa, Garrison, and Kathleen. Who knows, perhaps one of my grandchildren—Patrick, Kelly, Chas, Dylan, and Tori—will turn out to be a lobbyist. Stranger things happen.

CHAPTER 1

Introduction

It is not possible to conceive of American politics absent groups and lobbyists. James Madison, in the *Federalist Papers,* acknowledged that people organized themselves into factions to promote their passions and interests. For Madison, a faction—which we now refer to as an interest group or special interest—was "a number of citizens, whether amounting to a majority or minority of the whole, who are united and activated by some common impulse or passion, or of interest . . . ." Factions, according to Madison, are natural phenomena "sown in the nature of man."

The First Amendment to the U.S. Constitution reinforces what the Founding Fathers regarded as a natural basis of political society by guaranteeing the people freedom of speech and also the right "to petition the Government for a redress of grievances." On that clause hangs the power of interest groups in America and their lobbyists in Washington, D.C., and in the states. "The right to petition" means that citizens and groups can appeal to the government for fair or even special treatment. Where petitioning government is guaranteed, so is the right to lobby.

Lobbying is simply the practice of attempting to influence the decisions of government. Lobbying employs a variety of methods, including but not confined to oral and written communications with public officials. The word "lobby" has been around for some time, having first appeared in the English language in the middle of the sixteenth century. The word then referred to the halls and corridors of the House of Commons where those who were not in government made their case to those who were. The first recorded use of "lobby" in U.S. legislative circles was in 1808.[1] Since then it has been part of the lexicon of American politics.

The people who lobby are known as "lobbyists." They are regulated by government at the federal and state levels and are thus required to register. Lobbyists today represent every conceivable interest and are active at every level of government. The primary arenas for their efforts are the U.S. Congress and the state legislatures, where they work to promote and defend clients and causes. They are integral to lawmaking. A legislative process without lobbyists, according to journalist Robert Dvorchak, "is like having a road map with only interstate highways. They [lobbyists] are the access ramps, back roads, shortcuts, cutoffs and detours."[2] As evidence of their involvement and their influence, lobbyists in many places are known as the "third house" of the legislature. Along with the senate and the house of representatives, the lobby also has a role to play in the process by which a bill becomes (or fails to become) a law.

The Proliferation of Interests and the Growth of Lobbying

Lobbyists and interest groups have been part of the American scene from the beginning. Alexis de Tocqueville noted in the 1830s how disposed Americans were to organize into interest groups. In the 1960s James Deakin described the interest group scene in Washington, D.C.:

> There is an association, union, society, league, conference, institute, organi-
> zation, federation, chamber, foundation, congress, order, brotherhood,
> company, corporation, bureau, mutual cooperative, committee, council,
> plan, trusteeship, movement, district, assembly, club, board, service or tribe
> for every human need, desire, motive, ambition, goal, aim, drive, affiliation,
> occupation, industry, interest, incentive, fear, anxiety, greed, compulsion,
> frustration, hate, spirit, reform and cussedness in the United States.[3]

Since then, even more groups have formed, so that an "explosion of representation" is reverberating throughout the nation's capital. One commentator refers to the contemporary system as that of "hyperplural-ism," with a proliferation of interest groups, lobbies, and advocacy since the 1960s.[4] The level of political mobilization in the American system has risen dramatically, with an increase in the number and range of interests being represented and the number of issues being debated in Congress. Between 1960 and 1980, the growth in groups operating in Washington, D.C., was estimated to be about 30 percent. Many were formed in re-sponse to government initiatives. As government programs became larger and more numerous, organizations of recipients and service providers grew apace.[5]

Indeed, the increase in the number of interest groups lobbying in Wash-ington is in part the result of the rise of citizen groups, which include the so-called "public interest groups" and the "single-issue groups." Stimu-lated by Ralph Nader and the ineptitude of General Motors in its battle with the consumer advocate, citizen groups rose to prominence.[6] One group led to another, sometimes as a reaction and in opposition to, but also in emulation of the former's success. These new interests include consumers, environmentalists, women's groups, gays, pro-life and pro-choice organizations, as well as many others.[7]

Baumgartener and Leech have drawn on the *Encyclopedia of Associations* to provide a picture of the growth of groups overall and of various types of groups more specifically. In 1959 a total of 5,843 associations were listed; by 1970 the number was 10,308; by 1980 the total had risen to 14,726; by 1990 to 22,259; and by 1995 to 23,298. The growth of 100 percent and almost 50 percent in earlier decades had slowed in the 1990s. While trade, business, and commercial groups increased their numbers, the largest growth was by public affairs, hobby and avocational, social welfare, educational, and health and medical associations.[8]

The states followed the lead of the nation, exhibiting a similar explosion of interest group representation. As Thomas and Hrebenar recently concluded, on the basis of their continuing study of the subject: "There are more groups representing more people across the 50 states today than ever before."[9] Another interest group study, by Gray and Lowery, found that the average number of interest groups per state had increased from 195 in 1975 to 342 in 1980, and then to 617 in 1990, a tripling in fifteen years.[10] Take Iowa, for example: only the railroads, bankers, utility companies, and a few others used to be active in Des Moines. Now all kinds of groups are represented at the capitol. Pluralism is also triumphant in Kentucky, with coal, horse racing, liquor, and agriculture now having to share the stage with more recent arrivals on the scene. Nevada is no longer dominated by mining and railroads. Ohio, New Jersey, Minnesota—just about every state has witnessed a proliferation of interests.

The expansion of interest group organization and representation in the states results from a variety of developments. The scope of government is broader than it used to be. The states have moved into new fields and become active in consumer affairs, the environment, the workplace, and other areas dealing with social issues. Meanwhile, the federal government—through the Nixon, Ford, Carter, Reagan, Bush, and Clinton administrations—has been retreating from its earlier commitments to the states and localities. Devolution, as well as deregulation by the federal government has left a power vacuum for the states to fill. As a consequence, the states have started to impose their own regulations—on packaging, hazardous waste, automotive emissions, and so forth. Furthermore, with substantial cuts in federal aid but little letup in federal mandates, the ante has been raised in state capitols.

With states both choosing and having to take on new and greater responsibilities, interests groups have targeted their capitols. The cry used to be, "We don't need state government, we'll go to Washington." Not anymore. Groups today have to make their appeals state by state. Although it is true that policy has become nationalized and issues spread quickly across state lines (the media abet this process), this actually makes it more important for a group to establish a presence in each of the states.

As in the federal arena, the range of interests has broadened. Citizen groups concerned with social and public-interest issues are now active, as are single-issue organizations. They have been able to shape the agendas and policies of the legislature. With federal budget cuts and the advent of block grants, a number of the advocacy groups have to get their money from different coffers. Therefore, they are much more active at the state level than they once were. Some of these groups have not only challenged but also threatened the positions of more traditional groups.

In recent years, moreover, many traditional interests have been fragmenting. Cities no longer leave representation solely to a single municipal association. Their interests are more diverse than formerly, and narrower and narrower groups have formed to represent them. For example, the League of Minnesota Cities, which for years represented the state's municipalities, has been joined by the Association of Metropolitan Municipalities, the Coalition of Greater Minnesota Cities, the Municipal Legislative Commission, the League of Small Cities, the North Metro Mayors Association, and the Range Association of Municipalities and Schools.[11] Cities also represent themselves.

Companies that once relied exclusively on their membership in business and trade associations are no longer inclined to put all their eggs in such baskets. Because of keen competition and the differential effects of legislation on firms in the same industry, they are more likely today to provide for their own representation in addition to that furnished by an umbrella association. As a consequence, more interests, and more competitive interests within the same industry, are being articulated in the states.

Any group that can be touched by state government, or by a competitor using the auspices of state government, cannot afford to be without representation. That means having a lobbyist of one sort or another, someone to present the group's case and protect the group's interests at the capitol. A Florida legislator applied a legal analogy: "Before a judge makes a determination on something, he asks for briefs from opposing counsels. So do legislators, and the opposing counsels are lobbyists." Lobbyists had better be there to make the case for their organizations or clients.

If groups do not realize the need for a lobbyist at the outset, they soon learn their lesson. If one side has a lobbyist, the other side needs one. Even if there is no opposition, a lobbyist is necessary just to move a measure along. Florida's cities appealed to the legislature for the enactment of a program that would have facilitated urban development. The legislature was willing to accede but insisted that the cities come up with a revenue source to fund the program they wanted. Everyone searched for a source. They found it in the dry-cleaning business, one of the only groups without a lobbyist in Tallahassee. With no one in the legislature speaking against it, a sales tax was imposed on dry cleaning. Within a few days of the tax's enactment, the dry cleaners had gotten themselves a lobbyist. The distilled spirits industry was without a lobbyist in Santa Fe, but decided to hire one after the legislature increased liquor taxes by $18 million in 1993.

An Associated Press survey found that in 1990 there were more than 42,500 registered lobbyists at state capitals, an increase of 20 percent from just four years earlier. The growth has been modest since then, so that today the figure probably stands around 45,000 nationwide.[12] The number and the increase of lobbyists vary markedly by state. From 1989 to 1995, the increase in California lobbyists was 35.7 percent and the increase in lobbying firms was 28.9 percent.[13] Today, there are as many as 1,100 lobbyists registered in California, 2,000 in Florida, 3,500 in Illinois, 1,300 in Michigan and Minnesota, 2,000 in New York and Ohio, 1,200 in Texas, and 1,600 in Virginia. And Alaska, Delaware, Hawaii, and Maine have fewer than 300 lobbyists each.[14]

Today lobbying is a far different enterprise than in earlier days. Its exponential growth is described by a lobbyist in Minnesota: "Ten years ago you saw the same people day in and day out. It was like a small fraternity. Everyone had places where they stood around the rotunda. Now, I'm lucky if I know a fourth of the lobbyists." The styles and techniques of lobbyists at state capitols have also changed. State government relations at one time could be conducted with "a shake and a howdy," according to the vice president for government relations at a large company. No longer is that the practice. Long gone are the days when lobbyists, according to a veteran in the profession, set up card tables in the rear of the house chamber in Wyoming to pay for legislators' votes as they were cast.[15] Nowadays, lobbying is professional and sophisticated. New techniques have been developed, including coalition building, grassroots mobilization, public relations and mass media, and polling; and the older techniques of relationship building, political activity, and direct lobbying have undergone considerable refinement.

Lobbying is different today not only because there are so many interest groups and lobbyists on the scene, but also because legislatures have changed so markedly. Lobbying could not afford to lag far behind. Since the late 1960s and the period of state legislative reform, legislatures practically everywhere have modernized. The expansion of professional staffing has increased their capacity. Moreover, they have developed a sense of independence and do not routinely accept executive leadership. They are much improved and far more capable. As Jesse Unruh, the late speaker of the California assembly and state treasurer, said: "As legislatures improve, the third house tends to improve too."[16] Beyond this, power within legislatures is more dispersed than it used to be.

The action is at the state level. With legislatures developing, political careers and elections becoming more important, and partisan competition sharpening, the environment for lobbying has been undergoing further change. A New Jersey lobbyist, who earlier had served on the legislative staff, described this new environment: "There's just more lobbyist consumers because legislative staff has grown, because legislative agendas have become more encompassing, because legislators have gotten to be better politicians and focus more on the politics of it rather than the policy of it." Legislators nowadays introduce bills that are more aggressive, more wide ranging, and more headline grabbing. The process is more driven by politics than it used to be. Lobbyists cannot remain aloof from this new reality, because they are so integral to the process, a process that politicians, and not lobbyists, continue to command.

How Lobbyists Are Perceived

On the one hand, those who employ lobbyists—in-house or as consultants—recognize the importance of their services. Professional lobbyists of one type or another are vital to the representation of a client's interests before the legislature. On the other hand, those who deal with lobbyists—legislators and their staffs—depend upon them mainly for the information they communicate. In their capacity as lawmakers, legislators need to know where various groups stand on issues. And lobbyists represent the most intense and most affected interests, whose views would probably be sought out even if they were not offered.

From the perspective both of interest groups and of legislators them-selves, then, lobbyists play a necessary role in American democracy. From the public's perspective, however, lobbyists and those whom they repre-sent may be seen as a threat to American democracy. A typical view is expressed in a book by Kenneth G. Crawford, a journalist based in Wash-ington, D.C.: "Since the founding of the republic, the democratic process has been perverted to a greater or less[er] degree by cunning and power-ful minorities bent on serving their own interest."[17] Some evidence cer-tainly supports this view of greedy special interests subverting democracy. The Southern Pacific Railroad dominated California government until it was swept from power by the Progressive reform movement of the early twentieth century. Standard Oil was so influential in Pennsylvania that some claimed it had done everything to the Pennsylvania legislature except refine it. Historical examples of interest group power abound; con-temporary examples, while fewer and further between, are still not that difficult to find.

The word "lobbyist" is also loaded. The image of the lobbyist is probably a holdover from the past. For most people, the lobbyist today is like Artie Samish of California in the 1930s and 1940s. He represented liquor, ciga-rettes, railroads, racetracks, banking, and chemicals. No lobbyists then, and certainly not now, had the power of Samish who was said to "govern" California. He was a newspaper cartoonist's dream, with his straw hat, large cigar, big paunch, and loud tie. What made him known to the pub-lic in his heyday was an article in a 1949 issue of *Collier's* magazine, titled "The Secret Boss of California." The cover of the magazine was a color photo of Samish posed with a ventriloquist's dummy, "Mr. Legislature," sitting on his lap. The lobbyist was pulling the strings.[18]

Since the days of Samish, some lobbyists and some legislators have indeed exhibited scandalous behavior, which has led to public concern. In the late 1980s and early 1990s FBI or local law-enforcement stings revealed illegalities by lobbyists and legislators in California, Arizona, South Carolina, and Kentucky. Since then cases of a less serious nature have arisen in at least a dozen other states. Nonetheless, these cases have been extraordinarily few given the many, many interactions over the years among lobbyists and legislators.

People tend to generalize from the worst possible cases to all cases. The media almost ensure that the public will have as negative a view as possible. For the media, news is defined in negative terms—and the more nega-tive, the more sensational, the more scandalous, the greater the appeal to an audience. The media interpret much of what goes on between lobby-ists and legislators as the buying and selling of votes—for dinners, trips, gifts, campaign contributions, and whatever. In the media, lobbyists are "influence peddlers" for "special interests," and lawmakers are all too will-ing to do their bidding. As the *Columbus Dispatch* (February 6, 2000) put it, "lobbyists have slipped their tentacles inside state government. . . ." The media are dedicated to the axiom, "Follow the money," and rarely entertain the idea that anything else influences where legislators stand on issues. If, for example, Legislator A receives a campaign contribution of $1,000 from Lobbyist B and also votes in support of the interests of B's client, it is usually implied that A voted the way he or she did because of the contribution. The possibility that A would have voted that way in any case, and that the contribution was intended to help someone get reelected who was already in agreement with B's client, is seldom enter-tained, and hardly ever given serious consideration.

One needs only to look at a 1988 series by the *Akron Beacon Journal,* "Pay to Play," or the 1996 series by the *Indianapolis Star-News,* "State-house $ellout: How Special Interests Hijacked the Legislature," to see how the press suggests in its coverage of campaign finance that lobbyists and legislators are not to be trusted. Or take a 1992 series in the *St. Paul Pioneer Press.* Even in Minnesota—a state with squeaky-clean government and public financing of campaigns—the newspaper alleged that through campaign contributions the special interests had a tight grip on the legis-lature. A columnist, in commenting on the series, wrote:

> If you have been reading "Bankrolling the Legislature" . . . you know that the foul odor you have been smelling does not come from the Pig's Eye sewage plant, the Smith Street St. Paul stockyard or the garbage bins be-hind your neighborhood hamburger joint. The stench is coming from the hog wallow at the Capitol.[19]

Not only campaign finance, but socializing and, indeed, interaction of almost any kind between lobbyists and legislators is grist for the media mill. Florida has one of the largest and most talented capital press corps in the country. But its slant is negative. A 1995 series in the *Tampa Tribune* pointed out, ominously, that there were fourteen lobbyists for every one legislator in Tallahassee, more than three times the national average. Another story, which ran in a number of papers in Florida, reported that in a 1988 struggle, lobbyists for Alamo Rent A Car hosted a dinner for legislators at an expensive restaurant the night before a legislative com-mittee voted on an issue involving Alamo. The stories suggested that the free meal and the favorable vote for Alamo were linked. The *Pensacola Journal* later recounted the event (July 1990), concluding: "The next day, Alamo's side won. Coincidence?" Obviously the journalist writing the article did not believe so. The fact is, however, that Alamo had rounded up enough votes on the committee well in advance of the committee meeting, and the dinner itself had nothing to do with the outcome. Perhaps Alamo's significant economic presence in the state was the legislators' pivotal consideration. But that explanation received much less attention in the press than the dinner paid for by lobbyists.

Another Florida story about lobbyists and legislators focused on a lobster dinner bought for members of a legislative committee by lobbyists for a major industry. According to journalists, reporting on the lobster dinner was justified, not because anything illegal or untoward went on, but because the dinner served as a symbol that lobbyists and legislators were too close. One journalist admitted to feeling that lobbyists had money and access that ordinary citizens did not enjoy, and believed that highlighting the lobster dinner might help level the playing field. Another journalist likened the role of the press to that of a policeman: "If enough people go to these dinners and get slapped . . . , these meetings are going to happen a little less frequently. . . ."[20]

Given the actual instances of corruption and the treatment of lobbyists and legislators in the media, it is not surprising that the public is cynical and distrustful. From two-thirds to three-quarters of the people polled respond negatively when asked about special interests and lobbyists. When asked whether the government is pretty much run by major interests looking out for themselves or for the benefit of all the people, the respondents overwhelmingly choose the former. Three out of four people, moreover, believe that Congress is beholden to special interest groups and that lobbyists have too much power. And they do not use that power for the public benefit, as far as ordinary citizens are concerned.

One of the questions asked New Jerseyans by the Eagleton Poll of Rutgers University in February 1994 was "What percentage of state legislators do you believe are willing to sell out to lobbyists in return for free meals, free gifts, or campaign contributions?" Respondents could answer any percentage from 0 (which 3 percent chose) to 100 percent (which 6 percent chose). An actual 58 percent of New Jerseyans indicated that half or more of their state's legislators were willing to sell out.

A large majority of people believe that the role of lobbying is either a very serious or a somewhat serious threat to American democracy. In a 1997 survey conducted by the Pew Research Center for the People and the Press, the power of special interests was rated roughly even with "international terrorism" as the greatest threat to the nation's future.[21] And in Connecticut a poll in April 1996 by the Hartford *Courant*/Institute for Social Inquiry at the University of Connecticut found that four out of ten respondents said we would "be better off in all respects if there were no lobbyists."

What Americans who are so distrustful of and cynical about special interests and lobbyists fail to appreciate, however, is that today just about everyone is directly or indirectly represented by one or several interest groups and their lobbyists. In the words of Dennis Carpenter, a prominent California lobbyist, "the media call us special interests, but there isn't a person in the state who isn't represented by some lobbyist in Sacramento."[22] Or to paraphrase the comic-strip possum, Pogo, "We have met the special interests, and they are us."

The evidence of group membership and participation is clear. Despite a decline in voting turnout over the years, the political activity of Americans—as individuals and/or as members of groups—is high. And a good deal of their participation is aimed at influencing public policy. The General Social Survey, which includes questions about group membership, found that since the early 1970s approximately 70 percent of Americans had at least one membership. In their study of participation, Sidney Verba and colleagues found that 79 percent of Americans were members of some kind of voluntary association, with 61 percent associated with a group that took a stand in politics. And almost half of them made a contribution to these politically oriented groups. Just over 40 percent had four or more affiliations.[23]

Although people feel excluded, they are not. Their interests are represented directly by virtue of their affiliations and their views are also represented indirectly by groups with whom they agree. The groups with whom we are affiliated and with whom we agree are not special interests in our eyes. That is why on public opinion polls, when groups are identified specifically by name rather than lumped under the general epithet, "special interest," respondents rate them favorably. Only when people realize that they, too, have special interests, and that there is nothing wrong in that, will attitudes toward interest groups and lobbyists become more positive.

Observing Lobbyists and Lobbying

If people observe lobbyists and lobbying at all, they do it through the media. The media view lobbying mainly in terms of the exchange of monetary favors for political support—a quid for a quo. Lobbyists themselves talk about their striving to attain "access" simply so they can present their case. Some lobbyists go further, admitting to influence and hoping to reap benefits from their reputation. Legislators, who are on the receiving end, claim that most of what lobbyists do is provide useful information. They report that they are not swayed by lobbyists, although their colleagues may be.

There is a modicum of truth to each of these points of view. Lobbyists are looking for something in return for their generosity. But it is not usually a vote. Lobbyists want and work for access, but they also want, and work for, more than that. Legislators do get needed information from lobbyists, but that is not all they receive. An exploration of lobbyists and lobbying must go further than these one-dimensional views.

The approach taken in this book is distinct from that of most other political scientists who have focused on lobbying. We are attempting, on the one hand, to cover a broad area and, on the other, to provide detail on lobbyists at work. Just what do lobbyists do? How do they do it? In these pages, we shall survey the scene, but we shall also probe more thoroughly into many of the subjects introduced. By examining the types of people involved, the techniques they use, and the jobs they do, we hope to convey to the reader a sense of the lobbying enterprise and its part in the legislative process. Of interest here are matters of timing, targeting, cultivating, strategizing, coalescing, mobilizing, educating, and justifying.

Our examination of lobbying is located within the state legislative context. It is intended to apply generally, even though each state is not quite like any other and each legislative body in its particulars is unlike the rest. The first edition of this book, although generic in one sense, was rooted in the lobbying cultures and practices of six states—California, Colorado, Florida, Minnesota, New Jersey, and Texas. The principal source of information was lobbyists in these states—105 of them, of different types, who were interviewed during the period from July 1990 to May 1991. Lobbyists were also interviewed in Maryland and other places, and governmental affairs professionals were interviewed in Washington, D.C. The persons interviewed have been assured anonymity in order to encourage them to speak candidly; therefore the answers given in interviews are not attributed to specific individuals.[24]

In any study, it is necessary—and often difficult—to decide what to include and, more important, what to leave out. Our focus here is solely on the legislature, not the executive. We realize, of course, that the executive branch is also lobbied by lobbyists. Governors initiate programs and sign or veto bills enacted by the legislature. They are by no means exempt from lobbyists' attentions. Indeed, according to former Arizona governor Bruce Babbitt, "the ultimate lobbyist's coup is to plant an idea in a governor's agenda."[25] Few of them succeed, however. The access lobbyists have to governors is relatively limited. Departments and executive agencies, by contrast, receive an increasing amount of attention from lobbyists, particularly with the proliferation of rules and regulations that affect economic interests and other groups. Lawyer lobbyists, especially, devote substantial energies to the relatively invisible business of lobbying the bureaucracies.

Nevertheless, the legislature is still considered the stomping grounds for most lobbyists in the states. Normally, when lobbyists discuss their work, their conversations revolve around legislatures and not executive agencies. Most of their time is spent in the legislative arena. A survey of Kansas lobbyists, for example, found that about 70 percent of the respondents spent four-fifths or more of their time lobbying legislators, with activities involving the executive branch concentrated among representatives of regulated industries and professions. A study of lobbying in California, South Carolina, and Wisconsin confirms the point. In each of these states, the legislature is the primary target, although governors and executive agencies are also targets.[26]

A Preview of the Book

One objective in the chapters that follow is to put the reader in the lobbyist's shoes. That way the reader can see the process from the lobbyist's perspective. At the same time, it is important to keep in mind that although this book focuses on lobbying, the legislative process is not dominated by lobbyists. There are other influences at work, and in critical instances more important ones. The author's orientation is essentially positive toward, and understanding of, lobbyists and the lobbying process. That does not mean that critical analysis is absent in what follows. Another objective of the book is to analyze the behavior and practices of lobbyists as they interact with legislators, and to assess their role in the legislative system. The reader must decide whether these objectives have been met.

After this introduction, the book is divided into two main parts before the conclusion is reached. The first part, consisting of four chapters, deals with the players, the practices, the issues and interests, and the settings.

The second part, also consisting of four chapters, deals with the strategies and tactics of lobbying—what is done, why, and to whom.

We begin in chapter 2 with a description of the people who lobby. We consider the various kinds of lobbyists who operate at the capitol, who they are and what they are like, and why they are in the business that they are in.

Chapter 3 focuses on state government relations as conducted by national and state corporations and associations. It also assesses the advantages (and disadvantages) of contracting out for lobbying services.

Issues and interests at stake are discussed in chapter 4. An important distinction is made between the larger public-policy issues and the smaller special-interest issues. How lobbyists keep track of issues and legislation is described, as are the general battle lines when interests compete.

Chapter 5 goes on to explore the settings in which lobbying takes place, pointing out variations according to the rules of the game in each state. The structure of the legislature, the nature of the legislative process, and patterns of politics and power all make a difference. So does the capital culture and the ethical climates of each state.

One of the principal techniques employed by lobbyists, that of building relationships, is the subject of chapter 6. Relationships develop both naturally and by careful cultivation, and they undergo trial in legislative combat. The concepts of "access" and "connection" are considered here, and an assessment is made of how relationships benefit both legislators and lobbyists.

The involvement of lobbyists in political campaigns is another principal technique, which is explored in chapter 7. Lobbyist and political action committee (PAC) contributions and just what money can and does buy are addressed here. So is the more active participation of lobbyists and interest groups in political campaigns.

Chapter 8 explores the three major techniques used by lobbyists to generate widespread support. One is that of building coalitions, which is easier said than done. Another is that of grassroots mobilization, which is being used by more and more groups. The last is the use of public relations and the media, the first resort of a few groups and the last resort of most.

In the final analysis, lobbyists have to make their case in the legislature issue by issue. In chapter 9 we consider certain tried and proven principles of direct lobbying, differences between being on the defense and taking the offense, and the various targets of lobbyists in the legislative process. Most significant in direct lobbying are the education and information lobbyists provide members of the legislature and the functions that are thereby served. A discussion of the importance of compromise completes the chapter.

Chapter 10 concludes the book with an assessment of the influence of lobbyists, the power of clients and causes, how interests are represented in the American states, and the relationship of lobbying to representative democracy.

CHAPTER 2

The People Who Lobby

All of us have considerable experience of lobbying (and being lobbied), at least in the general sense of the word. Nearly every day we try to persuade someone to do what is in our interests or, conversely, *not* do what is contrary to our interests. Some of us have even lobbied government officials, our representatives in Congress, or the state legislature. The study by Verba and colleagues indicates that of a national sample of Americans, 13 percent reported contacts with elected officials at the national level and 25 percent with those at the state or local level within the previous twelve months.[1] When we contact elected officials, we want them to act or vote in a particular way, because it is in our interest for them to do so. However skillful we may be at lobbying, however, very few of us do it for a living—in the sense that we lobby in the state capital regularly, professionally, and officially.

Only a relative handful of people meet the legal definition of lobbyist. These individuals are required to register with the secretary of state, attorney general, secretary of the senate, or clerk of the house of representatives, depending on the state. Just how many people do register is a function both of the number of organized interests with policy agendas within a state and of the state's specific lobbying requirements. In Arizona, for instance, 5,500 lobbyists are registered in keeping with the state's broad registration requirements, but fewer than 100 are active in lobbying. Pennsylvania, by contrast, has fewer than 800 individuals registered. The principal reason for such disparities, which do not reflect the size of the population or the economic development of the states, is the definition of who lobbyists are according to how much time they devote to their jobs. In states where the definition is very narrow and does not include part-time volunteers for hundreds and hundreds of organizations, fewer individuals have to register. Other states prefer to be on the safe side, requiring registration of anyone who comes close to active lobbying. The California definition, for example, is relatively strict: individuals who have more than 20 contacts a month with legislators or staff are regarded as lobbyists. In places where any person having relatively few contacts with legislators is legally defined as a lobbyist, the registration lists tend to swell.

Florida statutes, for example, require the registration of all persons who seek to encourage the passage, defeat, or modification of any legislation (with the exceptions of legislators and legislative staff). Moreover, several states, Florida included, require state and local officials lobbying in their official capacities to register also. This accounts, in part, for the 2,000 lobbyists registered in this state.

One must proceed cautiously, therefore, in making comparisons among the states on the basis of lobbyist registration figures. Who a lobbyist is depends on when and where he or she is lobbying. Statutory definitions have changed in recent years, depending on the strength of reform movements or the incidence of scandal in the various states. Many of those who register, moreover, are not full time. For instance, a survey of lobbyists in California found that 60 percent of those responding said they did not consider lobbying to be their full-time occupation. Some were managers of associations, others practiced law, some ran businesses, and a number engaged in other occupations altogether.[2]

Most important, of those registered, only a few are considered "featured players" in the legislative process. Of 600 lobbyists in Colorado, for example, only about 100 show up every day the legislature is in session. In Ohio out of about 2,000 registered lobbyists of one kind or another, there are 65 contract lobbyists with ten or more clients. Out of 600 registered lobbyists in New Jersey, only 60 to 70 spend a good deal of time in Trenton and wield real influence. An even smaller proportion of these are "major players"—individuals who are involved either in a few issues that have statewide significance or in many issues of much narrower import. In this book, we shall be dealing mainly with registered lobbyists who have become very involved in the legislative process in the states.

Who They Are

Lobbyist is the label that people recognize, but lobbyists are called other things as well. Given the American system of federalism and the nature of statutory language, it is hardly a surprise that lobbyists are known by a number of appellations—legislative agent, legislative counsel, legislative advocate, professional advocate, and so forth. In the world of organized interests, they may be known as state governmental relations professionals, public affairs consultants, and state counsels.

Despite the variety of names, just about every lobbyist can be defined as "a person designated by an interest group to represent it to government for the purpose of influencing public policy in that group's favor."[3] The lobbyist's principal role is to represent group interests. It is in the interests of groups to use government to confer advantages upon themselves and disadvantages on rivals. Groups can reap gains or suffer losses at the hands of state government. As a consequence, they must be attentive to what the legislature is doing, or might do, to them or for them. One Texas lobbyist notes that, in his state, "groups such as bass fisherman, midwives, pawnbrokers, as well as oil and gas, utilities, truckers, chemical companies, and environmentalists, are all represented by lobbyists." As one contract lobbyist explained, "I'm trying to present a point of view for a group of people in a better way than they can do themselves."

Lobbyists are professionals who by virtue of knowledge and experience advise and represent clients. Another contract lobbyist describes his role as follows:

> A lobbyist is an advocate for his clients just like a lawyer. If he signs on with clients, he signs on to help them achieve their interests. It could be that they only want to protect themselves against adverse legislation. They are affected vitally in their daily lives and their welfare by what happens across the street [at the statehouse].

Just as individuals turn to attorneys for help on legal and other matters and to financial consultants for counsel on investments, so they turn to other professionals, that is, to lobbyists, when they require assistance in dealing with government.

As representatives or advocates of interests, lobbyists have as one of their principal roles that of communication. That is the thesis of one of the seminal studies of Washington lobbyists. This study defined lobbying as the "stimulation and transmission of a communication" by someone other than a citizen acting on his own behalf, with the hope of influencing a governmental decision.[4] In the business of lobbying, however, communication is a two-way street. The traffic runs from client to legislature and from legislature to client, as we shall explore further in chapter 3. One lobbyist explained: "I have a client on my left and the legislature on my right. I am the guy in the middle."

Although communication is an important part of the process, lobbying is not simply the transmission of information. The purpose of the endeavor is persuasion. Legislators must be persuaded to support the particular position being presented by a lobbyist. Persuasion is not necessarily conversion, however. "You don't change minds," explained a California lobbyist, "You find ways to make them think they agreed with you all along."

Friendship, assistance, pressure, along with argument and the providing of information, are among a lobbyist's repertoire of persuasive techniques. As we shall see, although many factors are taken into consideration, the bottom line in the relationship between lobbyist and client is success. And success depends, at least in part, on the lobbyist's ability to persuade.

When the media, in particular, think of lobbyists, they pay greatest attention to contract, or independent, lobbyists because of the size and variety of their clientele, their typically generous campaign contributions, and their reputation (however undeserved these days) as lavish entertainers. Yet several other kinds of lobbyists are active in state capitals and must therefore also be taken into account. Thomas and Hrebenar, for example, have placed lobbyists in five categories. They have also estimated the proportion of each group in the state capital lobbying community: contract, about a quarter; in-house, about a third; government and legislative liaison, between a quarter and a third; citizen or volunteer, about 10 percent; and private individual or self-appointed, 1 or 2 percent.[5] Others have made use of similar categories, such as the following.

Contract lobbyists are also known as independent lobbyists, "guns for hire," or state counsel (as they are referred to by national corporations or associations). What distinguishes these individuals is that they are not employees of a single organization, but instead have a number of clients, ranging from a half-dozen to thirty or forty. A few may even represent fifty to one hundred clients. Contract lobbyists may be sole practitioners, partners in larger firms, partners or associates in law firms, or members of other multiservice organizations. In this text, they are typically called contract lobbyists, although from time to time they are referred to as independent lobbyists.

Association lobbyists are just that. They represent business, labor, professional, and trade associations. These lobbyists work for a specific organization (thus, "in-house"), and they may have duties that extend beyond lobbying. National associations, headquartered in Washington, D.C. (for example, the Pharmaceutical Research and Manufacturers of America and the American Petroleum Institute), and state associations, located in the various capitals of the states, both employ full-time professionals who are responsible for dealing with legislation and the legislature.

Company lobbyists, like their cousins, association lobbyists, work in-house for a single organization, usually a business. A company may have interests in just one state, as do utilities, hospitals, many banks, and smaller corporations. Or it may have interests within a number of states and facilities in a few. In some cases—Anheuser-Busch is an example—a business will have interests that extend nationwide; but the larger the state, the greater a company's concern. Companies have their own government relations personnel, but are also likely to be represented by one or several business and trade associations.

Governmental lobbyists are employed by associations composed of local governments, including county and city officials, school boards, property appraisers, tax collectors, sheriffs, water districts, clerks, and other public officials. Also in this category are those who lobby for particular jurisdictions, such as Anne Arundel and Prince Georges counties in Maryland or the cities of Dallas and Houston in Texas and Tampa and Miami in Florida.

Cause lobbyists cover a broad spectrum of groups. They include citizen groups (or "white hat") lobbyists and those representing nonprofits and single-issue groups. Their clients normally have no commercial, material, or governmental interests—rather, their concerns are philosophical and ideological. They generally appeal to moral principle. These groups stand apart from others in claiming to represent interests that are not linked specifically to members of the group. Their organizations are not built on the vocational or professional interests of members, but rather on the more general ideas they share.[6] Among the most visible groups in this general category are those generally labeled "public interest," the focus of which is good government. The League of Women Voters, Ralph Nader's Public Citizen, and Common Cause are prominent examples. Also visible and active here are the environmentalists, such as the Environmental Defense Fund, Audubon, and the Sierra Club, and the various state public interest research groups (PIRGs), whose agendas include consumer as well as environmental issues. Hundreds of nonprofits are registered to lobby. Impact, for instance, is a Florida coalition sponsored by twenty-nine religious denominations to attend to social, economic, and poverty-related issues. In New Jersey the Council of Churches, Association of Jewish Federations, and Catholic Conference all have interests in legislation. In two-thirds of the states, groups, such as the California Children's Lobby, monitor children's issues.

Somewhat different are the groups with more ideological and, hence, controversial programs. They include organizations on the left: state affiliates of the National Organization of Women, National Abortion Rights Action League, and the American Civil Liberties Union. They also include organizations on the right: California's Right to Life League, Christian Action Council, and Concerned Women of America; Florida's Eagle

Forum, Minute Women, Pro Family Forum, and Clean Cable Coalition are other examples. And there are groups that bridge ideological positions, like Mothers Against Drunk Driving.

The Business of Lobbying

Individuals on an organization's payroll need not be concerned about selling their services. As will be discussed in chapter 3 below, they have other, equally pressing, concerns—dealing with an executive or chief executive officer, interpreting and helping to shape association or company policy, educating the membership, and employing and supervising independent lobbyists if they are needed. But these in-house lobbyists have essentially a single client. For them, lobbying is not a business, but an adjunct to some other enterprise. The independent or contract lobbyist, by contrast, is in a business, either as a sole practitioner or a member of a firm. This type of lobbyist must sell his or her services to a number of clients. Some of them are year-round, continue over time, and generally pay a basic retainer. Among other things, they want a watchdog at the state capital. Others employ the lobbyist on a one-shot basis to handle a particular issue during a certain legislative session. In some places, a few lobbyists will work bills for a contingency fee, taking a down payment with a promise of more if they succeed. In other places, contingency fees are illegal. There are almost as many arrangements as there are lobbyists.

The differences among these types of lobbyists are marked. Although they all are charged with promoting or opposing legislation, they vary in approach, style, and techniques because of who they are and whom they represent. The challenges they face are not at all the same. Indeed, the differences among contract, association, company, governmental, and cause lobbyists are substantially greater than the differences among lobbyists from various states. That is to say, contract lobbyists in Minnesota resemble contract lobbyists in Florida much more than they resemble cause lobbyists in their own state.

Types of Practice

Although the business of contract lobbying has grown larger and more complex, the sole practitioner is still the norm. Because the overhead is low, lobbyists can hang out their shingles when they have only a few clients lined up. Many of these independent lobbyists work for six or seven groups—the chiropractors, a medical center, travel agents, horse breeders, the burglar and fire alarm association, or a city in their state. Some carry as many as thirty or forty clients. A few specialize in certain kinds of issues or issue areas, but the large majority are diversified and carry mixed portfolios. (Occasionally, sole practitioners share suites of offices and secretarial support and may collaborate in the referral and handling of clients.)

More and more lobbyists of late have been entering into group practice with partners or working for larger lobbying firms or sometimes law firms. Significant advantages are offered by scale. First, multiple services can be offered a client. In addition to traditional lobbying, the larger firm can offer public relations, polling, direct mail, and grassroots services. New Jersey's Nancy Becker Associates, for instance, can assist clients with research, budget analysis, bill drafting, grassroots organizing, legislative and regulatory monitoring, workshops, receptions, media and newsletters, and association management. The Success Group in Ohio is another example of a firm that covers just about all the lobbying bases.

Second, greater support services are available, provided by assistants who specialize in arranging social events and assisting the lobbyists on specific issue areas and keeping in touch with clients. That allows lobbyists themselves to make more effective use of their own time.

Third, the lobbyists in a firm can more easily conduct "team lobbying," backing one another up with a senior lobbyist taking the lead on strategy. The former Florida firm of Haben, Culpepper, Dunbar & French illustrates the point. The partners included a former house speaker, a former counsel to Governor Bob Martinez, and a former member of the legislative staff with more than fifteen years of lobbying experience. "The first thing [the merger of lobbying talent] brings is an aura as much as anything," said John French, one of the partners. "When people see me, they know I've got Ralph [Haben] and Pete [Dunbar] backing me up."[7] In recent years, however, the partners have gone their separate ways.

Fourth, group practice permits better coverage of legislators. The more lobbyists, the broader their contacts with legislators are likely to be. One lobbyist may have close relationships with members of the house, another may have better relationships with members of the senate.

Fifth, a larger firm will, generally speaking, have the reputation for greater clout and therefore be more attractive to potential clients. A firm with a large staff, a formidable list of clients, and a war chest in PAC (political action committee) contributions has special appeal.

Sixth, whether working for a single firm or for several groups, team lobbying is becoming more and more important because of the weakening of legislative leaders, the higher turnover of members (especially in the nineteen states with term limits), and the loosening of party discipline. Increasingly, lobbyists will divide up responsibility for chambers, parties, leaders, and committees.

An example of a firm that offers a variety of services and a strong team of consultants is George R. Steffes, Inc., one of the top lobbying groups in Sacramento. Steffes started over twenty-five years ago, when he left his position in Governor Ronald Reagan's office to found the first multi-person lobbying firm in California. Now, George R. Steffes, Inc., employs eight professional lobbyists, who were formerly employed by either the executive or legislative branch of government. The firm's clients include 3M, American Express, Bechtel Power, California Healthcare Association, Enterprise Rent-A-Car, Exxon, IBM, Johnson & Johnson, and others.

A relatively recent development is the entry of large law firms on the scene. In many state capitals today, one can find a full-service law firm with the added service of lobbying. In some cases, lobbying has been in the repertoire of the firm from its establishment because of a founding partner's experience and interests. Joel Sterns had served as counsel to the governor of New Jersey and been involved in Democratic politics throughout his adult life. When he left public service in 1969 and opened up offices on West State Street across from the New Jersey State House, lobbying and law were both natural activities for him. In most cases, however, the phenomenon of law and lobbying under one roof postdates the emergence of the New Federalism and additional power being wielded by the states.

A law firm based in one of the larger cities of the state might locate an office in the capital. For example, the Miami-based firm of Steel, Hector & Davis also maintains a large operation in Tallahassee, just a few blocks from the capitol. Seven lobbyists, working in teams, represent a prestigious list of clients. Or a law firm, such as Faegre & Benson, has offices in downtown Minneapolis, not too far from the state legislature, as well as in Washington, D.C. It did not enter the lobbying field until 1983, and then did so somewhat reluctantly. But clients wanted a full-service law firm. The chief lobbyist at Faegre & Benson does a substantial amount of work for about eighteen clients, including a number of members of the Twin City corporate community, other business associations, and the City of Minneapolis and Hennepin County.

The law-lobbying phenomenon appears to have advanced furthest in Texas. In 1984, with the field getting crowded and competition stiffer, lobbyists began taking their place in law firms. The appeal of a law firm was that it could furnish administrative and secretarial support that contract lobbyists were unable to provide on their own. Moreover, a large law firm already had a clientele from which lobbying clients could be recruited. Finally, lobbyists were promised greater security; or as an early convert put it, joining a law firm was "a method of extending one's useful life."

But legal work and lobbying work generally do not overlap. And mainstream lawyers do not understand the profession of lobbying; like the public, they generally look down on it. The law-firm environment is not at all political and therefore not hospitable to those engaged in political work. Furthermore, lobbyists do not feel that they have benefited financially from their affiliations. The firms supply few clients and lobbyists themselves must continue to act as the rainmakers. Add to that the financial difficulties encountered by some of the major firms, and lobbyists are beginning to think about moving outside again. If a few go, others will likely follow, and the marriage of law firm and lobbyist will have run its course in Texas.

Competition and the Marketplace

Although contract lobbyists maintain friendships with one another and share professional norms, they are in a very competitive business. The competition is a friendly competition, but it is competition nonetheless. Even in good times, there is just so much business to go around. When it comes to wooing deep-pocketed clients, one lobbyist gets the contract and the other loses it. Indeed, if there is any trend discernible, it is toward more cut-throat relationships and less of a club-like atmosphere. In Austin, for example, no more than two dozen lobbyists dominate the marketplace and control the most profitable accounts. They are the power brokers, who have arranged a virtual cartel. Small lobbyists, who live precariously, resent the "big boys" who compete among themselves and share the spoils while keeping others at arm's length. Trade association and corporate lobbyists also appear to envy the hired guns, who make more money than they do. In addition, individual members of associations employ their own lobbyists, and this causes some concern to association directors.

Some lobbyists advertise their services, targeting mail to a select industry. The top lobbyists, however, seldom seek out clients in a public way but depend on their reputations, clients, contacts, and friends, and, of course, legislators. Little marketing takes place. It ordinarily takes a few years to establish oneself, with clients coming slowly as the word gets around. Lobbyists themselves make referrals to one another if their plates are too full or if the interests of a potential client threaten to conflict with those of a current one. And lobbyists do look out for their colleagues when it does not interfere with their own practices. Occasionally, if a client of theirs has an issue to push, they may alert friends, who then seek to be hired by the other side. They expect like treatment in return. It is reported in some places that here and there an issue is generated by lobbyists themselves as a way to stimulate business and a legislator is willing to introduce a bill that will send an industry or group scurrying for help.

In some instances, too, when it is late in the legislative session and too many balls have to be juggled at one time, a lobbyist may subcontract a piece of the action to a colleague. In fact, as the session proceeds with hundreds of issues rising to the surface, more groups and organizations emerge seeking representation. Under these circumstances, friendships count. If an influential legislator advises a group that "it would be a good idea to hire X," the message is seldom misinterpreted. This practice occurs in a number of states, although relatively few members engage in it. The governor of Louisiana used to recommended certain lobbyists to the major interests in the state, which then quickly retained them.

Those lobbyists with experience in the capital, particularly former legislators and legislative staff, have established themselves and their credentials over the course of years. They would maintain, along with a one-time member of the Colorado General Assembly, that "people have sought me out; I didn't go after clients. They knew my reputation." In lobbying, reputations grow over time, and certain lobbyists become known for their client lists, contacts, and clout. In lobbying, as in other domains of life, the rich get richer and the poor have trouble paying their bills.

Lobbyists will take on one-shot clients, those who need something done at that session and perhaps the next. But they are generally seeking long-termers as well—"anchor clients" who put them on retainer. These are companies, organizations, and groups that, in the words of a Colorado lobbyist, "want you to cover their tail." They form the core of the lobbyist's business and give it greater stability.

Many lobbyists take almost anything that comes their way. But others try to shape their practice. It is not easy to do. Some lobbyists are typecast, as are two women in Colorado whose experience was with advocacy groups and social service issues. Their initial clientele were the homeless, family doctors, and small pharmacists, and they had a difficult time when they tried to expand beyond the ranks of the powerless and do-gooders. Other lobbyists shape a specialized practice from the outset. A lawyer-lobbyist in Tallahassee, who represented developers among others, managed successfully to focus on relatively narrow environmental issues. A husband-and-wife team was just as successful working the other side of the street. They represented Florida's canoe liveries and outfitters, Audubon, the Trust for Public Lands, Environmental Education League, Fish Watch, and also voluntary hospitals.

Other contract lobbyists in Tallahassee also have chosen clients with discretion. One lobbyist turned down a bid from the tobacco industry, with which she had philosophical disagreements, and an oil company, which in her opinion had failed to clean up its act. A former legislator was similarly selective. He balanced his list, keeping a corporate base, but still got one-third of his clients and 10 percent of his income from nonprofits. Another Floridian, who both lobbied and practiced law in a larger firm, did not feel obliged to take on clients with whom he felt uncomfortable. Lobbying was only part of his living, and the other, legal, part afforded him a measure of independence. One of the most highly touted members of Tallahassee's lobbying community developed his practice by picking and choosing. He was particularly careful at the beginning not to take on clients, such as the pari-mutuel industry, whose reputations were tainted.

Why People Lobby

Students in college, graduate, or professional schools will think about careers in law, business, medicine, teaching, accounting, journalism, the arts, and government and politics. They often pursue a course of study that leads in one direction or another, and then respond to opportunities as they present themselves. A few, but a very precious few, entertain the idea of lobbying as an occupation or as a career. There is no course of study that trains one for an entry-level position as a lobbyist. And it is not at all like going into the family business, something that may be in the back of one's mind. Yet this too can happen. For example, Frank Hays, Sr., a former lieutenant governor of Colorado, in 1975 established what has become one of the largest contract-lobbying firms in the state. His son, Frank, Jr., a while later, went into partnership with his father.

Years ago Harmon Zeigler and Michael A. Baer noted that lobbying was a marginal occupation, characterized by ambiguous behavior and no clear images. Those who became lobbyists did not make a predetermined choice of profession but had drifted into the field.[8] The career path of most lobbyists has changed little since they wrote their book on lobbying.

The Career Paths of Contract Lobbyists

Different types of lobbyists tend to come to their jobs through different routes and for different reasons. The career paths of most contract lobbyists, and a number of the other types as well, are through government and politics. Until recently, government and politics, at the higher levels at least, have been a preserve of white males. Thus, a relatively small proportion of lobbyists in the states have been women; an even smaller proportion have been black. But in the past decade the number of women in the field has increased dramatically. A California survey shows that none of those registered as lobbyists before 1972 were women, but in 1983 one-third of the new registrants were female. By then, women comprised 14 percent of the total registrations in Sacramento,[9] and today the figure is higher. Colorado's legislature has one of the highest percentages of female members, 31 percent; similarly, almost a third of the state's registered lobbyists are women. Fewer women lobby in a state like Texas; but even so, 17 percent of the contract lobbyists in Texas who have five or more clients are women.[10] The latest estimate is that women now make up about 20 percent of state capital lobbyists, having grown markedly in representation since 1980.[11]

Some of these female lobbyists represent public interest groups and nonprofits, a number are in-house lobbyists for corporations, and quite a few are with associations. State government relations personnel headquartered in Washington have a particularly large proportion of women in their ranks. Some of the contract lobbyists are also women but, with occasional exceptions, the heavy-hitters in this field are still men.

Government and politics are the training ground for lobbyists, particularly for the so-called hired guns. In his study of Washington lobbyists, Robert Salisbury found that half of them had previously been employed by the federal government.[12] The California survey, mentioned above, showed 36 percent of the lobbyists there having state government experience, with 21 percent recruited from the ranks of legislative staff and about 5 percent from among legislators themselves.[13]

These are people who aspired to enter political life and hold public office, or who caught the bug along the way. A former chairman of Minnesota's Republican party, California governor Ronald Reagan's legislative liaison aide, the chief of staff to New Jersey governor Brendan Byrne, a top aide to Florida's governor Reuben Askew, the legislative assistant to Colorado's governor Richard Lamm—these are the kinds of individuals now lobbying the legislatures of their states. Some lobbyists have acquired expertise in a specific area of public policy. For example, a Florida lobbyist known as "Mr. Insurance" worked for two insurance commissioners and for twenty years lobbied for the insurance industry. A few lobbyists have journalistic backgrounds, such as the Trenton contract lobbyist who worked as a reporter for the *Newark Evening News* (and also as press aide to Governor Richard Hughes) and his one-time partner, who had been an editor on the *Trenton Times*. The latter had intended to take the knowledge he gleaned from lobbying back to a career in journalism. He got to like lobbying, however, and set up his own firm. An assistant city editor at the *Minneapolis Star* had his appetite for politics whetted, went on to law school, then handled legislative affairs for the attorney general, and finally went into lobbying.

Members of the legislative staff have a special affinity for lobbying. Nonpartisan research staffers are inclined to make a career of legislative service, or move over to the executive (what one partisan staffer referred to as "going into government"). But political and partisan staffs are more likely to see opportunities in the lobbying enterprise. A Maryland contract lobbyist served as a top aide to two senate presidents and then began lobbying. Another top aide to Maryland's senate president joined a law firm that lobbied. In fact of the ten highest-paid lobbyists in Annapolis, five used to hold key jobs in the statehouse.[14] In Texas, one of the contract lobbyists had gotten involved in politics right after graduation from college and took a job first on the staff of the house and then for one of the standing committees. Another was an aide to a house speaker and one was house parliamentarian through five speakers. In Florida, the staff director of a house committee, and subsequently chief of staff to the speaker, became a partner in a practice with his legislative boss after he had completed his speakership. Another Florida committee staff director also teamed up with his former chairman when the latter went into lobbying.

Former legislators are among the most effective lobbyists in the state capital and are certainly perceived to be among the most influential. But like everyone else, they did not have lobbying in their game plan when they ran for the legislature. While serving in the legislature, Florida's Sam Bell stood at the doors of the house chambers. Looking at the throng of lobbyists, he said to himself: "If that ever happens to me, shoot me." But in 1988 he lost a bid for reelection and, then, in 1991, after the two-year hiatus required by law, Bell was beginning to lobby. He was standing out-side the same doors of the house chambers, waiting to buttonhole mem-bers on their way in and out. "I may say the same thing," Bell now said. "If I ever go in again, shoot me."[15] "Lobbying was the last thing on my list," recalled a Texas legislator turned lobbyist. "As a house and senate member, I was tough on lobbyists." Whatever his earlier views, he carved out a career in lobbying. A former member of the Florida house, who was defeated in an election for Congress, joined a law firm in Tampa. Two years later the firm opened an office in Tallahassee, with one $5,000 contract. The former legislator handled that client and went out on his own when the law firm split up. His timing was good because the sales tax on services was the principal issue before the governor and the legislature. With all the groups fighting the tax, it could be considered a full-employment act for Tallahassee lobbyists.

The legislature is a natural training ground for lobbyists in many states. As of early 2000, Ohio's lobbyists included eight former members of the senate and nineteen former members of the house. About twenty former legislators, including several house speakers and a senate president, were registered in Colorado. Almost as many former legislators were registered as lobbyists in Nevada.[16] A similar situation existed in Florida, where four out of seven of the last speakers, among other former legislators, entered the lobbying practice. In Texas, too, a number of members wound up as lobbyists, and two former speakers went into the business. Legislators have also been overrepresented, proportionate to their ranks, in California and Minnesota. In some states, such as New Jersey, legislators have been rela-tively few and far between in the "third house." That may be because a number of legislators who lose elections or drop out are subsequently appointed to well-paying jobs in the executive branch or on boards and commissions.

Phil Isenberg is one among two dozen former legislators lobbying in California. After fourteen years in the assembly, Isenberg was term-limited and found new employment with a Sacramento law firm, for whom he now lobbies. Why not? He regards his new job as not very different from his old job; lobbying and legislating involve the same process—making deals happen.[17]

Legislators, and others who are members of the capital community, like politics. Some love it—are consumed by it; more than a few are addicted to it. A former staffer in the Texas legislature, who later lobbied for an association of local governments, commented: "It's all I do, all I really know—politics." Bruce Bereano, another former legislative staffer and one of Maryland's independent lobbyists, does not drink or smoke, has no hobbies, but is an avid sports fan. He functions on four or five hours of sleep a night, devoting the rest of his time to work. Lobbying is his life. A New Jersey lobbyist for teachers grew up in a political family, had an uncle who ran for Congress, and has a passion for politics. Although she has been a classroom teacher, she has spent most of her life dabbling in the political arena.

A number of these people have a consuming interest in public policy. They want to affect policy, and lobbying is one way to do so. Some have a thirst for knowledge about issues and problems, and lobbying affords them an opportunity to continue learning. Many of them, of course, like power, and that is one of the reasons they went into government and politics in the first place. Nearly all the lobbyists enjoy the game, although the women appear to be less infatuated with this aspect of lobbying than the men. A New Jersey contract lobbyist put it tersely: "I love the action. I thrive on it." A lobbyist for a Florida city describes the addictive quality of the work: "When you get what you want, it feels so good; you want to go back for more." There is little better, said a lobbyist for New Jersey's business community, than "getting something through or blocking something or knocking PIRG's block off on a clean water bill." Lobbyists exude heightened exhilaration during the closing days and hours of a legislative session. This is their last chance to get something through—and also their opponents'. They can win or lose, or come out a little ahead or a little behind. This is the lobbyist's moment of truth. Movement, action, and winning have special appeal for these political animals.

Lobbying is an appealing trade because political practitioners want to stay in politics and legislators and legislative staff want to continue playing roles in the process. Moreover, as legislatures and legislators have become more full time, members tend to sacrifice their outside occupations. No longer can they pursue two paths, as in earlier years. If they decide to, or have to, leave the legislature, there is not as much for them to return to as there was for the citizen-legislators of yesteryear. Some members are defeated, and others, with growing families or college tuitions in the offing, can no longer manage on a legislative salary. Members in two-fifths of the states are term limited and may not have other opportunities electorally. Where can they go, what can they do? Their greatest attributes are knowledge of the legislative process, familiarity with the issues, and friendship with many of the players. A number may be shocked that there is not widespread demand for their talents. Lobbying is, perhaps, the only endeavor that will put their talents to full use, and pay money besides.

Money is an important part of lobbying's appeal. Upon leaving the California senate, one individual was offered $350,000 by interests in Los Angeles to lobby a bill. How could he turn down such an offer? He discovered he liked lobbying and realized, as he put it, "I'm getting rich again." Another former legislator in Florida felt he was still involved in the legislative process. The difference was, in his words, "I used to do it for practically nothing, now I get paid well for it." One of New Jersey's presiding officers, who had announced that he was retiring from the legislature, was asked by a statehouse correspondent whether he intended to take up lobbying. The leader responded that he was tempted. "I think it would be very lucrative," he said. "The only problem," he added, "is that I would have to pay for the dinners, and I'm not used to that."

Not every lobbyist makes it big, but good money can be made, at least by a few—perhaps no more than the top five or ten lobbyists in a state capital. Maryland's Bereano used to have annual earnings of about $1 million thanks to his sixty or so clients and his twenty-hour days. The best lobbyists in Florida make over $500,000 a year. The very top lobbyists with the Austin law firms keep about 85 percent of the more than $1 million that they bring in. A number of their colleagues gross over $300,000. Incomes are not nearly as high in Colorado, where a few earn over $200,000, and several more make over $100,000. Some years ago, the highest-paid lobbyist in Little Rock, Arkansas, reportedly took in $200,000, while a number of others were said to have had incomes ranging from $50,000 to $100,000.[18]

The Career Paths of Other Lobbyists

Association lobbyists are less likely than contract lobbyists to have political backgrounds, although some of them do. Most come to their present positions from other associations. That is because so many of those who lobby for smaller associations also have other responsibilities as executive directors. They recruit members and provide them with services; lobbying therefore claims only part of their time. Of fifty lobbying executive directors of state associations of certified public accountants, for example, the majority have association backgrounds, while nine or ten come from the accounting profession and a few, such as Bruce Allen in California, once served on the staff of the legislature. Typical is the case of Tommy

Townsend of Texas, who earlier represented the realtors for thirteen years and wound up with the trial lawyers. Some individuals with associations come from lobbying positions with companies in the state.

Lobbyists for teacher associations illustrate a different career path. The large majority of them have prior experience as classroom teachers. Paul Hubbert, who served as executive secretary and "political genius" of the Alabama Education Association (AEA), started as a classroom teacher, became a superintendent in a small town, and then took over AEA in Montgomery.[19] Becky Brooks had sixteen years of classroom teaching, served as president of the Texas State Teachers Association, and then came to Colorado, where she lobbied for the Colorado Education Association. Dolores "Dee" Corona, a New Jersey classroom teacher, soon became active as president of a local chapter. Within a few years, she had a position as organizer with the New Jersey Education Association, and in 1985 became its lobbyist and director, a position she continues to hold. In some places, the education association recruits a person with a political, rather than educational, background to head their lobbying corps. Gene Mammenga taught at a state university, served in the Minnesota senate, and worked for the St. Paul School District before going to the Minnesota Education Association.

Many of those who work in state government relations or who lobby for companies also come to their jobs from politics. For example, Hank Fisher spent fifteen years in Minnesota politics. He chaired the Democratic Farmer Labor party, served on the staff of Walter Mondale, and ran a gubernatorial campaign for Wendell Anderson. When the savings and loan industry, which had been fighting legislation on a usury ceiling, asked him to take on their case, he contracted to do so, representing the industry and a few other clients for five years. In 1980 he was hired to head the public affairs division of a Minneapolis bank that was encountering problems with community groups. Tom Hagan of Texas is another good example. He had worked for lieutenant governors Ben Barnes and William Hobby and then for U.S. Senator Lloyd Bentsen as a legislative assistant in Washington. He came back to Austin in 1981 to take charge of state and federal relations for Central and Southwest Utilities.

Overall, most lobbyist personnel in corporations come from other departments in the company, not from outside. The pharmaceutical industry is illustrative. The national association's lobbying staff comes by way of government or association work. By contrast, the personnel of corporate members of the Pharmaceutical Research and Manufacturers of America comes mainly from within the companies themselves. Many are attorneys because the state-relations function often began in law departments and sometimes still reports to these units. There is a corporate belief, moreover, that lawyers are best suited for the job because they have been trained to interpret the language of legislation.[20] Those who do not make their way to lobbying from legal departments come from the corporation's marketing, sales, or human resources departments. They know the company and its products, and some think this knowledge may be more important in state government relations than an understanding of the legislative process and legislatures. This makes sense. Frequently the person responsible for a corporation's government relations does relatively little direct lobbying, but instead contracts out to independent lobbyists in target states.

Lobbyists for county and local governments and their associations have varied backgrounds. A few come right out of politics or government. They may have budget and fiscal experience. A number go from city to municipal association or from one association to another. Some have training in public administration and have been employed by local government. Michael Sittig's father was director of the Florida League of Cities, and since high school the son worked for the league. He grew up in the business and practically inherited the top position when his father left.

Cause lobbyists have taken very different routes, arriving at their positions by way of involvement in movements or with issues. Some are active in or have served on boards of the organizations that they later are hired to direct. They have generally confined their work to advocacy groups. Dolores Phillips, for example, was a nutritionist employed by hospitals. She took on being director of the New Jersey Animal Rights Alliance and then lobbied for the New Jersey Environmental Federation. Briggs Gamblin started with the Colorado Open Space Council, went with COPIRG a few years later, to Colorado Common Cause, and then to Common Cause in Washington, D.C. What distinguishes many of the good government, environmental, feminist, and even nonprofit lobbyists is that they are dedicated to a cause, a cluster of issues, or a vision of how society should function.

Not all the cause lobbyists continue in the same field. A few make a transition from organizational constraint to independence. Karen Woodall of Florida is an example. She spent from 1980 to 1990 as director of Florida Impact, serving the needs of the disadvantaged and homeless for a coalition of religious denominations. Then she opened her own lobbying firm while for the most part continuing to represent the same types of clients on a contractual basis. Nikki Beare of Florida provides a somewhat different example. A housewife, she joined the League of Women Voters and became a community activist. She came up to Tallahassee to lobby the issue of equal pay for equal work and then increased her lobbying efforts on behalf of the Equal Rights Amendment. When various groups noted that she was spending time in the capital, they would approach her and ask if she would watch a bill for them. In return they would pay her way to Tallahassee. Pretty soon she was getting paid for her work and some time later was lobbying for business as well as nonprofit and advocacy groups.

Qualities and Styles

No two lobbyists are identical in personality or in the qualities they bring to their jobs. There is clearly no single set of characteristics necessary for effective lobbying. People who range widely in their personal qualities all may ply their trades effectively. Yet there seem to be a number of qualities that are desirable if one hopes to be successful in this enterprise. Some of the qualities noted here apply far more to contract lobbyists at one end of the continuum than to cause lobbyists at the other end, but they are relevant across the board.

Characteristics of Lobbyists

Experience is important. The longer lobbyists are at it (up to a certain point), the more they seem to know. Furthermore, it takes time for integrity and honesty to be demonstrated, for victories to be won, and for reputations to develop. A New Jersey lobbyist, who had worked earlier as a reporter and for the Republicans in the legislature, put it simply: "Hanging around for twenty years gives you a lot of valuable experience." In the 1960s, Zeigler and Baer found that lobbyists in the four states they were studying averaged from eight to twelve years' experience.[21] Because of the growth of their industry, many contract lobbyists are relatively new to the scene. But the principal figures generally have ten to twenty years in lobbying, and prior political and governmental experience before that.

Like everyone else, contract lobbyists age and retire, and some burn out. A former Florida legislator insists, "I will do this as long as it's fun." By the closing weeks of every legislative session, he says, "I don't want to do this anymore." But he stays on because of the satisfaction he derives from doing good for clients, winning battles, and earning a nice income. Another lobbyist, from Minnesota, is about ready to leave. "You get worn out by banging into this stuff," he said. Another, who earlier had served in the Minnesota legislature, is less infatuated with the process than he used to be and leans on his colleagues a little more. However, voluntary departure by those who are successful is rather low (as it is in the legislature). The tenure of association and governmental lobbyists also appears lengthy. That is of particular benefit to the single client being represented in each case. It provides for continuity and memory, which give reassurance to legislators. Like the rest of us, legislators prefer stability in their relationships and, thus, a bit more predictability in their unpredictable lives.

In their study of Washington, D.C., lobbyists, Robert Salisbury and his colleagues found that experience provided knowledge about issues, familiarity with the decision-making process, and contacts.[22] Experience, in other words, leads to knowledge—of issues, process, and people. These are not separate commodities but warp and woof of the same fabric: "Everything in government . . . is interconnected," writes a folklorist who was working in the Delaware legislature. "Each new event, each new policy is connected to past events and the old boys have been around long enough to know the strands are woven together."[23]

Along with experience and knowledge as requisite qualities, "people skills" (as a Florida lobbyist dubs them) are essential. Few lobbyists can survive without a sense of and enjoyment in dealing with people. There are exceptions, such as one individual who represents an environmental group and lacks what we have come to call "interpersonal skills." But he has a client who cannot be ignored, advocates issues with political appeal, and works hard. So, he manages to survive. Intuition and instinct are also key. One observer has written that the chief stock in trade of the lobbyist is an intangible quality called "feel."[24] It certainly is. Also fundamental is the ability to figure out what path is best to take. An Illinois lobbyist expressed it succinctly: "I get hired for political judgment." Another pointed out that judgment is critical in the processes of negotiating. "You have to know how to close a deal," he said, "[and] what they are willing to buy."

Other attributes that seem to count are a willingness to work hard, tenacity, and persistence. Also important are communication skills, the ability to sell, and a hands-on style. Some people argue that a sense of humor is important, particularly the ability not to take oneself too seriously. Others, the lawyer-lobbyists, maintain that legal skills are important because, as they see it, "he who writes the language of a bill has control." Moreover, those who have learned to read statutory language "can make mumbo-jumbo arguments about legal problems that might arise from pro-posed legislation." Such arguments are difficult for laypersons to counter.

Intelligence is also required, particularly nowadays. Lobbyists often must have command of substance as well as of process. Contract lobbyists, who represent many clients and take on a range of subjects, have to be quick studies. Many of them are. Good judgment, of course, is requisite.

As important as any other quality is a lobbyist's attitude. It has to be positive. It helps tremendously if lobbyists are loyal to their clients and respect the process. To effectively represent a client it helps if a lobbyist can communicate a belief in that client's position. Indeed, it helps to believe in the client. Ginger Gold, a Rutgers University student, interned for Nancy Becker, a lobbyist who represented New Jersey's cable television industry. Ms. Gold embarked on her Trenton experience with nega-tive feelings toward the industry, but as part of her internship had to put together a report on cable's positions. She soon came to defend the indus-try and observed in a paper that she wrote, "I guess that lobbyists must love their clients or learn to love them to do the job effectively."[25] For lobbyists, work on an issue can produce attachment, if not commitment, to a cause. It is not difficult. Practically every client can make a reasonable argument for his or her case. Even if clients cannot, a lobbyist is likely to believe that everyone deserves representation. Either way, it is possible to sincerely advance clients and their causes.

For contract lobbyists in particular, the main thing is how they feel about the people whom they lobby. "You generally have to like legislators and the legislative process," according to a Florida lobbyist. People who do not exit relatively quickly. Most genuinely like legislative politics and politicians. Others have to work at it a bit. A lobbyist for one of Florida's cities explains that on one hand, "I spend a lot of my energy just trying to find something I like in each member" and, on the other, "I try not to *not* like people."

Corporate lobbyists may feel less ardor and their demeanor may be more formal. But if they are to manage state relations, their attitude must also be positive. Corporate lobbyists must have regard for the legislature and for legislators. "If they are disdainful or critical," a lobbyist for a major pharmaceutical firm suggested, "legislators will sense it and their effec-tiveness will be limited." Lobbyists therefore have to take the side of poli-tics and politicians. Specifically, they must understand and acknowledge the legitimacy of legislators' points of view, even if they and their company are opposed to their positions.

The qualities that count most in lobbyists are thought to be those normally possessed by legislators themselves. This is one reason why former legislators are among the most effective and influential members of the lobbying corps in the state capital. They know the issues, the process, and the people as well as, or better than, anybody. They have built up relationships and friendships, which takes time and requires proximity. For relationships to develop, people must be in close touch, as will be discussed later on. More than others, former legislators have established reputations for trust and credibility. A few, of course, may have made more enemies than friends, but most of those who go into lobbying have emerged from the legislature in good personal shape. Laurence Levitan is one of a number of former Maryland legislators who turned to lobbying. His success as a lobbyist derives in part, as he explains it, from the fact that "Over the years, I've been pretty fair and up-front with my colleagues and that comes back to help you."[26] Moreover, legislators have a perspective that is useful in a lobbying career. It derives from their experience negotiating, compromising, and usually settling for somewhat less than they would have liked.

The transition from being a legislator to being a lobbyist is not easy, however. A period of adjustment is required. A former member of the Florida legislature had to learn how to get a note to a lawmaker on the floor. He had always been called out of the chamber to talk to lobbyists, but now the shoe was on the other foot. He had difficulty getting to see a few legislators; it was frustrating. But he was able to manage the transition because he enjoyed the process and was being paid handsomely.

There is always the question of whether the ego can adjust, especially if, as many admit, ego is a substantial part of life in public office. When Massachusetts senate president William Bulger contemplated leaving the legislature after thirty years in office, he conferred with a friend, Kevin Harrington, his predecessor as senate president and then an independent lobbyist. How would he do if he became a lobbyist, Bulger asked. Harrington indicated that he would do well financially, in the mid six figures. This impressed a man whose income had always been limited, but whose family included nine children. But before you decide, Harrington went on, think about the following possibility. You've retired from the senate and are starting out as a lobbyist. You visit the office of Senator Smith to make the case for a client. His secretary looks up, greets you and asks, "Who shall I say would like to see the Senator?" You tell her, "Bill Bulger" (thinking, of course, why doesn't she know who you are), and thereupon she gets up from her desk and walks into her boss's inner office. A few minutes later she emerges to inform you, "Senator Smith is tied up this morning, but he will try to fit you in this afternoon, if you want to take a chance and drop by later." Do you still want to switch from the senate presidency to lobbying, Harrington asked? Bulger put off his retirement for several years, leaving the legislature only after his appointment as president of the University of Massachusetts.

A former leader in Colorado is perceived to have handled withdrawal very well: "I found out I didn't have a vote and I didn't have a parking place. You learn to be humble and you learn to wait." The pace of his life changed, and his wife suggested (in jest, one would believe) that he take up needlepoint. The adjustment is tougher for others. Some assume they are still insiders, even though they are not. Some try to "wing it," not mastering the issues they have to lobby. The most frequent criticism of former legislators, in fact, is that they are not used to working on detail and depend on relationships rather than substance. The most skillful and adaptable, by contrast, use their previous relationships but do not rely on them. Indeed, the less they rely on them, the more useful they are.

The Styles of Lobbyists

Various attempts have been made to categorize the styles of lobbyists. Among political scientists, Samuel C. Patterson distinguished among Oklahoma lobbyists as follows: the "contact man," who conceives of his job in terms of acquaintanceships and friendships with legislators; the "informant," who prepares information to support a client's case; and the "watchdog," who monitors the calendar in order to alert a client.[27] Among journalists, Lex McKeithen divided Florida lobbyists into four basic categories: "Pocos," the little guys with idealistic clients; "Cosmos," the bigger guys whose clients—doctors, lawyers, and accountants—have plenty of money; "Full-Court Pressers," the powerful lobbyists who represent organized industries or professions—such as realtors and optometrists—who take their legislative involvement very seriously; and "Big Boys," who have relationships with legislative leaders and make good use of campaign contributions.[28]

While acknowledging that the styles of lobbyists are highly individualistic, dependent largely on a person's peculiar personality and unique experience, it is still useful to differentiate among them. McKeithen's categorization is helpful because it distinguishes lobbyists principally on the basis of the clients they represent. For us, that is key, since the principal difference that can be observed among lobbyists is with respect to their identity. Contract or independent lobbyists have their own individual identities; other lobbyists mainly take on the identities of the company, association, government unit, or cause that employs them.

For the contract lobbyist only, influence is primarily personal. Legislators can identify the lobbyist first and foremost, the issue next, and then the client. "Unless you have had a big fight," said a New Jersey lobbyist, "probably half of them do not even know who you represent." That is partly because a contract lobbyist's client base may change over time but mostly because lobbyists represent twenty, thirty, or more clients during the course of a legislative session. On a single day, the lobbyist may concentrate on one specific issue rather than on others. "Today, I'm wearing my Blue Cross/Blue Shield hat," a Colorado lobbyist commented. Or on a single day, the lobbyist may focus on several issues for various clients. For instance, another Colorado lobbyist had represented as many as four clients before noon on a day early in the session. Even in a single conversation with a legislator, a lobbyist may deal with different issues, and on behalf of different clients.

It is no wonder, then, that legislators can identify the lobbyist more easily than they can identify the group that has contracted the lobbyist's services. To further strengthen their identities, contract lobbyists are more likely than others to develop relationships with legislators by means of entertaining, socializing, and engaging in political activity. Their interests are personal, extending beyond any client's. Their well-being in the business of lobbying depends on their connections with legislators even more than on their ties to any client.

To say that a contract lobbyist has his or her own very personal identity is not, however, to specify its precise nature. There are the "good ole boys," whose modus operandi is the three Bs—bourbon, broads, and beefsteaks. These lobbyists are known also as the "old bulls." Their approach is that of the "fixer." They are also "full service" lobbyists because they try to take care of the various needs of legislators. Not many of them smoke cigars anymore, as Artie Samish of California did; but a New York lobbyist, James Featherstonhaugh, is still portrayed as a cigar-chomping lobbyist. His explanation is that, "We represent the cigar manufacturers, so we applaud cigar chomping."[29] This "good ole boys" breed is on the decline, although a few pure types are still extant. In the ascendant nowadays are the "good new boys (and girls)," who make greater use of information and analysis, facts, and figures, but whose entertaining is more circumscribed than that of their predecessors. Even among the new breed, there are varying types. Some lobbyists are flamboyant types like Maryland's Bereano, described as a "consummate stroker, holding doors open for people, patting them on the back, buying them drinks."[30] He welcomes publicity, as do many of his colleagues. Others in Maryland prefer quiet and privacy. In Texas Neal T. "Buddy" Jones was once described as "a fraternity man in the corridors of power" who "lobbies lawmakers like it was rush week." But Texas also had Rusty Kelley, low-key and friendly, Don Adams, who neither smoked nor drank, and Dick Brown, who dealt primarily in information.[31]

Association and company lobbyists, who are on the payroll of a single organization, are a very different lot from the people they refer to (somewhat derogatorily) as "hired guns." They are known by the companies that keep them, and not by who they are. IBM, Johnson & Johnson, the chiropractors, dentists, trial lawyers, and retailers all are more identifiable than the persons who handle state governmental relations for them. Take an AT&T lobbyist on the subject of entertaining legislators, for instance. The purpose, she points out, is for them to "get to know us better as a company and leave them with a feel-good sense of AT&T." That is not the purpose of entertaining done by contract lobbyists, who are intent on strengthening personal—not company—relationships.

Companies and associations are in it for the long term; their issues are around session after session. In-house lobbyists are loyal to those who employ them. They have to be. Company lobbyists have to concern themselves with top management, while association lobbyists have to please the officers, an executive board, and the general membership. Contract lobbyists have divided loyalties, to legislators as well as to clients. While they have to worry about their clients, they are not dependent on any one of them. Even more important to them than clients are legislators and their web of capital relationships, upon which they depend for cooperation, success, a reputation for effectiveness, and future clients.

Those who lobby for counties, cities, special districts, and governmental groups resemble the in-house association and company lobbyists in many respects. Their identities are a function of their governmental affiliations. Moreover, they are even weaker when it comes to political and social relationships. They do little entertaining, have no PACs, and do not play favorites, although they do evoke political constituencies consisting of local government officials. The style of their lobbying tends to be straightforward and straitlaced and not overtly political. There are exceptions, of course. A lobbyist for the Texas Municipal League was an example of a governmental lobbyist who was totally involved with the legislative process, had a distinct political personality, and operated in much the same way as the hired guns.

The cause lobbyists are the antithesis of contract lobbyists. Their identities are shaped by the causes they espouse—Common Cause and campaign-finance reform, PIRG and the environment, NARAL and choice on abortions, ACLU and the First Amendment. People who represent these groups tend, more than other lobbyists, to be true believers. As they see it, theirs is a fight for truth and justice. Often they disdain compromise. How can one compromise the environment! They are willing to go to the wall for their beliefs and are less concerned than others about relationships with legislators now or in the future. Instead, in the critical words of one who represents the other side, they are "armed with a bucketful of righteousness" and a file folder of editorials.

Most of these lobbyists prefer to pursue "outside" strategies. They favor conducting research and dealing with the press and are, in the words of one cause lobbyist, uncomfortable with buttonholing legislators and "in-your-face" lobbying. Their personality types are different from that of the hired guns. There are, of course, exceptions. The public interest lobbyists in Colorado have often played an inside game, in part because of their own personalities and in part because of the Colorado legislature's culture.

Some of the cause lobbyists, especially those working for fringe groups, are not well regarded by legislators. One such lobbyist, for example, tends to harangue legislators, as if her outpouring of words could turn the tide. For the most part, these lobbyists and groups rely on the correctness of their arguments, the press, and veiled and not-so-veiled threats that legislators will be punished at the polls. They fear being co-opted by the system, so they try to stay at arm's length. As a lobbyist in New Jersey explained: "One of the dilemmas in public interest lobbying is the more successful you become and the more you get included in the system, then the more people expect you to play by the rules of that system." And that was not what he would have wanted to do. There are exceptions here, too. The lobbyist for the Texas Consumers' Union was described as aware of "when to hold a press conference and when to go into the back room." He could play the inside game as well as the outside one. Yet, as James Q. Wilson has pointed out, whereas most organizations have to conserve access and influence for a variety of policies, a single-issue group does not have to.[32] And cause groups are less likely to do so.

CHAPTER 3

State Government Relations

The relationships between contract lobbyists and their clients (or "principals," as the groups that employ lobbyists are known) are mediated by the numbers of clients they represent and their distance from them. The in-house lobbyists, by way of contrast, have but a single "client" and little if any distance. These lobbyists are the executive directors, presidents, and employees of varied organizations that include labor organizations, trade groups, and corporations, among others. They were the first type of lobbyists to appear on the scene, at about the time when big business was becoming such an important part of the economy. According to Thomas and Hrebenar's studies, in-house lobbyists as a group account for about a third of all lobbyists.[1] These men and women are not hired guns, and they have considerably less freedom of action. Their relations with top management, boards of directors, and organization members therefore receive nearly as much of their attention as their efforts at lobbying the legislatures. For them, lobbying and communications are two-way streets.

In-house lobbyists who work for corporations refer to their profession as "state government relations" or "state government affairs." Their ranks include vice presidents for public affairs, directors, and managers in the case of companies, and presidents, vice presidents, and, more commonly, executive directors and government relations directors of associations. In this chapter, we shall explore the role of these professionals within their organizations rather than their activities in the legislature. Their externally oriented tasks of direct lobbying, grassroots lobbying, coalition building, public relations, and political action are all vital. But just as vital are their internally oriented tasks of interpreting organizational views, helping to fashion organizational policy, communicating to executives and members, developing the necessary capacity, and building support within for the state government relations function. We shall also examine how these in-house professionals seek outside assistance from contract lobbyists and the ways in which contract lobbyists, their in-house cousins, and organizational clients all interact. The discussion here will emphasize (but is not confined to) business and professional organizations—interests that are present and active in virtually all the states.

The Culture of the Corporation

Corporations vary tremendously in the support they provide for their state government affairs department. Much depends on the type of industry, the size of the company, and the public policy questions involved.[2] Some companies have particularly close relationships with state and local communities; the utilities, telephone, and gas and electric are examples. These kinds of companies devote substantial resources to government affairs and community relations. Their approach would appear to be "go along and get along." "We don't get excited over little annoyances," were the words of a telephone company lobbyist who is adept at cultivating legislators. "We love them all," he says, "We have no enemies." Any companies that are deeply affected by state regulations will tend to opt for involvement. Indeed, they cannot easily avoid it. Even top management of these businesses may spend time and energy on lobbying in the state.

Andrew Baker was chief executive officer of MetPath, a subsidiary of Corning Inc., which operated clinical laboratories across the nation. He explained to a group of in-house lobbyists, "We're at the mercy of regulation, so I spend roughly one-third of my time involved in governmental affairs."[3] The level of government doing the regulating also matters. The liquor industry offers an illustration. Beer is regulated at the state level, spirits primarily at the federal level. Beer companies are well organized for working in the states because they have to be. Among spirits companies, however, only Seagrams has its own state government relations capacity. The others rely on their trade associations.

Companies may see state government relations as a way to improve profitability; they may consider it a way to minimize government interference with the functioning of the market mechanism; or they may view it as a means of accommodating the interests of business to the wider society. There are a number of reasons for corporations to pay attention. Yet a large number would prefer to avoid involvement with state government if this were at all possible. Although top management feels obliged to make some effort, as a rule its heart is not really in it. This lack of support is evident to corporation lobbyists, relatively few of whom express satisfaction with the level of commitment demonstrated by management.

In the view of many chief executives and senior management there is little incentive to become involved in government affairs. Executives have many other obligations. Some shy away from lobbying altogether because of their distaste for government and especially legislatures. Others are willing to pay some attention to government relations at the federal level, where public officials have higher status and Washington offers hotels and restaurants that are good, although still far below the levels of those in New York. These executives suffer from the "Rose Garden syndrome."[4] IBM's Thomas Watson, Jr., recognized the need to cultivate politicians in person but concluded that the worst way to do so was with a Washington office staffed with professional lobbyists.[5] Nonetheless, IBM has succumbed; nowadays it has a Washington office with its cadres of federal and state government relations personnel.

Relatively few business leaders are involved at the state level. Albany, Sacramento, Tallahassee, and Trenton have little appeal, and state legislators are too peculiar a breed. Top management is structurally and dispositionally removed from the political fray and, for the most part, not very accessible to the corporation lobbyist, who is likely to report, instead, to a general counsel or deputy general counsel within the company's legal department or to a vice president for public affairs.

In order for companies to go about their business with as few regulatory restraints and as light a tax burden as possible, state governmental relations staff is expected to defend company turf. Few companies have the luxury of thinking proactively. Instead, theirs is a holding action aimed at keeping government at arm's length. It is important, therefore, for their agents to monitor the political environment, be aware of threats, and design suitable defenses. Emphasis is on *not* making mistakes. Company strategies therefore tend to be conservative and cautious.

Of those companies surveyed by the Conference Board some years ago, nearly half reported important interests in one state only; these included utilities and banks. Most of the remainder had an interest in fewer than five states. Three-quarters of the largest companies, however, had an interest in ten or more states.[6] Depending in part on the intensity and extent of their interests, these larger companies organized their state government relations function in different ways. Targeting a single state is comparatively easy to do—fewer choices have to be made. The person employed by the company to be responsible for lobbying can simply be based in, or spend considerable time at, the state capital. If necessary, he or she can be supplemented by another staff member or by a contract lobbyist.

Companies with substantial interests in a number of states, by contrast, have to decide how to cover them all. This is particularly true since most corporations have very small state governmental relations staffs. In this respect, MetPath's state government relations efforts are instructive. Like many other companies, MetPath first established its presence at the federal level. Then it had to decide how to achieve influence at the state level. The challenge for management was to get representation in the states without spending huge sums of money. First, MetPath had to identify key issues and states. Second, it had to hire someone to run the company's state government relations operation. Third, it needed to devise a strategy for monitoring legislation. Management therefore posed two questions: "What legislation will hurt us?" and "How do we get into the act early enough?" MetPath knew it would not be possible to monitor every state, so it decided to keep an eye on New York and California, bellwether states, and to a lesser extent Michigan, Illinois, and Massachusetts. The final task was to hire, on a retainer basis, contract lobbyists in the targeted states, bring them to the company headquarters in Teeterboro, New Jersey, and let them "see, touch, and feel" the business.

Small companies have to rely on contract lobbyists in selected states. Frequently, they will count on line management—plant and facility managers—to play a part in their lobbying campaigns. Larger companies usually employ regional state government relations professionals, as is the case with AT&T. The regional directors in turn may employ contract lobbyists. Larger companies also tend to have larger staffs in their headquarters—five or even ten professionals. Johnson & Johnson, for example, has had six full-time staff members in its government relations department. These people shoulder responsibility for all fifty states but concentrate on fewer than half. But the pharmaceutical giant's main interests are in New Jersey, which its in-house lobbyists handle, and about fifteen other states where contract professionals are hired on retainer or as the need arises.

Anheuser-Busch, which has about 45 percent of the American beer market, is headquartered in St. Louis, and offers another example of a company that takes state government relations quite seriously. It has brewing plants in eleven states and an in-house state affairs group is supplemented by a network of independent, or contract, lobbyists in every state capital.[7]

Companies with little or no in-house government relations staff rely on trade associations; business associations also are relied on, though to a lesser extent, to represent their interests. In an earlier study the Conference Board found that about one-fifth of the companies surveyed, primarily smaller firms, reported reliance on associations.[8] Larger corporations also use trade and business associations. If their interests are more extensive than their government affairs budgets, they will not be able to retain contract lobbyists wherever they may be needed. They therefore have little alternative but to look to their associations for representation. Johnson & Johnson, again, is illustrative. Although it has in-house capacity, it also operates in its home state through the New Jersey Chamber of Commerce, the New Jersey Business and Industry Association, and the New Jersey Health Products Company Group. It pays dues to industry associations in California, Illinois, Massachusetts, and other states. Nationally, it works through the Pharmaceutical Research and Manufacturers of America, the Health Care Industry Manufacturers' Association, and other groups.

Even if companies could lobby an issue on their own, on some matters they may prefer the cover provided by an association. A lobbyist for a telephone company, for instance, chose not to wage single-handed combat with the legislature on the issue of parental leave; he let the state business association handle it. "There is no sense," he explained, "in having a battle of Armageddon over this policy," despite the strong views management had on the issue. Another national corporation had opposed the sales tax on professional services, which was passed by the Florida legislature in 1987 and repealed shortly thereafter. But because this company did not want to be identified as a strong opponent, several associations served the company's interests and permitted it to remain in the background. Corporations that take strong positions on certain issues run the risk of a boycott of their products. The director of state government relations for a Minnesota bank summed up: "To the extent that the trade association can deal with common issues, we support the industry and don't lead the way." That attitude is not uncommon.

Inevitably, however, there will be times that companies need to act independently of their trade associations. A large Minnesota bank could not depend on its association, which was dominated by all the small banks that were members. A large liquor company, with its own line of wines, was leery of the Wine Institute, which it believed was driven by the Gallo company. Another national company had doubts about its trade association, which it thought represented the lowest common denominator of membership and, thus, reacted defensively to governmental change instead of seeking to shape it beforehand. These companies, and many more, use their associations but reserve the right to act independently.

The Organization of Associations

Although most companies cannot afford to put all their eggs in the association basket, business associations, which are multi-industry groups, and trade associations, which are single-industry groups, still play an important role in the representation of interests. A recent survey in which 260 companies responded found that 98 percent of them belonged to business associations and 99 percent belonged to trade associations.[9] Several groups represent broad business constituencies in each state. In California, for example, businesses have membership in the following state organizations: Chamber of Commerce, Manufacturers Association, Business Alliance, Council for Environmental and Economic Balance, and Taxpayers Association. In addition, in each state there are hundreds of trade associations of every conceivable variety. Florida, for instance, lists among other associations the following:

Air Conditioning Contractors	Financial Services
Air Transport	Home Builders
American Insurance	Independent Gas Dealers
American Pet Products	Independent Petroleum Producers
American Publishers	Industrial Cogeneration
American Service	Manufacturers
Auto Dealers	Marine Manufacturers
Bankers	Mortgage Bankers
Beer Wholesalers	Municipal Electric
Broadcasters	Pawnbrokers
Broker/Dealers	Property Owners
Cable TV	Realtors
Cemetery	Recreational Vehicle Trade
Chemical Industry Council	Rental Dealers
Community Bankers	Restaurants
Credit Management	Retail Grocers
Direct Selling	Rural Electric Cooperative
Electronic Industries	Securities Industry
Energy Pipeline	Transportation Builders
Entertainment and Dining	

Or take Texas, which has more than 350 associations with offices in Austin, including even a Texas Society of Association Executives (TSAE), whose members are paid to manage associations. "Whatever you can think of in your wildest imagination," stated TSAE's president, "there will be an association to represent it."[10] The array of associations with a lobbying presence in Tallahassee, Sacramento, and other state capitals is staggering. Small wonder, then, that lobbyists are abundant in the legislative halls.

Associational Bases

Some associations are state based, others operate out of Washington but have interests in most of the states. Among the latter is the American Petroleum Institute, which has a large Washington staff, including regional managers, as well as a year-round presence in two-thirds of the state capitals. A much smaller organization is the Direct Selling Association, consisting of about a hundred member companies such as Avon, Tupperware, and Shaklee. This association manages to cover all fifty states with three professionals traveling around the country from Washington, and without any contract lobbyists. Many of the association's members, however, have their own state government relations capacity. Another example of a Washington-based group is the seven-hundred-member International Franchise Association, which includes as members Dunkin' Donuts, I Can't Believe It's Yogurt, MacDonald's, 7-Eleven, and H&R Block. The association, which deals only on matters specifically related to franchises, employed three professionals to cover federal and international as well as state government relations. Still another example is the Food Marketing Institute, whose membership includes 1,500 supermarkets and grocery wholesalers (of whom half are single-store operators) and 21,000 retail food stores. FMI's members account for about half of all grocery sales in the United States.

Although they may have Washington connections, the vast majority of associations are indigenous to particular states. Their activities encompass more than legislation and lobbying, with much of the staff time spent on membership services and the dissemination of information. Among the myriad of associations with ten or so lobbyists are the New Jersey Business and Industry Association, the California Chamber of Commerce, and the Minnesota Chamber of Commerce. The principal trade associations in Austin, Texas, are the trial lawyers, doctors, realtors, and automobile dealers.

Certified public accountants are organized state by state throughout the country. Of the CPAs' fifty state societies, only a few lack lobbyists. In some the executive director lobbies; in others the lobbyist is the director of governmental relations; contract lobbyists do the job in a number of states; and in a few, volunteers do the lobbying. In each of these associations a board of directors or comparable body has the responsibility for deciding on legislation.

State teacher associations, which are affiliated with the National Education Association, are major players practically everywhere. The New Jersey Education Association exemplifies these organizations. It has eight full-time lobbyists, a director of government relations and seven associates, who have to advance the interests of 162,000 members.

Citizens or public interest groups are associations of a different type. They are relatively new interests on the lobbying scene, having formed and multiplied since about 1960. Liberal groups, working on issues such as environmental protection, consumer affairs, civic rights, equality for women, and the Vietnam War, constituted the first large wave. Conservative citizen lobbies—the Christian Coalition, the National Rifle Association, and taxpayer associations—constituted a subsequent, albeit smaller, wave.

Citizen groups differ in that their basis of organization is not built on the vocational, professional, or financial interests of its members, but rather on their political and policy beliefs. While these groups do not have a monopoly on articulating "public" interests, they do claim to represent interests that are not linked specifically to their members.[11]

An array of citizen groups is active in just about every state. Take Minnesota, for example. Environmental groups, organized in the Clean Water Action Alliance in 1994, are particularly influential. Abortion groups are lined up on both sides. The Minnesota Family Council is active on the right and the Minnesota Alliance for Progressive Action and the Children's Defense Fund are active on the left. Religious groups also are organized and use their influence in support of the disadvantaged population in the state.[12]

MASSPIRG and New Jersey PIRG are examples of the Public Interest Research Groups that exist in about half the states. These groups, inspired by Ralph Nader, are funded largely by the student activities fees collected by universities and colleges. They claim to represent the interests of citizens and consumers. MASSPIRG legislative goals have included mail-in voter registration, closing of nuclear power plants, and the more intensive testing of drinking water.[13]

Organizations representing the interests of local-government officials also have state-relations expertise for lobbying the legislature. The California County Supervisors Association, the Florida League of Cities, and the Texas Municipal League each have about a half-dozen lobbyists. By contrast, New Jersey had only one full-time lobbyist for the association of counties, in addition to the executive director, who lobbied part time.

The associations mentioned above are well endowed compared with most groups organized at the state level. The latter typically have just a single professional whose duties range widely. The California Children's Lobby is such a group. The organization's director not only tracks one hundred or so bills on child care, health and safety, and other issues, but she also monitors four different budgets in two state agencies and handles the group's press, workshops, and fund-raising. The Sierra Club is another group short on lobbyists, relying heavily on volunteers. But recently it has managed to engage at least part-time lobbyists for the legislative sessions in all the states.

Internal Politics

Although the state government relations directors of associations are outward looking, they cannot neglect cultivating internal relationships. They have to attend to the overall views of the membership, the role of committees with which they work, and the organization's leaders to whom they relate on a regular basis.

The policies of business associations are made by a board of directors, usually on the advice of a legislative affairs committee. On many issues the organization already has a position, so it is not necessary to revisit the organizational decision. On other issues a position has to be developed. Staff members have considerable say in the policy-making process. Typically, they will explore the issues that the committee and board will be deciding. What is the issue about? How does it affect members? Who will gain and who will lose? Who are the supporters, who are the opponents? Are there other ways of dealing with the problem? What are the options—support, oppose, change? What priority does the issue merit?[14] Within limits established by their board, staff members have considerable leeway in interpreting and implementing organizational policy. They will usually touch base with a certain committee or check out strategy periodically with the board of directors. But during the course of a legislative session, staff has—and requires—freedom to act and react to events without requesting approval. Bills and amendments that suddenly arise may be inimical to association interests. Therefore, a rapid response often is necessary.

Other associations do not differ fundamentally from the business groups in how they make policy and oversee the conduct of state government relations. For municipal and county associations, a board of directors or the executive committee normally establishes the position. The staff must then advance that position and be given a relatively free rein. A group such as PIRG operates in a similar manner. Its board determines policy, but the staff makes recommendations to the board and then has discretion in following through on the board's position. Teacher associations encourage the broadest involvement in the development of policy. Their delegate assemblies decide on the recommendations of committees (on pensions, finance, and so on). Then the government relations committee, which is made up of local representatives, takes over. It establishes legislative priorities and formulates an action campaign. Strategy and tactics are up to staff, but staff keeps the committee informed through bulletins, meetings, and other contacts.

Despite the flexibility they have in advising on and carrying out organizational policy, state government relations personnel must attend to the care and feeding of leaders and members, whose confidence in them is essential. In most associations, the elected leadership turns over regularly, requiring the director of state government relations (and/or executive director of the association) to build confidence among newly elected leaders on an annual basis. Sometimes that may mean that one's every move must be measured, as in the case of an executive director who lamented, "You have to ask leadership if you want to cross the street." But if the director cultivates younger members of the organization at an early stage, he or she will have won their confidence before they ascend to leadership posts.

In the words of a Texas lobbyist, "You quickly learn in trade association work that membership is the most important thing—an active, supportive membership is absolutely vital."[15] Yet, in many organizations, the major problem is the membership's indifference. If an association has lost too many battles, members may withdraw from any activity. And as strange as it may seem, occasionally members become indifferent because an association has lost too *few* battles. "I have a lot of trouble getting my board of directors' attention," commented the director of an association based in Washington, D.C., "because they have become complacent." Involvement would probably increase if the organization were to suffer a loss. If there is too little real interest, members cannot be mobilized and the potential power of a group cannot be harnessed and directed. That is why considerable time is spent communicating to members by newsletter, action brief, and special report. By personalizing issues, staff members have a better chance of persuading and mobilizing members.

For those predisposed to buttonholing legislators, it is frustrating to have to deal with key association members who do not understand the issues of politics. But that is what they must do. They have to return their phone calls and initiate calls of their own. Whenever possible, too, they will travel through the state, visiting with leaders in their home communities instead of waiting for scheduled meetings or relying on the telephone. Although staff has to educate members and persuade them that their participation makes a difference, they also have to refrain from raising their expectations unrealistically. Moreover, they must mediate between the self-interested and parochial views of the organization and the imperatives of the legislative process. This is especially true for the cause groups, whose leaders can demonstrate great zeal and intensity and may not adapt to the bargain-and-compromise patterns of legislatures.[16] For example, leaders of one California organization, wanting to maintain an inviolate image in the gay-lesbian community, view compromise as being synonymous with evil. Their lobbyist engaged in a continuing educational campaign to get his members to "understand how the process works and what is probable, feasible, and impossible."[17]

Lobbyists understand that the legislature deals in increments, not big bites; but members of their associations may want big bites. The state government relations staff of teacher associations provides a good example of this dynamic. One teachers' lobbyist described her challenge as getting the association to compromise. "I'm in the middle," she explained, "My job is to keep the two sides working together." There are times, in her opinion, when teachers have to be understanding, but there are also times when she cannot ask them to compromise. "There are not many showdowns, but they are well selected," is how she described the relationship between her association and the legislature.

When an association is united on an issue, the lobbyist's problem may be in restraining members. A bigger problem occurs, however, when an association's members cannot agree on issues because their interests diverge. The fact is that fragmentation and internal conflict are frequently natural conditions of organizational life. Industries are split. Local banks and those aspiring to regional or nationwide status do not coexist comfortably within a single association. Nor do industries that emit pollutants and those that manufacture environmental equipment. In the category of alcoholic beverages, one finds distilled spirits at odds with beer and wine.

Frequently, large organizations are unwieldy. For example, the California Chemical Council's membership is highly diverse, ranging from Dow to small companies, and this tends to make agreement on organizational policy difficult. Among Florida's retail food stores are Albertson's and Waldbaum's, each with more than two hundred stores, and about five hundred small, independent retailers. "Outside of taxes, this industry cannot agree on anything," declares one lobbyist in Tallahassee. A group like the CPAs ought to be homogeneous; but that is not the case. Accountants differ in the services they provide. They differ in where they work; half the members work in industry, while the other half are in independent accounting firms. The latter are split between those in large firms and those in small ones. The horse-racing industry of Kentucky is divided, with the major horse breeders, owners, and trainers having different interests than the smaller ones.[18]

The oil industry, which is organized into state petroleum councils, may seem strong, but it is actually weak in all but the few states where oil is produced. Its members are a diverse lot, who are not affected similarly by the issues. The major companies have interests that differ from the smaller refiners. Likewise, the refiners and jobbers frequently have opposing interests. Service-station dealers have their own views on franchises, hours of operation, and rents, as do the oil companies. Because of their present image, the majors cannot take the lead on any issue, although they try to have their interests represented by other council members. In view of its fragmentation, the oil industry simply cannot define a course. "We're always on the verge of being neutralized," is how one petroleum council lobbyist described the industry's plight. In one state, oil faces a major fight, but the industry is so internally divided that even with a number of top-flight lobbyists in their employ they can do nothing. The lobbyists themselves are frustrated, waiting for marching orders. In the opinion of one of those involved, "it is like running with a bungee cord tied to your legs." Although citizens perceive oil interests to be large and powerful, at the state level the industry tends to be an ineffectual giant.

Also illustrative of fractionated groups are the associations of county and municipal government officials. The Texas Municipal League represents all the state's cities, but on certain issues Austin and Houston and Dallas will each go its own way. In New Jersey the split is between urban and suburban municipalities or urban and suburban counties, and also between the northern and southern parts of the state. The internal divisions of Maryland's association of counties reflect the differing legislative structures and roles within each of the state's twenty-four counties. That leads to varying local-state relationships, with members bringing substantially different perspectives to their association.

Such heterogeneity and lack of cohesion among members are burdensome for the staff of an organization and limit the organization's effectiveness. In order to achieve a consensus, some associations will adopt positions that reflect the lowest common denominator of membership views; or they address the issues in the broadest, most general terms so that exception will not be taken. If associations go too far in one direction or another, they risk losing members. Cigarette companies, for instance, pulled out of the New Jersey Business and Industry Association because of its support for antismoking legislation. (They later came back in.)

Another possibility is stalemate, whereby the association tries to adopt a position but simply cannot because it is internally rent. Among New Jersey's convenience stores, for instance, members who did not sell gas tended to support legislation authorizing self-service gas stations. Others, who sold gas but would have been at a disadvantage competing with the large service stations, were opposed. Their association could not take a position because of the split. On another issue, Public Service Electric and Gas Company backed a bill that would have taxed cogenerators, but most other members of the New Jersey Business and Industry Association were opposed. The association could not take a position. Indeed, it rarely took a position that favored one segment of its membership over another.

Contracting Out

Even companies and associations with in-house state government relations staff contract out to independent lobbyists for a good deal of the work. In this regard, the in-house professionals have the job of determining whether, when, and where contract lobbyists are required; employing them; and overseeing and assessing their work.

The Benefits of Employing Contract Lobbyists

The use of outside lobbyists has grown over the years, particularly among business companies and associations, but also among other groups as well. Indeed, some in-house lobbyists do not lobby directly anymore, but rather oversee contract lobbyists who do the job for them. The reasons are several.

First, as we noted earlier, a national company or association may have a small staff and still have to cover many or all of the states. It will therefore allocate a percentage of the state relations budget for hiring independent lobbyists. Companies and associations within a single state may also seek outside help because their own staff is spread thin. Societies of

CPAs (for instance, the one in Florida) do all the lobbying themselves. Many of the smaller societies, however, use contract lobbyists because their executive directors cannot carry the load.

Second, outsourcing has become fashionable in many aspects of company operations. Lobbying is merely one of them. The objective is to keep the staff and the central budget smaller—or at least to have it appear smaller.

Third, even if in-house capacity exists, it may lead, not to self-reliance, but to seeking outside support. According to the Conference Board survey, the more state-relations professionals in a company, the greater the likelihood it will hire contract lobbyists.[19] This is partly because the size of the in-house staff reflects the company's or the association's acknowledgment of how important lobbying can be. Thus, the more—up to a point—the more.

Fourth, a presence in the state capital is desirable, if not requisite. "It helps," said one state-relations professional from Washington, D.C., "if you live with them [legislators] and drink with them." Not all national organizations are situated in the U.S. capital, nor are all single-state organizations in the state capital. Again, the CPAs provide an example. Most state societies are located in the capital; a few are not. The Florida society used to be in Gainesville; but the CPAs decided this made no sense. "We'd better be located where the action takes place," was the feeling expressed by one lobbyist. So the society moved and took up quarters two blocks from the capitol building in Tallahassee. The in-house lobbyists, who "parachute in" when the legislature is in session, are at a great disadvantage, not possessing the kind of relationships and trust with legislators and their staffs that residential lobbyists develop. Moreover, by the time they arrive, the informal process is well advanced and the outcome may already be determined. Someone has to be on the scene all, or most, of the time.

Fifth, contract lobbyists are not only on the spot, but they are also usually in the fray. By way of contrast, state government relations professionals tend to be more aloof and distant, sometimes taking on the semblance of bureaucrats. Independent lobbyists have greater standing as individuals and potentially greater influence. Indeed, as one state government relations professional observed, "Sometimes you need a well-connected lobbyist so that legislators will take you seriously." Retaining a hired gun signals the client's concern; the act resembles anteing up in a game of poker.

Sixth, if a state is critical for a national organization, it will require and retain counsel there. If an issue arises where no one is on retainer, the organization will employ a lobbyist on an as-needed basis and for the issue's duration. In New Jersey, for example, a proposal was introduced to ban the manufacture and sale of plastic tampon applicators because they washed up with other garbage on the beaches. Although it had its own staff, International Playtex hired two contract lobbyists in Trenton to kill the legislation. The latter devised the strategy and led the assault, while company staff provided knowledge of the interest involved and, of course, paid the bill.

The disadvantage of engaging an independent lobbyist is that the principal loses much of its identity. Although the group may win in the short term, it has built little equity in the longer term. Some state government relations professionals therefore conclude that they have to do the lobbying themselves. This entails developing relationships with legislators, offering testimony, and establishing, insofar as possible, an organizational presence and, hence, an organizational identity.

Managing Contract Lobbyists

Once an organization decides to employ an independent lobbyist to represent its interests in a state, the government relations staff is then responsible for recruiting the individual. If they are not familiar with the state, they may employ on a consultative basis firms such as MultiState Associates or Stateside Associates, which have contacts throughout the nation. These firms, which were established in the late 1980s, are headquartered in the Washington, D.C., area. They work for a fee, helping companies locate lobbyists in particular states and tracking issues for them. Their clients are trade and professional associations and corporations. Multi-States, for example, has a network of 1,500 lobbyists throughout the United States. State government relations personnel also have their own networks by virtue of their company's or association's membership in groups like the Public Affairs Council (PAC) or the State Government Affairs Council (SGAC). It is not difficult, by working through these councils to obtain recommendations concerning contract lobbyists, examine the lobbyists' client lists, check out reputations, and even interview several candidates.

Throughout the process the staff members must have in mind just what kind of lobbyist is needed for the task at hand. A former legislator? One of high or low visibility? A good ole boy or one of the new breed? And so forth. An organization's reputation is shaped in part by that of the lobbyist it hires. Putting one of the most influential contract lobbyists on the payroll can provide instant status to an interest group. That may not be what a group has in mind, in which case one of the newer, less political lobbyists may be preferable. And there is always the problem of having to share time with a contract lobbyist's other clients, as was pointed out by a staff member of a Washington-based association: "The bigger the contract lobbyist, the more likely they have bigger clients. They have conflicts. And when push comes to shove, your interests get lost." From the point of view of the contract lobbyist, "You have to conserve chits; you can't use all your bullets." That means that not every client's interests can be represented equally, and certainly not at the same session.

In many cases—particularly in the more partisan states—a choice has to be made about employing someone with mainly Democratic or Republican contacts. A bank in Minnesota, for instance, retained a lobbyist with a Democratic background because it already had standing with the Republicans. The Greater Miami Opera first hired a lobbyist with Democratic credentials to lobby the Florida legislature. After a member of the opera board suggested hiring a Republican close to Governor Bob Martinez, a second lobbyist was also employed.

Clearly, the more lobbyists, the more bases can be covered. Some interests therefore hire several lobbyists to represent them year-round. Others hire multiple lobbyists to represent them on key issues, which usually involve fights between large companies or industries. In Texas they are known euphemistically as "bluebird" issues (as in the "bluebird of happiness") because so many contract lobbyists are employed on one side or the other, usually at substantial fees, resulting in happiness for them. Electricity deregulation, which was on state legislative agendas in 1998 and 1999, witnessed the employment of many lobbyists. For example, twenty-five registered lobbyists were working for Northeast Utilities on deregulation in Connecticut.

This large-scale lobbying gives rise to what is called "team lobbying," with five, ten, or more professionals on each side. Team lobbying permits a high degree of specialization. That is to say, the more lobbyists working an issue, the better the contact with members of the legislature. One lobbyist has close contacts in the senate, another in the house. One has an in with Republicans, another with Democrats. One knows the speaker well. Another has a long-standing relationship with the chairman of the standing committee that has jurisdiction. An African American lobbyist may have better access to African American members, and a female lobbyist may have greater rapport with women members.

Certain issues have generated battles between lobbying teams throughout the states. Tort reform and product liability, which involve business on one side and trial lawyers on the other, are such issues. Another fight between teams involves car-rental companies, with Hertz and Avis against Alamo and other smaller companies. The main issue here is that Alamo and its allies depend on collision damage waivers (CDW) for a large percentage of their business.[20] Hertz and Avis support legislation that would restrict the CDW practice, thus hurting their competitors. Although the fight has been waged in many states, perhaps the biggest battle was in Florida, Alamo's home base. Almost fifty lobbyists were involved, including a team of eighteen working exclusively for Alamo. Dayton-Hudson's contract-lobbyist law firm had fifteen lobbyists representing the company's interests on legislation that would have prevented a hostile takeover. One reason for hiring these lobbyists was so that they would not sign up with the opposition.

Team lobbying is used, to some extent at least, practically everywhere. But it is a prominent part of the legislative environment in Texas, where it came into style in the 1980s. In the period since, the automobile manufacturers have hired several lobbyists to pass a seatbelt law. Then, tort reform and product liability engaged the services of a number of Austin's top guns, who were retained by the Texas Civil Justice League. One session of the Texas legislature found AT&T pitted against U.S. Sprint and MCI, with thirteen lobbyists signed up on one side and twelve on the other.

A major battle was fought between Texaco and Pennzoil. Texaco came into Texas first and hired every major lobbyist in Austin but one; Pennzoil hired him. Before it was over, about twenty-five contract lobbyists were on the payrolls of the two companies. One prominent lobbyist commented in retrospect, "It was almost an insult not to be hired." Another remembered the experience clearly, "That was the biggest fee I ever made in my life." The lobbyists on each side would meet together regularly to compare notes and update strategies. "It was a zoo," recalled one of them, "like the bar scene in *Star Wars*."

Surely for those who do it, team lobbying has payoffs. Indeed, it has been labeled the "Lobbyists' Full Employment Act." And it may also be fun for lobbyists to share campaigns with colleagues, engaging in a form of lobbyist bonding. Given the connections each lobbyist brings to the enterprise, it can be effective as well, although one side can cancel out the other. Questions have been raised, however, about whether team lobbying has gone too far in Texas. Given the number of power-broker lobbyists involved, an issue may be receiving too high a profile. Furthermore, the amount of money being spent in fees may leave a bad taste in the mouth of the press and public. Under such circumstances, team lobbying may become counterproductive.

Once companies and associations contract with lobbyists, they can choose either to direct and monitor their efforts closely or to trust in their competence and take a good deal on faith. The relationship varies by lobbyist and client. If a lobbyist has worked for a client long enough, a relationship of mutual confidence is likely to have developed, and the need for frequent contact lessens. Some clients are more politically astute than others and want to be involved, and the lobbyist acquiesces. The more bills clients have at stake, too, the more involved they are apt to be. Obviously, companies or associations that are located out of state have to limit their involvement. Their in-house lobbyists may want to be kept informed, but they are rarely on the scene. It is not likely that they will try to micromanage, and even less likely that they will be able to do so.

The situation tends to differ when the relationship between lobbyist and client is new. One of New Jersey's top independent lobbyists described his approach with a new client:

> We sit down in a room with a prospective client and we explain what our staff capabilities are. We first advise them on how we will handle the issue, on who will handle the account, and on who will take the lead. Then we try to get a feel for where the minefields will be and what resources we have to work with. Next, we break it down legislatively according to where our strengths and weaknesses are going to be.

Sometimes a company's concern is so great that top management involves itself in orienting a new contract lobbyist. That was the case with a bill, which was being pushed by Anheuser-Busch, to change Florida's regulations governing how beer companies conducted business with their distributors. Augustus Busch himself brought a Tallahassee lobbyist to St. Louis to tell him how important it was to the company. After that, it was up to the lobbyist to get the bill passed, and he managed to do so.

One of the principal jobs of the contract lobbyist is that of lobbying the client. "Communicating," "educating," "explaining" is how contract lobbyists describe their efforts. They keep track of what is happening, alert their clients to developments, and propose strategies of response or adaptation.[21] One Massachusetts lobbyist described his job: "I spend 90 percent of my time lobbying my clients, and 10 percent legislators." The job requires helping the clients figure out what they want, and what they can realistically expect to get. "The biggest hurdle is to convince your clients what is doable," explains the Massachusetts lobbyist. "Your position, A, won't sell. B, however, is possible. But, if you want a sure thing, go to C." That kind of talk is often necessary. Typically, the client wants to win, while the lobbyist realizes the value of compromise. One lobbyist described the fight between the engineers and the architects over professional turf:

> The engineers, who were one of our clients, would not compromise or change the bill that they wanted. We got the bill passed by both houses. . . . It was a crazy bill. They were lashing back at the architects, who they thought had wronged them.

The governor vetoed the bill. The lobbyist went back to the engineers and asked them to compromise. They finally agreed. But they could have held out and said, "We're paying you good money to get what we want done, and not what you want done." That would have been unfortunate for the client-lobbyist relationship.

Compromise is a major tool of a lobbyist trying to get a job done and to stay in the game to play another day. Those who depend on their relationships with legislators would much rather work things out so that everyone wins something and no one loses too much. The question, as posed by one lobbyist, is "When do you shoot the bullets?" The answer for most contract lobbyists is "As seldom as possible." And given the legislative process, that is not only in the interest of the lobbyist but probably of the client as well.

CHAPTER 4

The Interests at Stake

S tudying the individuals who lobby, and their strategies and tactics, is certainly important. But "without an adequate understanding of the interests involved," as political scientist Robert Salisbury writes, "an analysis of institution, process, or policy choice will not get it right."[1] In line with Salisbury's advice, in this chapter we shall look more closely at the interests at stake, the issues involved, and the conflicts that arise.

Issues Big and Small

State government today makes major public policy decisions. These are no longer the exclusive province of the federal government. State legislatures have therefore come to play an increasingly important role. In the past, major state policy was mainly the prerogative of governors; no longer. The distribution of taxes and tax rates, interstate banking, education reform, school funding, highways and mass transit, sentencing and prisons, Medicaid cost containment, economic development, electric deregulation, and workers' compensation all are on the legislative agendas of the states.

Take the agenda for legislatures in the fifty states during the 1999 session. Health was the most active policy domain that year, with 37,270 bills introduced and 6,231 enacted. Education came in second, with 21,997 introductions and 3,380 enactments, followed by transportation with 17,855 introductions and 3,030 enactments. Legislative activity in the environmental area had declined from earlier years to 8,201 bills introduced and 1,433 enacted.[2]

There are also the so-called hot issues, emotional and moral questions that arouse special furor among competing groups and make legislators particularly uncomfortable. Abortion is the most obvious "hot" issue at present. But gun control, the death penalty, sex education, pornography, home schooling, and the use of animals in research are others. Such issues bring out groups that range from feminists and liberals on one end of the spectrum to the religious right and conservatives on the other, including such diverse groups as sportsmen, animal-rights advocates, and the pharmaceutical industry.

The important issues mentioned above constitute some of the agenda of major items addressed by the legislatures of the fifty states. But other issues—and hundreds of other bills—are not major by any stretch of the imagination. How many of the 5,418 bills introduced in the 1996 and 1997 regular and special sessions of the California legislature were important statewide? Of the 1,229 introduced in Colorado, the 5,132 in Florida, the 6,742 in Minnesota, and 5,561 in Texas, how many had significant implications for public policy? The answer is, relatively few. Even among these enacted—2,136 in California, 683 in Colorado, 853 in Florida, 433 in Minnesota, and 1,487 in Texas—few had policy significance.[3]

Many of these bills are relatively inconsequential and do not attract the attention of any group. More "housekeeping" than anything else, they are introduced in response to a request by an administrative agency. Or they are sponsored by legislators to please constituents of no organizational hue. Beyond these, many others are promoted (and/or opposed) by interest groups, managed by lobbyists, and introduced by legislators on their behalf. A contract lobbyist in Texas categorized the legislation introduced at a typical session: about 100 had statewide implications and perhaps an additional 100 had impact on members' districts. "Another 4,800 don't appear on my radar screen at all," he said. From the perspective of statewide policy, these bills are minor; but from the perspective of one group or another, they are of tremendous import.

Generally, one-third to one-half the bills addressed by a legislature relate to "private" or "special interest" issues, but they will be debated in public policy terms. These bills have only indirect relevance, however, to statewide policy. Although most everything has public policy ramifications, they primarily affect the welfare or pocketbooks of various business and professional groups. These interests try to manipulate the regulatory environment or defend themselves against or gain ground from their rivals by seeking state intervention favorable to their cause. For every group looking for some advantage, some other group is resisting being taken advantage of. Moreover, if evidence of some abuse is brought to the surface, executive and legislative officials will seek to impose a remedy on their own.

Like individuals, groups have the constitutional right to petition their government. (Government, of course, does not have to give them what they petition for.) One contract lobbyist summed up as follows: "Frankly, the legislature in New Jersey exists for the lobbyist." What he meant was that the governor wanted five or six bills a year, legislators wished for one each, and the rest were desired by lobbyists and the interests they represented. "The fact is," he said, "that we are here because it is our right to be here." Lobbyists and their clients are the "squeaky wheels"; they expect to get the grease.

There is no way for groups to ignore the legislature entirely. The impact on interests large and small is too great. Corporations and associations can be affected by many of the bills that are introduced. A public utility company, such as gas or electric, is affected by almost anything government does. It is a big taxpayer, so a change in tax policy can be critical. Moreover, there are times when electricity issues are in the forefront as was deregulation in the 1998 and 1999 sessions. Millions of dollars were at stake for manufacturers, independent power producers, and public utilities, while environmental and consumer groups had their own concerns.

Take the situation of the nation's cemeteries and crematoriums. They are being challenged by those who question whether buried bodies could contaminate underground water or if cremation could be a source of toxic air pollutants. The umbrella group representing the interests of crematoriums expressed concern because some states had environmental laws that lumped crematoriums together with other incinerators; that did not make sense. The issue for cemeteries and/or funeral directors was that just as cremation was becoming popular (it is used in about 26 percent of deaths), it began to suffer from antipollution laws. And the laws differed significantly from state to state.

The 2000–2001 agenda of the New Jersey Business and Industry Association (NJBIA) is illustrative of the breadth of some agendas. The association took a position of either support or opposition in ten policy areas. On issues of labor relations and human resources, it backed a few measures and lined up against a few others. On the environment, it supported three bills and opposed three more. On health care, it supported three and opposed five, and on economic development and taxation, it supported four and opposed two. In the regulatory domain NJBIA endorsed six measures and in education it endorsed five. It took positions on one bill in each of the following areas: transportation, solid waste, energy, and government.

The executive director for the retail food association in one state pointed out that members were required to identify, label, and announce everything on their shelves. "We have more damned laws that require signs," she complained. "We are being regulated to death." New legislation can be overwhelming, as is frequently the case with the insurance industry. A lobbyist for a large company noted that at one annual session, the Florida legislature passed 140 measures affecting his company. He observed that "It will take the company six months to figure the legislation out. It will take the legislature a year to figure it out. But we'll have to start complying in two months." It is little wonder that business thinks it is under siege. Nor is relief in sight.

Legislative agendas are by no means confined to the business sector. Professional associations are also heavily affected. Certified public accountants, for instance, have a proprietary interest in educational requirements and the accountancy laws that license CPAs. They range further afield, alert to many other issues that can affect their profession—sales taxes on services, investment advisor regulations, real-estate-appraisal regulations, and legal liability and tort reform. Teacher organizations are also enmeshed in the process, depending as they do on the legislature for salaries and benefits, conditions of work, and collective-bargaining negotiations. Although teacher concerns are very focused, much that comes before the legislature can affect teachers and the schools. In Colorado, for example, of about six hundred bills introduced in one session of the legislature, about seventy-five had implications for education, including one that would have abolished tenure.

Organizations of local public officials also have their hands full with all the bills introduced in the typical legislature. The Texas Municipal League attends to more than a thousand bills during a typical session, not just monitoring them, as one lobbyist explains, but "really trying to screw with them." The County Supervisors Association of California has to pay attention to anywhere from two thousand to three thousand introductions during a session.

Keeping Track

The lobbyists' mill gets its grist in all sorts of ways. A few issues will come up once and then vanish from the scene. Many have been around for ages, however, and continue to crop up, year after year. Rarely can a group fold up its tent on the assumption that "this issue is won, let's move on to the next one." There is always the next session. Every bill that failed the previous year tends to be prefiled again, almost as a matter of course. An issues manager for one of the country's large insurance companies stressed that "issues tend not to go away; issues are around forever." This is because one or both sides are never fully satisfied with an outcome. Issues may be redefined as time passes, but in the struggle among groups, they are never truly resolved.

Initiating Issues

Many issues are brought to the fore by a business or professional association in an effort to maximize advantage for itself or its members. Sometimes an industry will appeal for state regulation in order to eliminate the varying local regulations. Polystyrene as a packaging material had been banned by local authorities in a number of New Jersey municipalities. Because the industry lacked resources to contest the issue town by town, it tried to get preemptive legislation. The tobacco industry also sought to have the legislature preempt local authority to limit smoking. That is because the antismoking movement has a great advantage at the local level, and, in the words of one journalist, "city and county councils are passing local restrictions faster than the tobacco industry can count them."[4]

A number of initiatives come from the many cause-oriented groups. The environmentalists have been particularly effective in raising issues that lobbyists and their clients have been forced to confront. In addition, the issues will never be completely settled for the environmental groups; the cause and the issues are their raison d'être.

Despite the intense involvement of various interest groups, however, it is incorrect to think that public officials merely respond to lobbyist initiatives. Governors, other state officials, and legislators raise issues of their own and take leadership in steering their passage. They have their own agendas, which are related to, but still independent of, those of business, labor, teachers, environmentalists, and the rest. Indeed, the more crucial the matter, the more important the role of public officials.

Upon taking office, New Jersey Governor Jim Florio proposed a restructuring of automobile rates. Insurance reform had been a promise of his campaign for governor the year before. The New Jersey Business and Industry Association opposed the shifting of costs that the legislation entailed. A Maryland securities commissioner initiated legislation that would have required CPAs to register and be regulated as financial planners. The local society fought the proposal. Minnesota's commissioner of commerce and attorney general undertook to regulate mortgage bankers. Predictably, the mortgage bankers fought back. A New Jersey state senator for some years pushed an ethics code for local government officials. The New Jersey League of Municipalities expressed concern and did all that it could to waylay what it considered to be an unworkable plan, and one that would make life difficult for local public officials.

However issues arise, chances are that they will spread from one state to another. Solid waste, hazardous waste, recycling plastics all make the calendars of more than a few legislatures. Until recently, the bottle bill, which required that consumers pay a deposit on cans and bottles, was an issue that had traveled widely. It has been enacted as a recycling measure in a number of states but is now relatively dormant in others. As Common Cause succeeds with campaign-finance reform in certain places, its chapters elsewhere press especially hard, and especially in states that allow for the initiative, whereby voters through petition can place an issue on the ballot.

Legislation tends to spread like wildfire because legislators today travel out-of-state to meetings and discussions sponsored by the National Conference of State Legislatures, the Council of State Governments, and other organizations. Legislators have their antennae out, constantly on the lookout for bills to introduce when they get home. Moreover, national organizations of public officials themselves suggest legislation by adopting model laws. For example, a Model Franchise Investment Law was adopted by the North American Securities Administrators Association. The next year, with the backing of state securities commissions, that proposal was introduced in several states. Public officials in one state will discuss possibilities with those in another. "What did you do? How much flack did you take?" they ask. If the answers are satisfactory, then they go for it.

Monitoring Issues

Given the numbers of bills introduced and the pace of legislative activity, how do lobbyists and state government relations staff keep track of what is going on? The answer is, not easily. Nevertheless, tracking legislation is a large part—and perhaps the largest part—of what lobbyists do. In-house lobbyists and hired guns alike must be on the lookout for any bill that might affect their organization or client. One hundred, two hundred, or five hundred bills may need watching, although fewer are likely to have significant impact, and even fewer are likely to get very far. The lobbyist has to have a sense of whether a bill is going to move and whether it can go anywhere. A specialist in solid-waste management and government relations likened four thousand or so pieces of legislation to icebergs. Some can be nudged and they move away. "Others," he noted, "have a great deal of ice under them and can sink your boat if you're not careful." The image is apt. Legislation must be navigated with caution.[5]

State government relations professionals, who are not resident at the state capital, have to range widely in order to keep up with legislation that may affect their organization's interests. They subscribe to multistate computerized information services, use their network of colleagues, and touch base with other organizations and associations. If they have contract lobbyists in specific states, they naturally depend on them for timely information.

The sheer volume of legislation makes tracking by computer particularly welcome. Most large companies and associations have in the past subscribed to one of the two major tracking services, the Commerce Clearing House and Public Affairs Information. With key words and phrases provided by clients, bills on subjects of interest could be identified and followed.[6] Procter & Gamble, for instance, used Public Affairs Information. It received and reviewed about three thousand bills a year, taking a position on two hundred to three hundred of them, while following another six or seven hundred.[7] But before the computer age, monitoring was a hit-or-miss proposition. It is now far easier to keep up with bills and amendments. And computer-generated tracking information can be supplemented from other sources—association members, other associations, legislator allies, or lobbyists looking for business.

Some associations have developed their own computerized systems. Associated Industries of Florida (AIF) developed one of the most advanced monitoring systems, which members and even nonmembers were able to use for a fee. Subscribers could search for key words and phrases and get a list of bills on the topic. AIF did not track every single bill, but more than 80 percent of bills introduced were tracked routinely.

The Internet, of course, has enabled lobbyists to find out quickly about issues emerging from practically anywhere.[8] "If you're not on the Net in this day and age," said Eric Rabe of Bell Atlantic, "you might as well be working out of a cave." In the past, lobbyists had to depend on clipping services for information. Now they are privy to the communications among groups and their e-mail alerts. It is possible to monitor Web sites, chat rooms, e-mail services, and other Internet sources. An Internet-based, password-protected service is being provided for members by the Ohio Chamber of Commerce. It identifies bills that are of importance to its members and notifies them by e-mail whenever the bill is being considered. A chamber member can search for a bill, check its status, see the chamber's position and comments, and can even e-mail the chamber or lobbyist with additional questions. The Ohio chamber's members do not have to track down their lobbyists. "We've used our Web site to bottle those lobbyists, capture information and put it online," explained the chamber's communications director.

Lobbyists on the spot will try to identify bills of importance to clients as early as possible. Sometimes they can access everything on the legislature's computer system. Their job is to anticipate who has a stake in particular issues; and when, where, and how they are likely to push them. They are on the lookout for early-warning signs regarding crucial bills. "You have to have your ear to the ground," advises one contract lobbyist in Trenton. The worst thing that can happen is for lobbyists to be surprised by an issue they never thought would arise. But at every session each lobbyist is caught off guard by a bill or two. Inside sources are useful. One lobbyist visits a contact in the state attorney general's office to find out what issues will be coming up in his field. Another useful practice is to watch for indicators. For example, when Hertz started to hire a cadre of heavy-duty lobbyists in Tallahassee, Alamo knew an assault on its interests might be imminent.

In addition to preliminary screening, lobbyists monitor the course of legislation after it is introduced. Although they may have computer systems to assist them, most lobbyists at the capitol have a hands-on monitoring operation. A Florida lobbyist describes his procedure:[9]

1. Preliminary screening
   - Reviews titles in presession interim calendars or journals.
   - Examines various legislative sources.
   - Watches for alerts by associations, legislators, legislative staff, and other lobbyists.
   - Checks with committee staff.
2. Review
   - Reads titles and summaries of printed bills.
   - Studies full text of bills on pertinent subjects.
   - Checks with clients for review and comments.

Moreover, when lobbyists are monitoring areas, their concerns are made known and legislators, legislative staff, and colleagues may alert them to noteworthy developments.

Lobbyists not only have to figure out which bills affect their clients, but they also have to determine priorities. How great an effect is a bill likely to have? What are the chances of its enactment? What should a client's position be? And what action should be taken? If a lobbyist has determined that a number of issues affect a client organization, then he needs to decide what action, if any, to take on each. A Colorado lobbyist's rule of thumb is, "If it's going the way my client wants it to go, I stand back." A state government relations professional for a large New Jersey company says he makes careful calculations about when to intervene. Otherwise, he says, effort is wasted on legislators who can say: "We gave you that one, so we cannot give you this one." Lobbyists need to have a precise understanding of when to lobby an issue and how far to go with it.

It is said in legislative circles that there are bills for "show," bills for "go," and bills for "no." The first group of bills is introduced by legislators but no one expects them to go anywhere. The second group includes those that the lobbyist wants to get enacted. The third group comprises legislation the lobbyist wants to defeat. Many more bills fall in the third category than in the other two, particularly as far as business groups are concerned. Business is more apt to be on the defensive, its lobbyists constantly alert to bills that will impose taxes, regulations, or other hardships. Years ago, Zeigler and Baer noted that business lobbyists were inclined to define their role as one of stopping "bad bills" rather than pushing for passage of "good bills."[10] More recently Hamm and his associates, in a study of California, Iowa, and Texas, found that although groups generally were more likely to support than oppose legislation, business was the least proactive.[11]

The business community's major objective is to be left alone. It wants to keep state government from restricting its freedom of action. Whether fat and happy or lean and mean, business does not want government on its back (although it will appeal to government for subsidies of various sorts).

Several examples illustrate the defensive posture taken by business. First, the liquor industry is in trouble because of the health and sobriety attitudes now pervading American society. It is also facing serious liability issues and feels it is being taxed to death. A Minnesota lobbyist who represents liquor put it this way: "They pound on you time and time again. It is futile to try to make major gains. I try to keep [the industry] from being destroyed." The tobacco industry is in worse shape, having been hurt severely by various bans on smoking in public places and increasing excise taxes. For tobacco lobbyists, too, the game is almost entirely a defensive one.

A giant company, which operates in Minnesota as well as elsewhere, is principally concerned with workplace issues. According to its contract lobbyist the Minnesota legislature is trying to solve social problems by regulating the workplace with respect to such issues as parental leave, drug testimony, and privacy. His job for this client is to keep government from interfering.

Contract lobbyists spend much of their energy defensively because most of their clients are from the ranks of business. A veteran New Jersey lobbyist estimates that about 70 percent of his work is defensive, and much of that involves monitoring legislation. A Florida lobbyist characterized his job as trying to protect the people he represents. "If nothing comes up," he says, "it's a victory."

Business is not the only group that wants to manage its own affairs without interference. Professional groups also want to limit government involvement, although they, too, depend on government for laws and regulations that benefit them. The certified public accountants were taken by surprise when Georgia passed a law requiring those who provided financial-planning services to register as investment advisers. The regulatory movement spread to other states because the financial planners, in order to professionalize, wanted to be regulated. The CPAs were already regulated. They claimed they provided only generic advice and sought an exemption in the law, but state securities commissioners resisted. The issue put the accountants on the defensive.

County and local governments would like a larger share of state revenues, or at least the ability to raise some revenue on their own; otherwise, they too want to be left alone. In California about a third of the bills introduced in a session affect county government. Most of them require a defensive posture by the association of county supervisors in an effort to "protect ourselves from the state's intrusion in our lives." The problem with the legislature, according to the Florida League of Cities, is its disposition to give employee benefits, particularly pensions, that entail delayed costs to the cities. In the view of one in-house lobbyist, "the legislature runs out of money before it runs out of good ideas." Although money is not the primary issue in Texas, the situation is similar. The Texas Municipal League's emphasis is mainly defensive. In a typical session of the legislature, it tries to get about twenty-five bills passed and about a thousand killed. "If we didn't pass a single thing and nothing bad passed," said one league lobbyist, "we would have a good session."

Given the nature of the legislative process, it is ordinarily easier for lobbyists to play defensive ball. But not always. Some measures have broad public appeal, making them difficult to fight. A proposal for an indigent-care trust fund, paid for by a special tax on business, would have broad appeal. A business lobbyist could not oppose the principle of caring for the indigent but would probably argue that this was society's responsibility and should therefore be paid for out of general revenues. Some environmental and consumer bills are difficult for business lobbyists to oppose head-on. The strategy, then, is to deflect, amend, water down, or at least get the most objectionable elements removed. But for the most part, the bills that lobbyists fight are of narrower scope and lesser interest to the public.

Lobbyists usually try to hold up the bills they oppose as long as possible so that they expire without final action by the time the legislature adjourns sine die. As the session progresses, the lobbyist's workload shifts; many of the bills are for all realistic purposes dead. One lobbyist estimated that at the outset of the legislative session in Texas, he had an interest in 150 to 200 bills, and was defending against 125 to 150 of them. By the time the session was drawing to a close, he was trying to get three passed and five or six killed.

Despite the importance of defense, particularly for those who desire to preserve the status quo, offense is also part of the lobbying game. Those who advocate a cause or who are seeking state support will obviously take a proactive stance. Environmentalists, for example, spend most of their time on the offensive. They can do so in part because of a sympathetic public and the press. For example, a Trenton contract lobbyist, who has as a client an environmental group, focuses on land-use issues that include the Pinelands (a protected area of the state), stormwater management, freshwater wetlands, farmland preservation, and funding. Her principal job is to develop and promote legislation.

Cities, too, from time to time have to go to the legislature for enabling authority. In Florida they sought a bill that would permit municipalities to levy a sales tax without resort to referendum. Then there are the groups that go on the offense in order to gain an advantage in the marketplace and/or to damage rivals and competitors. The nationwide push of Hertz and Avis to change the collision damage waiver system is one example. Another example is the effort of trial lawyers to limit protective orders, which protect the trade secrets of pharmaceutical companies during the discovery process in civil litigation.

Business, too, will take the offensive, either to prevent a governmental solution, modify regulations, preempt local action, or simply to be able to win a victory. In Minnesota, oil companies were able to cooperate with jobbers, dealers, and state agencies on a program to clean up underground storage tanks, whereby industry agreed to tax itself. Oil's attitude was that it had better clean its own house because a government-dictated alternative would be much worse. Tobacco has been under siege for years, unable to hold the line on taxes and regulation. However, it did take the offensive in a number of states, sponsoring legislation barring employment discrimination against smokers. Among other things, the industry wanted an issue on which it could win.

A permanent defensive posture, furthermore, can be debilitating over the longer run. A Florida lobbyist, who represented human services groups making claims on the budget, said she had switched from being reactive to proactive. It gives a group greater stature, she said, "People learn that they have to deal with you." A national association of businesses also had traditionally assumed a defensive posture in order to maintain the status quo. But the goodwill others felt for the group, according to its state government relations director, seemed to be dissipating. The enactment of regulations adverse to his association's interests was, in his view, imminent. He therefore developed a proactive strategy that involved consumer education, support of enforcement of antifraud provisions, and alternative means of conflict resolution.

"If you continue to only play defense, eventually someone's going to kick a field goal right by you" observed the executive director of the Pennsylvania trial lawyers group.[12] Despite such advice, business is not normally proactive. One of New Jersey's top contract lobbyists encouraged clients to be proactive, telling them to go through the laws and regulations that affect them and then come up with a wish list of things they want changed. This lobbyist's largest clients rarely provided him with a list.

Fighting It Out

In view of the hundreds, even thousands, of bills introduced in a legislature each session, it is not surprising that many are uncontested. We have already seen that a number are sponsored by administrative agencies and pertain to narrow, housekeeping matters. Others are for the benefit (usually symbolic) of unorganized constituencies. And still others are being monitored, but have so little support that their chances of going anywhere are minimal. On these, lobbyists need not declare a position.

Moreover, many bills stimulate no opposition. James Q. Wilson refers to them as measures that concentrate benefits and distribute costs. They benefit a well-defined special interest but impose no visible costs on any other interests.[13] They may not be controversial, but these bills still require a lobbyist to manage them. While legislators may have agreed to sponsor these bills, they often have to be reminded of the obligation they have taken on. Otherwise, they will turn their attention to more immediate matters and higher priorities, and the bills in question may fall through the cracks. Lobbyists remind legislators continuously. It is not pressure, but rather it is nudging. Everything is competing for attention and the lobbyist's job, with respect to unopposed measures, is to make sure that they get the legislator's attention. Each lobbyist will have more than a few bills to pass that are not controversial and have no opponents. On a minor matter, if no one objects, the legislature's tendency is to go along and satisfy the group. Perhaps also, as we shall see below, the parties that had a concern were able to reach an agreement beforehand.

Occasionally, achieving consensus can be a fairly easy matter. An example of such a "consensual" issue is a bill that permitted New Jersey dentists to diagnose and treat patients in the hospital. The legislation was initiated because the New Jersey Department of Health prohibited dentists from taking medical histories or treating patients in a hospital setting. The bill authorized dental work as long as a physician was consulted and the dentist's credentials were approved by the hospital. Supported by the dental, medical, and hospital associations, the bill won unanimous approval in each house of the legislature.

Allowing for bills that are relatively inconsequential and those where consensus can be reached beforehand, there still remains much for groups to fight about in the legislature. Wilson refers to such measures as ones that concentrate benefits and costs, but not in the same place. These proposals, benefiting a well-defined special interest, at a cost to another equally well defined special interest, generate organized conflict.[14]

Group conflict on legislative terrain is by no means new. There has always been substantial conflict, at least as legislators view it. But the incidence of conflictual issues appears to have increased during recent decades as legislatures have enlarged their scope and more and more issues have been fought out. That is the experience of veteran lobbyists. According to Ralph Haben, a contract lobbyist in Tallahassee: "Ten years ago there was nobody on the other side, and now you can assume 90 percent of the time some other lobbyist will object to what you want to do."[15] A Maryland lobbyist held the same view. He could not think of one recent case where he was not competing with some lobbyist on the other side of an issue. Often, although there was no active and direct opposition, his client would be competing with others—and even with members of the legislature— for budgetary resources.

It is important to realize that, even if competition is not always direct, one group may still be pitted against another group. Some groups make claims on the state budget, competing with other claims and constrained by finite revenues and the legislature's unwillingness to raise taxes. For these groups, the appropriations process is a principal target. But as much as they want budgetary benefits, groups also want to avoid paying more than what they consider their fair share of the bill. A good part of business's agenda, therefore, is related to the structure of state tax systems and the incidence of taxes on business.

Even school children, who are being taught to engage in politics by their teachers, are in competition for limited resources. For example, a group of third-graders in Massachusetts undertook to lobby a legislative committee for a bill that would designate the chocolate chip cookie as the official state cookie. But another group of youngsters was pushing a rival bill, one that would give the honor to the Fig Newton. Neither group, it should be noted, retained the services of a registered lobbyist.

Looking for Bucks

"The real action is in the budget," remarked a California lobbyist for a nonprofit association. A Colorado lobbyist had a similar perspective: "A lot of it is how to get money, where to get it, and who will pay." Pro-choice groups lobby to make funds available to family-planning clinics. The pharmaceutical industry lobbies in the budgetary process to ensure that money is allocated to Medicaid, particularly to pay for the drugs that the industry markets.

Groups, such as teachers, cannot ignore the budget, as is illustrated by the experience of the Colorado Education Association (CEA) during one legislative session. Discounting funds essentially committed by prior budgets, only $125 million of new money was available for all the state's needs. CEA wanted $81 million of that amount for education. It lobbied the joint budget committee, the legislature's most powerful body, but came away with much less than it wanted. So CEA appealed to the group that would determine the fate of the budget bill (the so-called long bill) in the house, the majority party caucus of Republican representatives. Sitting around the room at each of the open caucus meetings were not only lobbyists from the CEA, the rest of the education community, and some of the large local school districts, but also those for the counties, cities, and special districts, and those wanting more money for prisons, highways, mass transportation, and whatever else. The caucus room was crowded.

The Association for Retarded Citizens (ARC) is organized in forty-six states. The New Jersey ARC was established in 1950 by a group of parents whose children were receiving institutional care. Its six thousand members depend largely on the state budget for appropriations to meet the needs of retarded children. In the governor's proposed budget for fiscal year 1997, it was proposed in the legislature that funds be cut by 2 percent, not a large cut, but one that meant $4.8 million less for retarded children. New Jersey ARC had its job cut out for it.[16]

Health and social welfare groups, in particular, also lay claim to funds in the state budget and participate in the appropriations process. So do local government groups, such as the New Jersey League of Municipalities and the California Association of Counties. While the budget is the principal provider, it is not the only one. The tax system offers further opportunities. In New Jersey, for example, a large developer proposed a tax-increment financing bill. It would have allowed up to one-half of sales tax revenue received as a result of a particular project to be used for grants to the developer or for other infrastructure improvements. One argument in favor of the proposal was that such a program existed in forty-six other states.[17]

Avoiding the Bill

Everyone wants to avoid paying more taxes, and most of us would like to pay less. Those who have, or who generate, money are in greater and more frequent peril than the rest of us. That means business interests. A Florida legislator, addressing a gathering of state government relations representatives of large companies and associations, advised that when the state needs money "you are all at risk." Business groups agree; taxes are the major issue facing them. Here, they are not in combat with any other group but rather with government itself. Every year, according to one government relations specialist, the tax departments of major national companies "go crazy just analyzing the impact of tax legislation in the various states."

When legislatures are looking for ways to balance the budget, the so-called sin taxes on alcohol and tobacco are always leading possibilities. The affected industries will argue that the proposed hikes are not fair and, furthermore, that retailers will be hurt because neighboring states tax these commodities less. But the political risks of reaching into the pockets of these industries are negligible. The position of Anheuser-Busch, in a battle that took place in one state, was that alcohol should not be singled out, but the company would consent to pay more if the legislature wanted to increase the sales tax and put it on everyone. Increasingly, also, efforts are being made to increase taxes on alcohol and tobacco and then earmark the funds for social-welfare causes, such as drug abuse, alcohol education, and cancer research. Business lobbyists much prefer that taxes remain a revenue issue and not become associated with a cause.

The distilled spirits, wine, and beer interests are in a continuing struggle over taxes. Spirits argues that wine and beer are favored when it comes to taxation. When a bill threatens to raise "sin taxes," the Distilled Spirits Council of the U.S., Inc. (DISCUS), has as its first objective its defeat. If the tax bill can not be defeated, the association argues for tax equity—a level playing field—for spirits, wine, and beer.

Another revenue measure that now and again arouses the ire of both business and professional groups in recent years is the sales tax on services. One of the epic battles was in Florida where many groups fought against a tax on services, but lost initially. The tax was enacted in 1987, but the groups did not give up. They succeeded in getting it repealed the following year. Since then legislatures have been leery but, nonetheless, have tried to extend sales taxes to additional goods and services. Attorneys, real estate agents, and certified public accountants all have engaged in the battle. The CPAs, for instance, have tried to defeat taxes on services or to gain a provision, as they did in Massachusetts, exempting small business. In New Jersey, Governor Florio presented a sales-tax package that included a 7 percent tax on telecommunications. The cable television association argued that it would have cost their 1.7 million subscribers an extra $25 per year, causing a decline in subscribers and harming the industry. One of the current issues confronting business is that of health insurance, with the prospect that legislatures will impose a payroll tax on business to finance indigent care. All of these issues ensure the continued employment of the most skillful lobbyists at the state capitals.

Just as groups seek to avoid greater tax burdens, they also look for tax breaks and exemptions wherever they can. It may be a tax break for art collectors or a box to be checked on a return that allows the taxpayer to earmark an amount for the homeless. Or it may be a tax credit for solar-electricity producers in California. The Maryland General Assembly helped a trade association representing linen and uniform rental companies by exempting it from paying a sales tax on cleaning materials and equipment.

Local officials are strongly concerned about tax policy, as well as budgets. In Texas the big issue for cities is taxes because the state provides so little local aid. Whereas the per capita national average of state aid to cities is more than two hundred dollars, in Texas it is about three dollars. Property, sales, and franchise taxes all are at the top of the Texas Municipal League's legislative agenda.

Getting an Edge

Groups are engaged in a never-ending quest to pull even with or gain on their competitors. If possible, they would like to force them off the field entirely. The legislature is being asked to decide between competing private interests, cloaking its decision, whenever possible, in terms of broader values, such as equity or the public interest. Whatever the rationalization or rhetoric, however, the underlying issue is that of group advantage. Local Bell telephone companies endeavor to get from under state regulation; AT&T wants them to remain regulated. Florida tracks compete for racing dates for pari-mutuels; whoever gets the prime dates comes out ahead.

Oil jobbers press for legislation requiring retail marketing divorcement, which would force oil companies to give up local dealerships they own. The measure would weaken big oil. The petroleum industry is opposed. On the other hand, the New Jersey Petroleum Council continues to press for repeal of the ban on self-service gasoline stations in the states. An underlying reason is that conversion to self-service would force many of the independent stations out of business, thus strengthening the position of the large oil companies. The New Jersey Gasoline Retailers Association, as might be expected, strongly supports the ban.

The biggest running battles by far of recent years are those over tort reform, insurance, product liability, and workers' compensation, with the trial lawyers on one side and business, insurance, and doctors on the other. These issues have been at the top of the agenda in many states. The ongoing conflict has been described in Texas as one in which the trial lawyers have managed, through their strength in the legislature, to preserve a civil justice system to their liking. It has benefited their plaintiff clients in personal injury, medical malpractice, product liability, and other civil cases. It has also benefited trial lawyers themselves, who collect contingency fees of up to 30 percent of jury awards to their clients. In recent years, however, business and organized medicine in Texas have been able to effectively challenge the trial lawyers.

As we noted earlier, one of the fiercest economic battles to be fought in recent years was that between car rental companies—Hertz and Avis versus Alamo and some of the smaller firms. Known to lobbyists as "Car Wars," the principal issue was the collision damage waiver (CDW), a contract provision in which the rent-a-car company waives its right to recover damages against the renter. Alamo and the smaller companies, which rented mainly to individuals, profited from the fees for such waivers, while Hertz and Avis, which dealt mainly with self-insured companies, had less of an investment in the practice. If they could have CDWs prohibited, their competitors would be put at a disadvantage. The Hertz-Avis onslaught was nationwide. Legislation to abolish CDWs was proposed in at least thirty-five states, passing first in Illinois and New York. Elsewhere either Hertz and Avis were repulsed or, by way of compromise, car rental companies were limited in the amount of money they could charge per day.

In Florida much of the top lobbying talent was hired to represent one side or the other. Yet legislators neither understood nor cared about the issue. It could hardly be called a public policy question of great moment. It was nevertheless highly political, and the factor that probably determined the outcome in favor of CDWs was that Florida was Alamo's home base. Since the first battle in Florida, the combatants have continued, in the words of one of Tallahassee's lobbyists, "trying to stick it to one another." In California the battle between car rental companies was also intense; and it included issues besides CDW. As in Tallahassee, practically every top contract lobbyist was retained. Legislation to ban collision damage waivers was suggested by Hertz and Avis, initiated by the state attorney general, and carried by a reform-minded member of the assembly. It passed the assembly, but the opposition had organized by the time the bill reached the senate judiciary committee. Hertz and Avis maintained that the consumer was being ripped off by CDWs; their opponents framed the issue in David-and-Goliath terms. Hertz and Avis, their lobbyists suggested, were simply trying to kill off the competition. They argued, moreover, that if the bill passed, car-rental rates would go up because collision damage would be included in the regular rate. The outcome was a compromise—caps on collision damage waivers.

Hertz and Avis have also attacked their competitors on issues of airport-access fees and advertising. The two largest companies are usually located on airport grounds, for which they pay premium rents. They supported legislation requiring that companies not similarly situated pay a special access fee for transporting car renters to and from the terminals. Hertz and Avis won the round. They also challenged Alamo on its advertising, declaring its rates were misleadingly low because their ads did not truly reflect the charges. They won here as well.

Combat between professions over turf may not match the car wars in terms of the number of lobbyists employed. But they do provide relatively permanent employment to some of the capital's lobbying corps. Competing professional groups seek to expand or defend their economic turf. A classic battle, one that has been waged just about everywhere, matches optometrists against ophthalmologists. It began when optometrists, who had been limited to giving eye examinations and prescribing glasses, tried to obtain the authority to use diagnostic drugs. They were opposed by ophthalmologists, eye doctors who had attended medical school, and had the monopoly on treatment. The optometrists gained the authority in almost every state. Moreover, they have expanded their authority, so that three-quarters of the states now allow them to use drugs for the treatment of serious eye diseases, like glaucoma.

The continuing struggle, which has become known as "Eye Wars" now finds the two groups fighting over a new laser procedure that corrects nearsightedness by slightly flattening the cornea. Optometrists insist that they, as well as ophthalmologists, should be authorized to perform this procedure. Whoever wins, of course, will derive substantial financial benefits.[18]

Another face-off finds the orthopedic surgeons on one side of the line and podiatrists on the other. The struggle is over ankle injuries, and the issue is whether or not podiatrists should be permitted to work on ankles. Critical to their practice is the definition, established by law, of where the foot stops and the ankle begins. When the issue was fought out in Colorado, the medical association was distracted by the other, numerous items on its agenda. In contrast, the podiatrists had the ankle high on their priority list. The podiatrists prevailed; the law that was enacted defined the ankle as part of the foot. Dog groomers have also battled veterinarians, trying to acquire the right to brush a dog's teeth. Is this the beginning of the "Canine Wars?"

A group seeking to establish itself professionally will normally seek the sanction of the state through regulation. Groups such as acupuncturists and massage therapists can achieve recognition if the legislature enacts a law regulating them. And they can gain greater control of their own destinies rather than be controlled by doctors on a board of medical examiners.[19] When groups such as these turn to the legislature for help, other groups rise to defend their domains. The battle is joined. As one contract lobbyist describes the situation: "The toughest legislation to get passed is legislation that annoys another group. The engineers annoy the architects, the occupational therapists annoy the physical therapists." These controversies, in this lobbyist's view, have little to do with the good of the public in general. Therefore, he contends, most of the bills that lobbyists work on do not bear on public policy issues on such. "The public," he concludes, "is not the consideration."

CHAPTER 5

The Rules of the Game

In a report offering advice to lobbyists, the director of state relations at the Sun Company wrote: "Every state capital has a personality all its own. Never go out on a limb until you know exactly how the game is played."[1] This is sound advice. Political scientists recognize the importance of political culture. One of the classic studies in the field, a comparative exploration of legislative systems, found it to be significant in determining the modes and styles of pressure politics in four states.[2] Each capital, indeed, each of the fifty states, possesses a distinct political culture. With a tradition of progressivism, California's state government is known for its professionalism and policy initiatives. Colorado has a more populist reputation, and this can be seen in its persistent distrust for big government and big business. Florida's cultural roots are traditionalist, but today it has no coherent identity. Progressivism and populism are at the core of Minnesota politics, and the sense of a civic community there, while weaker than it used to be, still remains relatively strong. By contrast, politics in New Jersey is characterized by individualism, pragmatism, and, until the 1970s, a localism that dominated state politics. The political culture of Texas is more individualistic, even Darwinian, with power relationships and hardball politics the mode of interaction among elites. Politics is personalistic and the preference is for limited government.

Just as political scientists differentiate states according to political culture, they also categorize them according to the strength of their interest groups. They no longer find one or two interests, such as the Southern Pacific Railroad in California, running a state, although gaming is still very influential in Nevada, oil in Texas and Louisiana, and agriculture in a number of the farm states. Otherwise, political pluralism has been expanding, with interest groups sharing power among themselves and with others. Naturally, the impact of interest groups on government differs from place to place. According to a series of studies nationwide, their impact in the late 1990s was greatest in Florida, somewhat less in California and Texas, still less in Colorado and New Jersey, and least in Minnesota.[3]

While political culture and interest group environment are rather abstract concepts, the state's economy is a more concrete phenomenon.

Its effects on lobbying may be indirect, but largesse or budgetary constraint can be felt by almost everyone involved in the governmental process. The climate of looming deficits and shrinking budgets, particularly in places like California, Florida, New Jersey, and Texas, can dominate a legislature's agenda, as it did in the 1980s, a decade of fiscal crisis. Much of what the legislature and many interest groups did reflected economic conditions and tight budgets. The contrast with the late 1990s is striking. With economies growing steadily, legislatures did not have to worry about raising revenues but instead had to figure out whether or how to spend them.

The frameworks established by a state's political culture, interest groups, and economy are important to the functioning of the political system. How do they affect the work of lobbyists? What are the rules of the lobbying game, and how have they been changing?

The Legislative Arena

Lobbyists must adapt to a particular legislative environment. What works in the Colorado General Assembly might not work in the Texas legislature. Lobbyists must also adapt to peculiar circumstances, which change from session to session and vary with the change of personnel. That means that what works in the New Jersey legislature today might not have worked there five years ago. It means that Florida with Lawton Chiles as governor is quite different from Florida governed by Jeb Bush. The structure of the legislature, how the legislative process works, the patterns of politics, and the distribution of power all affect how lobbying is carried on in the states.

The Structure of the Legislature

State legislatures have changed. They were transformed during the legislative modernization and reform period, which began after the reapportionments of the 1960s and lasted through the 1970s. Legislatures added skilled professional staff, raised salaries for members, and improved facilities. As legislatures became more developed, their collective sense of independence increased. The legislative branch became more powerful vis-à-vis the executive. As legislatures became professionalized, legislative office became more attractive, and different types of people were recruited to candidacy.[4]

The professionalization of legislatures and the careerism of recent generations of members have had substantial effects on state politics and on lobbying as well. California, the first of the nation's legislatures to professionalize, became a full-time body with a large staff and a membership committed to careers in public office. In the 1950s, before the structural transformation, twenty-five full-time lobbyists stationed in Sacramento could visit members in their home districts. There was time and opportunity for the most personal interaction. Such relationships no longer exist, and today the dominant locale for California lobbyists and legislators to meet is the fund-raiser.[5]

Professionalization and careerism are also influential in Colorado, Florida, Michigan, Minnesota, New Jersey, Ohio, and Texas, albeit to varying extents. In each of these states legislators are devoting more and more time to the job, especially if constituent service and political stroking in their districts are considered part of the job. Legislatures as institutions are spending more time in either regular or special sessions and more time between sessions, doing interim work through standing and special committees. In each of these states, many members are devoting from half- to full-time to their work as legislators and otherwise behaving like careerists. In Michigan, for example, members are essentially full time, putting in fifty or so hours a week. That includes three days a week for nine months and four to five days a week during the height of the session. If their districts are safe, Michigan legislators can hold down another job on a part-time basis. Ohio is similar, with more than half the members essentially full time, having given up much, if not all, of their outside incomes. Of the states mentioned above, only Colorado seems determined to maintain a citizen legislature and, so far, has managed to do so. The others have moved inexorably in the direction of full-time professional bodies.

Careerist legislators are intent on remaining in their current office, at least until they can run for higher office. With hanging onto their jobs as an objective, the guiding questions for them are: "How do I stay in office?" and "Is this going to cost me votes?" Thus, many legislators are almost always campaigning. All of this alters relationships that members have with one another and with lobbyists. Many legislators today have less time to develop personal relationships than did their predecessors. Instead, they are concerned about who will be opposing them in the next election, what groups will be giving them support, and how the necessary funds can be raised.

The new breed of legislator tends to have held prior government or political jobs. In California, even with term limits, one out of three members fits this description. A good number of them have ascended to legislative office after having served on congressional or legislative staffs. Fewer attorneys sit in the legislature nowadays, and this has weakened the position of trial lawyers and their agents. There are also fewer people who work for large corporations or in business generally. This has not helped the agendas of business lobbyists in the legislature. Quite the contrary; business has been hurt by the change from a citizen legislature to a career-ist legislature dominated by individuals having no other occupations and by school teachers and government workers, but few businessmen. In Minnesota, where this has been the trend, one contract lobbyist com-mented that he and his colleagues "can feel the difference in the working of the legislature."

The emergence of women in state legislatures during the past twenty years has also changed the environment. One consequence is that more women have been able to make their way as lobbyists. Another conse-quence is that the legislative culture has changed. Take Colorado, where one-third of the legislators are women. The "good ole boy" atmosphere is practically gone in Colorado and is no longer as pervasive even in Florida and Texas. The emergence of minorities has also made a difference. African American and Latino or Hispanic legislators (the latter in Califor-nia, Florida, and Texas) not only provide special access for ethnic lobby-ists, but also, like women, have put new items on the legislature's agenda.

Although the Colorado General Assembly still maintains its citizen-legislature status, it has undergone substantial enough change to alter the environment for lobbying. Here, too, legislators have come to spend quite a bit of time in Denver, both in session and on interim and ad hoc com-mittees. The composition of the legislature's membership has shifted markedly. The ranchers, farmers, lawyers, and businessmen who used to predominate are no longer willing to sacrifice the time or income required by legislative service. Moreover, few companies are willing to underwrite employees who take time off for the legislature. Therefore, according to one contract lobbyist, "not many legislators nowadays know what it means to meet a payroll."

Fewer members in Colorado are between the ages of thirty-five to fifty. Instead young men and women, recently out of school and with no steady occupational experience intervening, and retired people are finding their way to legislative office. The increasing number of women have included many who have been housewives and now are earning a second income in their families. One lobbyist characterized the membership of the Colorado General Assembly as follows: "Half of them don't have work. If they lost their seats, they wouldn't know what to do."

The nature of the legislative staff also makes a difference in how lobbying is conducted. Certainly staff members offer legislators a source of information, although they have hardly eliminated legislators' dependence on lobbyists in this regard. Legislators still rely on lobbyists for both technical and political information, but at least nowadays their staff serves as an alternative source. Staff has independent input, particularly on bills where substantial policy questions are involved; its input diminishes, however, on questions that are less significant to the public and the states and where special interests competing for advantage are the principal actors.

In any case, where legislative staff does play a central role, lobbyists may have to lobby them as well as their legislator masters. Although the California legislature does not approach the congressional system, where everything has to go through staff, it comes closer than any other state. Lobbyists must reckon with committee consultants, individual aides, and leadership staff. In Florida, staff in the offices of the speaker of the house and president of the senate are key players, as are committee staff. New Jersey's key staff personnel are in the majority-party offices of the two houses. Any Trenton lobbyist would be fortunate to have preferred access to the executive directors of the assembly and senate majority parties. In Texas the staffs of the members themselves have to be cultivated, particularly in the senate.

Only in a state like Colorado is staffing no problem for lobbyists. The Colorado legislature has a centralized, nonpartisan agency that provides basic service to committees and members. But the staff of the Office of Legislative Council keeps its distance from political and partisan matters and can devote little attention to many of the special-interest issues that lobbyists care about. In Colorado legislators have no alternative; they must rely on lobbyists for both sides of many issues. Despite variations in the size and patterns of staffing among the states, however, the similarities in lobbyist-legislator interaction outweigh the differences. Not only in Colorado, but in California, Florida, Minnesota, New Jersey, Texas, and other states, lobbyists enjoy access to legislators, leaders, and rank and file alike. They may have to work a little harder in some places, lobbying key staff as well as members, but their positions and their messages manage to get through if they have a case to make and a client to represent.

Elements of the Process

Lobbyists have to know the legislative process in a particular state inside and out. When it comes to the interstices of process, no two places are alike. Each has its own procedures and routines, and lobbyists learn and adapt to them.

For one thing, the house and senate are very different institutions just about everywhere. Often, as has been the case in Florida, the rivalry between the two chambers is even greater than that between the two parties. Senates are smaller, more individualistic, and usually the leadership is weaker. Senators are generally more experienced than their colleagues in the house, the pattern being that a number of senators have served previously in the house. This is especially true in states with term limits, like California where house members frequently run for the senate when their terms expire or even sooner. Thus it makes sense for a lobbyist there to work especially hard building relationships with house members, some of whom will move on to the senate. Lobbyists, however, may find that they have to touch more bases in senates than in houses, because although there are fewer members, power is more broadly distributed among them. They may also find, as in the case of Texas, that the way the senate conducts business encourages compromise. If their tasks are primarily defensive, they need to win over just one house. Yet lobbyists cannot afford to neglect either chamber. There is no telling when they will have to get a bill passed, and no assurance that a particular house will acquiesce in killing a measure they oppose.

For another thing, the work schedules of legislatures vary markedly. California meets in regular session almost the entire year, breaking during the summer months and during the fall of even-numbered years when members are up for reelection. Colorado meets for 120 calendar days.[6] Texas is one of only seven states in the nation that still meets biennially, for 140 calendar days, but special sessions are not at all unusual. New Jersey meets year-round, but members travel to Trenton only 30 or 40 days a year; sessions are held on Mondays, and perhaps on Thursdays too, each week except for budget recesses, the summer months, and the fall of odd-numbered years when legislative elections are held.

Whatever the schedule and whichever the state, one thing is dead certain. As the session nears the date for adjournment sine die, the pace quickens. The last week, and especially the final days of the session, are usually frenzied. This is the make-or-break period for legislators and lobbyists alike. The schedule and metabolism of lobbyists must keep pace with that of the legislature.

Even when the session ends, legislative activity continues. Special sessions are becoming more common and committee work during the interim period is the practice nearly everywhere. For the lobbyist, the legislature is rarely dormant. Something is always going on, although a client's interests are only directly at stake when the legislature is meeting.

The process by which bills are considered and voted on also varies from place to place. This naturally affects how lobbyists do their jobs. Well-connected lobbyists can usually find a legislator willing to sponsor a bill that they are pushing. For many legislators in most places, introducing a bill on behalf of a constituent or group is not considered heavy-duty work. For them, sponsorship does not necessarily imply ardent support. The bill may not get far, but at least a lobbyist has a bill introduction to show for his or her efforts. Legislators in some states are limited, however, by rule or custom as to the number of bills they may introduce at a session. Such restrictions force them to be far more discriminating, thus making it more difficult for lobbyists who are on the offensive and seeking a sponsor. It is not unusual to have a legislator beg off when asked by a lobbyist to sponsor a bill. "I've already used up all my titles" is a frequent reply. The lobbyist then has to scramble and look elsewhere.

A bill limitation, as practiced in Colorado and also in Florida, helps interests on the defense. So does the process generally. In Texas, according to several lobbyists, the process is designed to protect the establishment. On the house side of the capitol, the speaker has the power to refer a bill to whatever committee he chooses. And the State Affairs Committee in each chamber has traditionally been known as the graveyard for legislation. Nor are standing committees in Texas required to take up or report out bills. Furthermore, if legislation is reported out, the House Calendar Committee serves to kill bills opposed by leadership. On the senate side, an extraordinary two-thirds majority of the members present is required to put a bill on the calendar. Therefore, only eleven out of thirty-one members of the Texas senate are needed to kill anything. That is one reason why certain groups, such as the trial lawyers, have contributed generously to senate races and why their cause has achieved strength within that body. In Texas, to be on the defense is to have a head start. Nonetheless, a head start is not everything. The system also works to get legislation through, but only after both sides have had their say. The very size of the senate and the way the body does its business work to encourage compromise. To a large extent, much of the process in Texas as elsewhere is one of devising language in legislation with which both sides can live.

New Jersey's process balances defensive and offensive considerations. On the one hand, a constitutional majority is necessary to pass a bill, so members who abstain or take a walk are essentially voting "no." In the eighty-member assembly, for instance, a bill needs forty-one votes to pass.

It does not matter how many red lights appear on the tally board, but only whether forty-one green lights come on. On the other hand, during a two-year legislature, a bill is never dead, even if it seems to have been dispatched on several occasions. "A bill never loses in New Jersey," commented a contract lobbyist, "it just does not win." Once on third reading, the bill remains on third reading and in a position for a vote. So the defensive lobbyist always has to be on guard with respect to bills he or she thinks are dead, but may still breathe some life. The safest tactic is to have a bill that does not pass referred back to committee, where it can at least be bottled up if not killed.

Just about everywhere, the moment of truth for lobbyists comes during the final days or hours of the session. That is their last chance to score, or be scored against. The hope, and the fear, then is an amendment. Colorado lobbyists, who are up against a stringent limit on bill introductions, can get a legislator to introduce a measure as an amendment to another bill on the floor. The Colorado requirement is that an amendment to a bill be germane, but germaneness can cover a wide swath. And if the bill's sponsor agrees to an amendment, the measure favored by a lobbyist has a better chance of adoption. In Florida, the process of amendment dominates the close of the session. Legislators and lobbyists here are constantly on the lookout for "vehicles," that is, bills to which they can attach amendments when the time is appropriate. Thus during the final days, a number of bills become "trains," going from one house to another, with the original bill functioning as the engine that picks up car after car of amendments. These trains may include bills that passed one house but not the other or that never had a hearing in either house. Each lobbyist is intent on ensuring that the train on which his or her measure is riding does not get derailed. At the same time, each lobbyist is working assiduously to wreck the train that runs against his or her client's interests.

Politics and Power

Any lobbyist who ignores the politics of the state and of the legislature cannot possibly succeed at the job. Politics drives the process, although partisanship is more acute in some states than others, and in some competition is harder. Partisanship is a growing phenomenon in legislative bodies, in large part because competition between Democrats and Republicans is keen. Either party has a real chance (albeit not always a good chance) of winning a majority in about two-thirds of the nation's ninety-nine legislative chambers. Partisanship dominates in states like New Jersey, where there is keen competition for control of the legislature. It is also strong in states like California, where Republicans do not now pose a serious threat, and in Ohio, where Democrats do not now pose a serious threat, and it counts in Minnesota, even though independents have had success with the election of Jesse Ventura as governor. In the past decade partisanship increased enormously in states like Florida and Virginia, where Republicans surged from far behind to somewhat ahead in both chambers. Republicans captured the Texas senate and made impressive gains in the Texas house, but partisanship still is not a dominant factor.

Naturally, partisanship is exacerbated in an election year. But the campaign in competitive states never ends, and so there is no such thing as an "election year." Fund-raising goes on year in and year out, and lobbyists above all others feel the pinch. The incentives for individuals to win reelection and for parties to maintain or gain control are so powerful that lobbyists cannot help but be squeezed. When electoral politics takes over in the legislature, as in New Jersey with the assembly speaker and senate president for a period of time both unofficial candidates for governor in 2001 (as was also the case in 1989), the lobbyist's agenda must adjust accordingly. The legislature's course becomes even more overwhelmed by political considerations.

As far as lobbyists are concerned, the office of governor is critical. As governor of Minnesota, for instance, Democrat Rudy Perpich vetoed business-sponsored bills on workers' compensation. His Republican successor, Arne Carlson, however, was more sympathetic to business's position. Reform governor Jesse Ventura is more difficult for lobbyists to read. The change in governors from Thomas Kean, a Republican, to Jim Florio, a Democrat, had a clear impact on the New Jersey Business and Industry Association. With Kean, the association made headway on product liability, tort reform, and antitakeover legislation. With Florio (and a Democratic legislature) the association had to adopt a more defensive posture, especially in the environmental area. The election of Christine Whitman brought a far more sympathetic ear for business.

Who controls the senate and the house is even more critical for most lobbyists than who holds the office of governor. Tort reform and product liability, for example, tend to find Republicans siding with business interests and Democrats siding with trial lawyers and consumer groups. On these issues, the lawyers have a better chance when Democrats are in the majority and business has the edge when Republicans are on top. This is the situation in Minnesota, where the trial lawyers were able to hold the line with Democratic majorities in the legislature, but would be in trouble if Republicans won the two houses. Colorado's Republican legislature blocked proposals adverse to business, kept taxes low, and ensured that government's role remained relatively minor.

Organized teachers groups in the states also fare differently depending on which party controls the legislature. In states such as Illinois, Indiana, Michigan, Pennsylvania, and Wisconsin, unions have had to fight Republican measures designed to limit teachers' ability to strike, their tenure, and their bargaining power. Republicans, disenchanted with the performance of the public schools, have been the strongest proponents of school choice plans, which the teachers have resisted strongly. When Republicans gained control of the Illinois legislature, they joined with Republican governor Jim Edgar to outlaw a strike for eighteen months, eliminate the right to bargain over issues such as class size, and give principals broader authority to dismiss teachers.[7] In New Jersey, when the Republicans controlled the assembly, environmentalists failed to pass the Clean Water Enforcement Act. Soon after the Democrats took control the act was passed and signed into law. In 1992 the Republicans took firm control of both houses, and the lobbying situation reversed itself.

Different lobbyists rise with each new group of leaders. The inner circle of lobbyists therefore changes as the top political establishment does. A Florida lobbyist explained it tersely "Had Martinez won [the governorship] and beaten Gwen Margolis [for the presidency of the senate], we'd be closed." As it was, however, this particular lobbyist was very much open for business because of his earlier career and relationships. A connection with leadership certainly helps, but it is not sufficient. In state legislatures, as in the Congress, it is no longer possible to make one's case with a powerful few. Instead, the lobbyist now has to contact a wider group of members and touch more bases.[8] One lobbyist said it was a "different ballgame compared to when I first came on the scene." Apparently, things used to be a lot simpler—only the speaker, the committee chairman, and one or two others counted. "Today, you get your votes one at a time," this lobbyist explained, "no power brokers. It's a much more fluid situation. . . . Even when you think you've got a situation well in hand, you're never quite sure until the vote is over."[9]

Power is more dispersed just about everywhere today. In the New York legislature, where power still is concentrated in top leadership, it is not as concentrated as it used to be. Indeed, in 2000 insurgent Democrats tried to oust Speaker Sheldon Silver in the middle of his term. Once the rank and file tastes power, it is not apt to give it up. In earlier days members could not get a copy of the bills they were considering on the floor. In contrast, today information is available to everyone and each member has a copy of every bill and every amendment. Joe Doria, the minority leader of the New Jersey assembly, explained the difference between now and then. "When I was a freshman," he said, "they treated you like a mushroom. They kept you in the dark and fed you bullshit." No longer.

In part because everyone is informed, power in the Minnesota legislature is diffused, and both leaders and committee chairs have a tougher time controlling legislation. Lobbyists have to deal with every legislator, and not just the powerful few. Texas has moved in a similar direction. In the 1970s everything was decided by the leadership. One lobbyist recalls: "If you played ball with Gus Mutscher [the speaker] and Lieutenant Governor Ben Barnes, their lieutenants would carry a lobbyist's bill, work the floor, and get it through unscathed."[10] Since then, however, the power of leaders has diminished and lobbyists now have to work the members as well.

In California and Florida leaders used to have significant power, particularly in the assembly and house. The power of Florida's speaker and senate president was limited by the tradition of rotating leadership, which usually limited terms to two years. With term limits in both states, as well as in Colorado, Maine, Michigan, Ohio, and Washington, leadership power is likely to be even more restricted. Since term limits took effect, California has had a new speaker every year or two. The terms of presiding officers of both house and senate are likely to be shorter than before in practically every state affected. This means that lobbyists cannot afford to put all their eggs in leadership's basket. Doing business at the capitol requires dealing with a laundry list of members besides the leaders—and probably staffs as well.

A book detailing the dos and don'ts of lobbying in Washington, D.C., notes that "lobbyists must adapt to the prevailing rigors and mores of the institution."[11] As in Congress, so too in state legislatures. In the states, as well as in the nation, political and institutional change has been accompanied by change in legislative norms. Many lobbyists believe the norms are eroding, indeed that the institutional fabric of the legislature has deteriorated. They attribute this, in part, to the individualism of members preoccupied with their careers, reelections, constituencies, and pet policies. The intense struggle among single-issue groups and between the political parties is also believed to be at blame.

One historically paramount norm, keeping one's word, also appears to have weakened. A former Michigan legislator writes that if a legislature is to function, there has to be some degree of natural trust among members. "A legislator who does not keep her or his word . . . is likely to lose credibility swiftly as a result of violating legislative norms." Trust, in his view, may be based on expertise or ability, but its firmest base is friendship. And that appears to be on the decline, as more highly educated, hardworking, ambitious, career-minded, entrepreneurial men and women take seats, particularly in the more professionalized legislatures.[12] New members are less respectful and less trusting.

Legislators have to give their word to one another, but renege more often now than earlier. Lobbyists cannot count on commitments from legislators, and some do not even ask anymore. "If someone gives you his word, it's a definite maybe," observes one Florida contract lobbyist and former legislator. Another Florida lobbyist, employed by an association, explains: "You can't depend on what they tell you. In terms of commitment, it depends on who was there last." He therefore advises that, when counting votes, lobbyists should have substantial margins to allow for switches. Otherwise, they will be in serious trouble. In earlier days people in Minnesota made a deal on a handshake. Nowadays, according to a lobbyist for an association, "You can go into a legislative office and you think you have a deal, and then you're surprised in committee."

Recent political and institutional developments have not made life happier for veteran lobbyists. Newcomers may welcome change that breaks up the closed circles of established insiders. But the old-timers, who look back to the 1970s, are of a very different mind. For them, lobbying is less fulfilling now. Alan Marcus, a veteran contract lobbyist in New Jersey, spoke for many of his colleagues when he said "it's getting harder and harder to work in the political process. . . . It's become too partisan, too mean-spirited."[13]

Partisanship, ideological warfare, polarization, fragmentation all are taking their toil on the community of lobbyists. Take Colorado and Minnesota, two states with progressive traditions and strong and effective legislatures. A Colorado lobbyist related how he started in politics at a time when legislators and lobbyists together were truly trying to solve problems and made the compromises necessary in order to do so. That system, in his opinion, does not operate anymore. Now so many interests are affected by a problem that there is no real incentive to solve it. Furthermore, legislators are more preoccupied with reelection and fund-raisers, and lobbyists are concerned about their clients and businesses. The environment has deteriorated because of more interests and more players and less leadership. Minnesota's increasingly careerist legislature has also dismayed veteran lobbyists. What used to be a very compromising legislature is now much more rigid. Single-issue politics and ideological convictions are causing greater polarization—business versus labor, conservatives versus liberals, Democratic Farm Laborites versus Republicans, and even one wing of the Chamber of Commerce versus the other. According to one lobbyist, people are so uptight that "you can't go over there and not get engaged in conversation over abortion." For that and other reasons, old-school lobbyists do not regard it as fun anymore. But neither do old-school legislators.

The Capitol Community

Every day the Florida legislature is in session, lobbyists will gather between the two chambers on the capitol's fourth floor. This area, known as Ulcer Alley, is where lobbyists can send a note into the chamber asking a senator or representative to leave the floor and confer with them for a moment. This is where lobbyists can watch deliberations on television monitors, discuss amendments and bills with allies, and use their cellular telephones to contact their offices and their clients. In Connecticut lobbyists hang out in the atrium of the Legislative Office Building or roam the floors. In every capitol, they congregate in one place or another.

Given modern technology—bill tracking by computer; cellular phones and pagers—contemporary lobbyists are far better informed and more immediately in touch than their predecessors. With respect to the place and role of lobbyists in the capitol community, change is also taking place, but it is more gradual than the change in technology.

Within each capital city, legislators, staff, lobbyists, and journalists can be thought of as members of the capitol community. This community, according to the director of state government relations for the Sun Company, is a "loose-knit fraternity of independent individuals who share common interests."[14] Like the legislative arena itself, the capitol community shapes the interactions between lobbyists and legislators.

Traditional Social Life

During the sixty days when the legislature is in session, the city of Tallahassee is transformed from a quiet place, albeit the site of state government and two major state universities, to a buzzing, swirling swarm of legislators and lobbyists. The city's very size and design shape the social lives of members of the political community. People hang around the capitol, they socialize, and they enjoy one another's company. The culture is such that legislators find themselves in the closest proximity to lobbyists. Austin is much larger than Tallahassee, but it exerts similar charm for members of the political community. With Austin thought to be a more delightful spot than any other place in Texas, neither legislators nor lobbyists (with the possible exception of those from Dallas and Houston) are eager to return home when the session ends. The culture in Austin also encourages legislators and lobbyists to get together.

Except during the end-of-the-session crush, socializing is interrupted on weekends when legislators go home to their districts. Florida's legislators arrive in Tallahassee Sunday evening and normally leave Thursday evening. They stay in the capital the last two weeks of the session, but then they have little time for socializing. In New Jersey, socializing is limited by the fact that every legislator commutes to Trenton one or two days a week. In a commuter legislature, social life is necessarily limited; only those members who live relatively close to Trenton are likely to stick around after hours. Although Colorado and Minnesota do not have commuter legislatures, many members come from the metropolitan areas of Denver and Minneapolis–St. Paul. They drive between their houses and the capitol on a daily basis. About three out of five of Colorado's legislators live in Denver or its suburbs. They seldom remain for any but obligatory political and social activities. About half the members in Oregon are within commuting distance of Salem and about half in New Mexico live in the Santa Fe or Albuquerque area. In states like Delaware and Rhode Island everyone commutes.

Nonetheless, opportunities still exist for lobbyists to come together with legislators in social rather than business settings. Many, but by no means all, lobbyists take advantage of such opportunities, seeking to get as much informal time with legislators as possible. This is their way of building and sustaining relationships, and of getting in some business besides. For example, during one six-month session members of the Colorado house were invited to forty-eight cocktail parties, forty-four lunches, forty breakfasts, nineteen dinners, and twenty-three other functions.[15]

Many receptions are held for legislators at a hotel or restaurant or sometimes in the capitol building itself. These are sponsored and hosted by groups that range from tavern owners to cable television to health care to the education association. Almost every major association uses the reception as an occasion to bring in group members, as well as their lobbyists, and chat casually with as many legislators as possible. During a sixty-day session of the Florida legislature, for instance, about eighty receptions or similar functions were held during the day or night—on Tuesdays, Wednesdays, and Thursdays, but not during the final week.

When receptions were hosted by only a few groups, they served to get the legislature's attention. But nowadays, with everyone doing it, receptions may be losing their impact. Moreover, the large galas of yesteryear are now a little outmoded. But legislators feel obliged to attend receptions, especially if any of their constituents are present. Sometimes they do so mechanically or grudgingly, because they are obliged to show up at three or four events in the same evening. On occasion legislators send their aides, whose main mission is to simply pick up their boss's nametag from the registration table and make it appear that the legislator has put in an appearance. Most legislators try to attend as a courtesy and perhaps to show support for the lobbyist who is responsible for the function. At one reception, of the Colorado Education Association, which was held from 5 to 7 p.m., about half the legislators showed up. One, from the Denver area, who stopped by, said, "I came because it was right downtown, and I could do it on my way home."

Lobbyists have scant chance to mingle with legislators who are on the run at a group's receptions. They have to settle for "pigs in a blanket" and white wine, and a little networking and schmoozing. They may not do much better at fund-raisers; but these too are practically obligatory. In California, where entertaining lobbyists is severely limited by law, fund-raisers have become the major social (as well as political) events. They have taken the place of entertaining in Sacramento, where during some periods there may be six different fund-raisers on the same night. "Afterwards, if you want to go to dinner," said a contract lobbyist, "you go dutch." The crowds at fund-raisers are large and legislators have little time to talk with any single individual. Still, lobbyists feel they ought to attend, to be seen and to shake hands. It is their way of showing support for the particular legislator and for the process. Not only in California, but in many states, ethics laws now make private entertaining and receptions problematic. The result is that opportunities to socialize—or more likely, to show one's face—are provided by fund-raisers held by legislators.

A variation on the customary reception is the annual New Jersey State Chamber of Commerce train trip from Newark to Washington, D.C. Dating to the 1930s, the event brings together more than a thousand of New Jersey's politicians, lobbyists, business leaders, and lawyers, who all work the train and make and renew contacts. The trip is not the occasion it used to be, but it does permit lobbyists to ply their trade.

Lobbyists do better, as far as "quality time" is concerned, in the watering holes, clubs, restaurants, and even in their homes. They pick up the tab for drinks and dinner and, in return, have the company of one or several legislators for an hour or two. The watering hole, however, is a shadow of its former self. There is still Clyde's, an old-fashioned gin mill, only a few steps from the capitol building in Tallahassee. "I can talk to ten people there," says one lobbyist, "and know what's going on." However, many more lobbyists than legislators do their fraternizing at Clyde's; even in Tallahassee the tradition is dying.

Then there are the restaurants where lobbyists used to treat legislators to lunch or dinner. Lorenzo's in Trenton once had a large legislator-lobbyist clientele on session days. Frank Fats used to be the place in Sacramento. Now one trendy restaurant after another gets a business that is highly dispersed, with most legislators in most places paying their own way. In Denver, lobbyists may take legislators to breakfast at Racine's or to lunch at the Profile, but evenings are ordinarily a time for receptions. A number of Colorado's lobbyists, particularly those representing localities, nonprofits, and cause groups, do their entertaining in the capitol cafeteria. In Austin, where the Petroleum Club is popular with high flyers, the capitol's basement cafeteria—known as the Linoleum Club—is for those with limited expense accounts. Both the basement and fifth-floor cafeterias at the capitol in Tallahassee also do a thriving business. Legislators and lobbyists, and lobbyists and lobbyists, deal with one another over a quick breakfast or lunch in fast, if not furious, fashion. No longer, however, do lobbyists ordinarily pick up the tab for both meals.

To some extent, too, lobbyists convene with legislators at sporting events. In New Jersey, some watch professional football from a field box at Giants Stadium. In St. Paul some get together for a home game of the Minnesota Twins. In Florida it may be a football or basketball game hosted by the University of Florida or by Florida State. In most states, college football and basketball are the favored activities. There are few poker games anymore, but lobbyists will find a way to jog or play tennis with a legislator. For a number of them, the best form of entertainment is golf. In Austin, "the biggest deal is golf and Barton Creek is the best golf club—so you take members to play golf."

Changing Times

The capitol community is not what it was years ago. The old days are dimly remembered now. Few people remain who can recall lobbyists dispensing patronage to supplicant legislators. Nor are the clubs in Sacramento still the centers of life they once were. "Moose Milk," the Derby Club, "Clam and Corral," all paid for by a number of lobbyists and attended by legislators, are either history or irrelevant to the political process. In Denver the poker table in the press room and the refrigerator stacked with beer have vanished. No longer does the clerk of the house in Florida maintain a secret lounge under a stairway in the capitol where legislators can take a few snorts from a stash of liquor donated by the liquor lobby.

Just about everywhere parties are fewer, wining and dining has diminished, and spending is down. Not too long ago a $1,000 dinner bill at the end of a legislative day in Trenton was not unusual. A large contingent of members would go out, eat, and drink on some lobbyist's tab. Not anymore. The Profile in Denver used to be packed with legislators, but no longer. In St. Paul the hangouts like the Gopher Grill of the St. Paul Hotel, the Criterion, or Galvin's are gone. There is no single place where one can find a group of legislators after hours. In Annapolis everyone used to be at Fran O'Brien's on Monday nights. That doesn't happen nowadays. The hotels where members and lobbyists booked rooms are gone. Now members are dispersed, staying at different places, no longer a sitting target for lobbyists and no longer as likely to socialize with one another.

A lobbyist, who covered the Rocky Mountain states for AT&T several years ago explained that even in Wyoming, the capitol community was undergoing significant change:

> Wyoming may be one of the last states where almost everybody stays in the same hotel, but we're starting to see the change. The Hitching Post [hotel] is no longer a place where you can find a mail box for every legislator and just walk in and put notes. . . . People are starting to rent homes during the legislative session and some members are finding other motels. . . . It's much harder for lobbyists when members are in session right straight through the day and then split for the day.[16]

Ohio offers an illustration of what has been going on. Legislators once stayed at the Neill House or Sheraton when they were in Columbus. Now they are all over. When Vern Riffe was speaker, he held forth at the Galleria, which was the legislative watering hole. After the Galleria closed and Riffe retired, no other establishment succeeded in taking the Galleria's place. Although there were several places where people got watered, there was no watering hole as such. One important reason is that the legislative leaders of the 1990s, House Speaker JoAnn Davidson and Senate President Richard Finan, were not watering-hole types. Both took their work home from the office evenings. Davidson took hers to her house in Columbus and Finan took his to his hotel room.

The culture is different today. So are the people. There are more like Davidson and Finan and fewer like Riffe. On the whole, state legislators are a less colorful, but a harder working, bunch than a generation or two ago. Take Oregon's former speaker of the house, Vera Katz, who is described as "almost religious in her devotion to catching the 5 p.m. commuter bus so she could get home to walk her golden retriever."[17] Just about everyone in the cast of characters has changed. Even on Beacon Hill, where the Massachusetts General Court (legislature) sits, the old stalwarts are gone. There used to be people around the Statehouse named "Knocko" (Edward "Knocko" McCormack) and "Onions" (William "Onions" Burke), but they are gone.[18]

Lifestyles are very different. Legislators, like many other people in our society, are conscious of their health. They eat less and drink less. A lobbyist who wants to take a legislator to lunch may find that he or she spends lunchtime at an athletic club. At night, members who live nearby want to go home; the rest will take work back to their hotel rooms, apartments, or condominiums where they live when in the capital. Oftentimes, a committee will be meeting in the evening or some other work session will be taking place. Most legislators are too busy for dinners and lunch. Moreover, when legislators have time free they often reserve it for their colleagues.

Families and work dominate not only for legislators, but for lobbyists too. Nearly everyone is turning away from entertaining. A lobbyist in Texas loves the game of golf, but had not played once with a member during the session. He was simply too busy. A Minnesota contract lobbyist indicated that he would take lawmakers to lunch or dinner if they were old friends or if it was the only time they could meet. But he did not hang around in the evenings to take legislators out. In any case, the pickings would be too slim; no one would be around. A veteran association lobbyist in New Jersey believes his age and experience preclude the need for socializing. He wants to see his family in the evenings. "By the end of the day, I'm ready to go home," said a Florida contract lobbyist, "and I take a pile of paper with me." Wining and dining, furthermore, is not the preferred style of many contemporary lobbyists. "If I get to the capitol early, spend my time wisely, and leave when I'm ready, that's what it takes," commented a lobbyist in Tallahassee. "A lot of the other stuff is folderol," she continued, "they stand around the same cheeseball, but nothing happens." The ethics laws, which prohibit, limit, or restrict the entertaining of legislators by lobbyists, have had an impact. They have given lobbyists a rationale for getting home earlier. One Maryland lobbyist described entertaining in Annapolis as having "fallen off a cliff." Due to ethics regulations enacted in the 1990s he can get home early and coach his son's Little League team. "Ethics laws," in his view, "improve family life for lobbyists."

Indeed, ethics legislation has probably had as great an impact on entertaining and socializing as lobbyists' tools as anything else.

Changes in the ethical climates of statehouses have been precipitated by a tidal wave of ethics legislation throughout the country. This legislation results from a variety of factors: public expectations that are less tolerant of free-wheeling ethical behavior by public officials, on the one hand, and abuses that lead to scandalous situations, on the other hand. The media, and in particular the print media that report on the statehouse, have helped shape new public standards and have encouraged the regulation of legislative ethics.

For a long time Wisconsin has had restrictive laws, which virtually prohibit legislators from accepting gifts, including entertainment, from lobbyists. Except in limited circumstances, a Wisconsin legislator may not accept anything of pecuniary value—travel, a meal, even a cup of coffee—from a lobbyist or a principal. Legislators are advised by their staffs that, to protect themselves from inadvertent violations, they should ask any person who offers them something of value whether or not that person is listed as a lobbyist or principal in the registry maintained by the office of the secretary of state. They are also advised to review the list, which is filed regularly, to know who the lobbyists are.

One of the first states to enact ethics reform legislation in recent decades was California. The Political Reform Act of 1974, known as Proposition 9, was passed on a vote of the electorate. This law effectively ended the entertainment era in Sacramento by prohibiting gifts larger than $10 to any public official in a single month and requiring detailed disclosure. The ethics law in California was tightened in 1990 with the passage of Proposition 112, along with a law enacted by the legislature. That law barred honoraria, limited gifts further, applied gift limitations to principals as well as to lobbyists, virtually eliminated free trips, curtailed the postemployment of legislators as lobbyists for one year, and required that legislators, staff, and lobbyists all take periodic ethics training.

Since the 1970s the nationwide trend has been toward the prohibition, limitation, and/or the disclosure of gifts from lobbyists to legislators. These laws have been intended "to isolate legislators from the generous expense accounts of people who want to influence them."[19] A number of states enacted such laws after scandals like "Shrimpgate" in California,

"Operation Lost Trust" in South Carolina, "AzScam" in Arizona, "Boptrot" in Kentucky, as well as untitled scandals in Connecticut, Florida, Minnesota, New Jersey, New Mexico, and Ohio, and other places. All have led to laws that further regulated the interaction between lobbyists and legislators. Recently Philip Morris was fined because its chief Albany lobbyist failed to disclose all that the corporation was spending on meals and gifts for dozens of lawmakers. The lobbyist was barred from lobbying state government for three years and the pressure for additional regulation proved difficult for the legislature to resist.

New York already limited gift-taking by legislators, if the total amounted to $75 or more. But with the Philip Morris revelations, the Senate Majority Leader, Joseph Bruno, introduced a bill to ban gifts over $25, with some exceptions. Although the assembly did not go along, the senate in 2000 adopted a voluntary ban on gifts worth more than $25.[20]

Where gifts are prohibited—as in California, Iowa, Massachusetts, Minnesota, South Carolina, and Wisconsin—exceptions are ordinarily made for receptions. In Wisconsin, for example, no lobbyist or principal may furnish anything of value to a legislator unless it is also furnished to the general public. Thus, the city of Superior, Wisconsin, which puts on a feed in Madison for the legislature has to open the event to the public. In South Carolina, receptions are excepted if all members of the legislature, the senate or house, or a committee are invited; the public does not have to be. In Minnesota, the exception provides that legislators who speak at a gathering can accept food and beverage.

Washington's limitation on gifts makes an exception for unsolicited flowers, plants, and floral arrangements; unsolicited advertising or promotional items of nominal value, such as pens and notepads; unsolicited tokens or awards of appreciation in the form of a plaque, trophy, desk item, or wall memento; informational material, publications, or subscriptions related to the recipient's performance of official duties; food and beverages consumed at hosted receptions where attendance is related to the state officer's official duties; and admission to, and the cost of food and beverages consumed at, events sponsored by or in conjunction with a civic, charitable, governmental, or community organization. Each legislature, and each legislator as well, will have to decide just where to draw the line on gifts.[21]

The regulation of lobbyist spending on legislators has had a variety of effects. Some consequences are trivial and even foolish. There is always a question of what items legislators can actually accept as gifts. What about plaques, which legislators may be awarded by groups in honor of their service? Representative Phyllis Kahn requested an opinion from Minnesota's Ethical Practices Board, because she had received plaques from a member of groups honoring her legislative service. The board ruled that the plaques were of more than nominal value, since they cost over $100 each. Kahn argued that, whatever the cost originally, once inscribed the plaques had little commercial value. The board, however, stuck to its ruling.

Kahn tested Minnesota's gift law in another appeal to the board. In 1995 she wrote that she and her husband traditionally celebrate Passover with friends, one of whom was a registered lobbyist. She wanted to know how the law applied if she went to the lobbyist's house: does she have to pay for the value of what is served her or for the value of what is served to both her and her husband? "If we supply part of the ceremonial table, i.e., the haggadahs or the haroset, and appropriate desserts, is that considered an even exchange? If we are the host house one year and she the next, is that considered an even exchange? If she makes the gefilte fish for our Seder, is that an inappropriate gift?" The letter, dated April 10, asked for a quick reply, since the first Seder was on April 14 and the second the following day. The Ethical Practices Board responded that same day with the chair's opinion that the board "is not authorized to address the matter of a religious ceremony in a private home because of the separation of church and state."[22]

The Effects of Regulation

In many capital cities, where the legislature has been a prominent presence, restrictions on entertainment have been unkind to the restaurant business. Sacramento's restaurants suffered much earlier, but have since rebounded. In Tallahassee, Trenton, Columbus, and St. Paul, some of the established eateries took a hit. Most recently, pricey restaurants in Albany, such as Ogden's, lost business because of the senate's ban on accepting lobbyists' meals. In fact, Albany restaurant owners claimed the loss of one-third to one-half of their business on weeknights. Meanwhile senators munched sandwiches at their desks for lunch and made do with pizza and Chinese take-out for dinner. One senator, it was reported, lost twenty pounds in four months.[23]

The abuses of the past—an electric company lobbyist who spent $175,000 on Florida legislators during a two-year period, quail-hunting trips in Georgia, poker games in Texas where legislators never lost—are extremely rare today. A Maryland legislator recalled how one or the other of his colleagues used to say, "Who's got a sponsor? Let's go out to dinner."

Now, he never hears the work "sponsor" with reference to a lobbyist. The capital culture of Annapolis is totally different than earlier, as are capital cultures in most states. Legislators are wary of taking gifts from lobbyists even if the law permits it. And they can never be absolutely sure just what is allowed and what is not allowed. "If anybody can say exactly where the dividing line between legality and illegality is, they are wrong," said a California lobbyist. "The situation is too fluid." Even if they do not stumble over the law, legislators risk having whatever they disclose used against them in an election, if it is reported in the media and exploited by an opponent. Legislators now maintain more of a distance from lobbyists, lest their dealings be misconstrued. The gulf between lobbyists and legislators is such that, "The two are now waltzing at arm's length . . . instead of dancing cheek-to-cheek."[24]

Entertainment, at least that which is furnished by lobbyists, is down all over. Hunting and fishing trips are becoming extinct. Since enactment of ethics reform in Texas, the amount that lobbyists spent on legislators decreased significantly. Legislators are still inclined to ask the Texas Ethics Commission whether they condone the practice of going hunting at the invitation of lobbyists, which they had been doing for years. The advice they get is to go dutch. "Anybody can go hunting with anybody," as one commission member put it. "You only get into a problem when people aren't paying their own way."[25] In Florida, trips to Disney World and gala parties are relics of the past. A few members still go hunting and fishing with lobbyist friends, but they pay for their lodgings. Fewer and fewer people in states like Connecticut and Maryland want to risk disclosure if a lobbyist picks up the tab for a meal. So legislators do not go out to dinner at all, dine only with colleagues, or simply pay their own way if lobbyists are present.

New Jersey's experience illustrates the decline of "benefit passing." Current disclosure requirements were passed by the legislature in 1991 and went into effect at the beginning of the next year. The amounts spent by lobbyists on legislatures dropped steadily for the first few years and by 1995 leveled off at about $75,000 to $80,000 a year (with the exception of 1998 when $114,532 was spent, the rise attributable to a few trips taken by a few legislators).[26]

Resourceful legislators and lobbyists can find ways to get around some of the restrictions. Lobbyists can no longer pay for golf with legislators in a state such as Ohio. So, each golfer pays his or her own way. But they can make a bet on the eighteenth hole (which approximates the cost of the legislator's round), and the legislator would always win. Nonetheless, entertainment and socializing are exceptions to the new norms. The consequences of this highly regulated environment are several.

First, there is less socializing, less informal contact, not only among lobbyists and legislators, but among legislators themselves. Lobbyists used to serve to bring legislators together, many of whom were from different chambers, different parties, and different ideological persuasions. These social occasions made it easier for legislators to develop trusting relationships with one another, as well as with their hosts. Such relationships helped in the exchange of information and the bargaining for votes. In the words of a Maryland legislator, "the system was greased by socializing." Lobbyists no longer perform such a function, and nowadays usually choose to dine with colleagues with whom they have much in common rather than with those who are quite unlike themselves. Their relationships, therefore, tend to be narrower than they were before restrictions on gifts.

Second, much of the socializing that does take place occurs at receptions, where legislators run less risk in attending. They go to receptions that are held by associations and groups of all sorts to see any constituents who might be there. And they also go to see one another. During the course of the legislative session there may be one or more receptions three or four nights of the week. But the opportunities for socializing at an event, where people mill about and approach one another continuously, are a far cry from opportunities at smaller dinners. In some states, ethics regulations have discouraged legislators from attending receptions. In Minnesota, for example, the number of receptions held in St. Paul is way down and legislators are wary of attending them; they are even hesitant to go to receptions in their home districts. People simply get together face-to-face less often.

Third, the last major arena of contact in the highly regulated states is the fund-raiser. In California, for example, it is *the* place for lobbyists to touch base with legislators who are diligently raising funds for the next election campaign. Lobbyists can pay their respects, but there is little time for much more. Relationship building—outside the context of campaign contributions—is not really possible.

Fourth, a stricter regulatory environment affects the way lobbyists live their lives and do business. Those who want to get home earlier in order to spend time with their families have more chance to do so. Many of the newer, younger lobbyists seem to be of this disposition. As far as building relationships with legislators is concerned, the job would appear to be tougher for practically all lobbyists. The few for whom entertaining and socializing were critical probably are at a greater disadvantage nowadays than the rest. But there is no evidence that any kind of lobbyist has suffered much more than another kind. Indeed, one survey of California lobbyists after Proposition 9 was passed showed that only one out of twenty felt that the $10-per-month gift limit had either greatly enhanced or reduced his or her effectiveness.[27] Lobbyists adapt to the environments in which they operate, relying on alternative techniques of communication and influence when traditional ones are no longer as useful.

Lobbyist Ethics

Lobbying is a far different profession today. Two political scientists, both experienced students of interest group politics in the states, observe that the lobbying communities have become much more professional during the last twenty years.[28] They are correct. Moreover, part of the professional character of the community is attributable to higher ethical standards and more ethical behavior. "They are much more honest as a profession than they were twenty or thirty years ago," is the assessment of Bob Stern, executive director of the Council on Governmental Ethics Laws.

With a much larger lobbying community and increasing competition in each state capital, it has become harder to agree on norms, and the profession may be attracting marginal members. Some of these members make mischief, it is said, in order to stay employed. A few hold to the belief, in the words of one lobbyist, that "You should never kill a bill so bad that [the opposition] can't come back next year, or you'll be out of business." The competition for clients among contract lobbyists is fierce, and it is not unusual for some of them to try to discredit their competition as they aggressively grow their businesses.

Contract lobbyists make choices of an ethical nature in the clients they take on. Some take the position, like that of an attorney, that everyone is entitled to representation, and are willing to work for just about anyone. Most draw the line somewhere, refusing to represent certain interests. Harold Hodes in New Jersey was involved with the enactment of Pinelands preservation legislation when he was chief of staff to Governor Brendan Byrne. He will not accept a client whose goal is development in the Pinelands. Phil Isenberg in California says that to him tobacco and guns are off limits: "But having said that, you can't be alive very long before you realize that issues aren't as simple as you thought when you were young."[29] Just about everyone who needs and can afford representation by a lobbyist gets it.

A thorny ethical problem for contract lobbyists is conflict of interests. A conflict occurs when two or more of a lobbyist's clients have competing interests. Conflicts come in many different forms. The interests of one client may be directly adverse to the interests of another. One client, a health insurer, favors an increase in cigarette taxes to fund smoking cessation programs, while another client, a cigarette company, opposes the increase. Or the client a lobbyist represents on one issue may be opposed to the position taken by another client on an unrelated issue. Or it may be difficult to represent two clients simultaneously because of strategic factors, as when a legislator is only willing to lend support on one of the lobbyist's issues.

The more clients a lobbyist or a lobbying firm has, the greater the likelihood of conflicts. If a lobbyist has fifty or sixty clients, as some do, and is involved in a hundred or more different pieces of legislation, as some are, it is difficult to avoid such conflict. Or if a law firm, with both legal and lobbying clients, has a large portfolio, a conflict is almost sure to crop up. Lobbyists with fewer clients—say, ten or so—are less likely to encounter conflicts, particularly if they screen potential clients. Screening is necessary. A Colorado lobbyist, for instance, will not take on a client whose interest might conflict with that of a current client. He will refer such an account to a colleague. A Texas law firm with a lobbying practice does a computer check of all clients to identify situations of possible conflict. Many lobbyists leave the decision up to the clients. They inform clients of a possible conflict, and, if the clients have no objection, the lobbyist represents them both.

Sometimes, of course, a conflict may come up unexpectedly during the course of the legislative session. An ethical lobbyist will notify both clients and then choose one or the other to continue representing on the issue. It may be the first client or the one who provides better business. The real issue, however, is the lobbyist's perception of a conflict, which is not always evident or clear cut. These judgments are difficult judgments, as a Colorado lobbyist says, "[deciding] where you draw the line is not an easy thing to do."

Lobbyists are facing the challenges of rapidly changing rules and ethics laws and a highly critical press. The question is, can the profession respond? Even in the 1960s lobbyists had a sense of belonging to a distinct profession, according to the study of lobbyists in Oregon, Massachusetts, North Carolina, and Utah.[30] Over the past thirty years that sense has grown along with the professionalization of state legislatures. Today, most lobbyists take pride in what they do and believe they are vital elements in the legislative process and representative democracy.

The professionalization of lobbying has been facilitated by the organization at the national level of state government relations personnel and, in a number of states, the organization of lobbyists. The Public Affairs Council (PAC), an association of professionals who are responsible for government relations at the federal and state levels, has been providing continuing education for lobbyists. In 1975, the State Government Affairs Council (SGAC) formed. Its purposes were similar to those of PAC, but its focus was on state lobbying exclusively.

Organizations have also sprung up on the state level. The Minnesota Governmental Relations Council was founded in 1978. Its purpose was to raise ethical standards and enhance the professionalism of its approximately 250 members. The Arkansas Society of Professional Lobbyists was formed in 1990, in large part to offset intense media criticism, notably by opinion columnists in two statewide newspapers who "pretty much bash lobbyists and legislators and everyone else." The society set about to tackle the problem of image through educating its members and the public. The Florida League of Professional Lobbyists formed in 1989 to upgrade the ethics of lobbyists. One of its first tasks was to adopt a voluntary code, which encouraged members to avoid conflicts of interest, not tell lies, and comply with all state laws governing lobbying.

Organization does not work everywhere. There is none in New Jersey, although a lobbyist's club used to exist in Trenton. A similar group, called "The Third House," existed in Denver. But as the ranks of lobbyists grew, the Denver group turned into an exclusive club and soon dissolved. According to one Colorado lobbyist, the group was very effective in straightening out the occasional errant lobbyist, but Colorado lobbyists have shown little interest in forming a successor organization.

In Texas organization appears to meet the needs of one part of the lobbying community but not the other. More than two hundred associations in the Austin area belong to the American Society of Association Executives. Many in-house lobbyists are active in this association. But Texas contract lobbyists have no group of their own, perhaps because of their varied interests and keen rivalries.

Lobbying is a highly regulated industry, and there is no indication that regulation will be relaxed in the years ahead. Several states now provide ethics training for legislators, and a few require it for lobbyists as well. Since 1990 California has required that anyone who registers to lobby also sign up for a day's ethics training conducted by the senate or assembly, and including a review of statutory law on bribery, extortion, gifts, and so forth. At the session in June 1999, for instance, 137 lobbyists attended the training given at the Sacramento convention center.

Partially in response to regulatory pressures, lobbyists themselves have begun to formulate codes of ethics to guide their behavior. The Institute of Governmental Advocates in California has such a code, as does the Capitol Club, Inc., of Oregon. At the national level, the American League of Lobbyists adopted a set of guidelines for professional conduct in 1987. It encourages lobbyists to temper their advocacy role with consideration for the public interest, fairly present all points of view, protect confidences, avoid conflicts of interests, and not bring discredit to the profession because of personal conduct. The professional lobbyist, according to the guidelines, should always "deal in accurate, current and factual information" and "not engage in misrepresentation of any nature." The American Society of Association Executives (ASEA) guidelines employ the same standards.

The Minnesota Governmental Relations Council (MGRC) has a code of standards that specifies that

> members should not knowingly make any false or misleading statements to clients or employers or other advocates, employees of the legislature or administrative staff, or anyone else involved in the governmental process.

At the same time, Rule 76 of the Minnesota senate calls for essentially the same behavior as does the lobbyists' own code:

> A lobbyist shall not knowingly furnish false or misleading information or make a false or misleading statement that is relevant and material to a matter before the Senate or any of its committees when the lobbyist knows or should know it will influence the judgment or action of the Senate or any of its committees thereon.

The senate rule, like the MGRC provision in its code of ethics, establishes a standard according to which lobbyists are expected to behave. The rule and the standard however, were never invoked until recently.

In the past the sanctions against lobbyists who misled legislators in Minnesota—as well as everywhere else—were informal, not formal. If someone deceived a legislator, the word got around. And in the relatively small community of the capitol a reputation for lack of integrity or untruthfulness could be fatal. The few lobbyists whose reputations were questionable would lose their effectiveness. The constraints on lobbyists thus were powerful.

In the Minnesota senate's deliberations in 1998 over a proposal to reduce the drunken-driving standard from 0.10 to 0.08 percent blood-alcohol level, John Berglund, a lobbyist for the Minnesota Licensed Beverage Association, was charged with misrepresenting statistics on drunk-driving arrests. He had distributed a flyer that said most drivers who register at 0.08 and 0.09 percent drive safely home after being pulled over. State officials said that such drivers are almost always arrested and almost never drive home.[31] An official of the Department of Public Safety denied statements that had been attributed to her on the flyer and said that, "I feel that Mr. Berglund intentionally used my name and reputation to provide false information."[32] Berglund apologized for what he claimed was an unintentional error.

The dispute might have ended then, with possible effects on Berglund's reputation. But John Marty, a member of the senate considered by his colleagues to be self-righteous with a "holier than thou" attitude and also a strong proponent of reducing the drunken-driving blood-alcohol level standard, filed a complaint of a possible violation of Rule 76. The ethics subcommittee would have preferred to leave things to the informal process. The chairs checked with legal counsel to determine if the complaint included sufficient grounds to proceed under the rule, and were informed that the grounds were there. The subcommittee had no choice but to move forward on Marty's complaint.

After investigation, it could not be proved that Berglund knowingly misled the senate. But the committee decided that he was "careless and negligent" in not verifying the statements he had attributed to the director of Driver and Vehicle Services. The committee resolved that Berglund acknowledged that he should have verified the statements and, in not doing so, he was careless and negligent. Upon receipt of his acknowledgment by the senate, the committee recommended that the complaint be dismissed.

Berglund's case became a cause for Minnesota lobbyists. As a lobbyist, Berglund personally did not think that he should have been bound by senate rules. Furthermore, he objected to being judged by senators, who were political, rather than by a court or ethics board.[33] The Minnesota Governmental Relations Council went further, challenging the constitutionality of the process. According to its review, state statutes make it a felony to "corruptly" influence legislators by "deception." The Berglund case, therefore, should have been pursued through the criminal process where more constitutional protections were available to the accused. MGRC also pointed out that appropriate procedures and rights were not articulated in ethics subcommittee rules and that Rule 76, in proscribing behavior that would bring the senate into "dishonor or disrepute," was too vague and imprecise to satisfy due process requirements. It suggested that the criminalization of lobbyist conduct was not the direction to pursue. In MGRC's judgment a disturbing precedent had been set "as to how the mistakes of members and lobbyists will be handled by the Senate, even after sincere apologies have been offered." It suggested that if a problem cannot be resolved informally between the individuals involved, it ought to be brought to MGRC, which has a code of ethics for lobbyists.[34]

The lobbyists' association tried to get the Minnesota senate to exempt lobbyists from Rule 76, but without success. In Minnesota, as in other states, the conduct of lobbyists falls within the jurisdiction of the legislature. In Minnesota a single member can trigger an ethics inquiry. In other states, barring a Rule 76 equivalent, it would be harder to do. But under pressure from the media and the public, the trend is probably running toward more formal mechanisms of regulation.

For a brief period Berglund had become something of a folk hero with the St. Paul lobbying community. But he was concerned with how the issue might have affected his reputation with legislators and the longer-term implications for his career. Shortly thereafter, Berglund left Minnesota for a position elsewhere.

CHAPTER 6

Building Relationships

W hat I do requires me to get my clients a fair hearing," says James Featherstonbaugh, a New York lobbyist. "And my relationship with all these people helps me to do that."[1] Much of what happens in the state capitals comes down to basic human relationships. If, as Tip O'Neill says, "All politics are local," it is also true that all legislative politics are, at least in good part, personal. Whatever the political system or culture, the lobbyist's goal is to make connections and develop close relationships with as many legislators (and, in some states, as many of their legislative staff) as possible. One of Florida's contract lobbyists put it baldly: "Everything must be seen in terms of relationships." Not all lobbyists subscribe to this goal, and of those who do, not all subscribe equally. Contract lobbyists are the truest believers. Citizen group lobbyists are less concerned with the "inside" work of developing relationships. They have their issues, their members, and a sympathetic press; they mainly play an outside game. That probably suits their personalities, budgets, and philosophies as well. Occasionally, as in the case of the public interest groups in Colorado, citizen lobbyists find the inside game clean and appealing. So one can also often find them building personal relationships like most of their colleagues.

Some lobbyists believe they spend more time developing relationships than they do on direct lobbying. In the words of a Florida lobbyist and former speaker of the house, "Lobbying really is friendship more than anything else." "If you've got the wrong chemistry," according to a Colorado association lobbyist, "it's hard to do business." A New Jersey lobbyist for a university explains, "Before I ask for anything from them, I try to make friends."

The significance of personal relationships should be obvious to anyone familiar with the legislative process. Without trust, credibility, and veracity in the dealings among individuals, the process could hardly work at all. So, lobbyists try to develop relationships that allow them to demonstrate the worthy attributes they themselves possess, which is prerequisite for promoting their client's wares. Personal ties make it easier for legislators to develop trust and confidence in, and a liking for, those who are trying to influence them. Legislators, like the rest of us, are more apt to do things for individuals they like and trust. No greater commendation can be paid a lobbyist than that paid by an admiring California legislator. In his summation, the lobbyist was "completely honest," "very well informed," and "projected complete frankness, yet never appeared disloyal to his clients."[2] But it takes time for people to develop trust in one another. If, through a relationship, a lobbyist proves to be a credible, reliable, loyal, empathetic, and likable person, he or she will have made the grade; the path of direct lobbying will have been made smooth.

Natural Development

Relationships are not difficult to forge in a legislative setting. Indeed, as one Florida lobbyist and former legislator said: "It's hard up here not to develop friendships." Legislators and lobbyists naturally gravitate toward one another. Because they share a stake in the legislative system, they can commiserate and celebrate with each other.

But some lobbyists have a head start, especially when they have relationships with legislators that go back a long way. Friendships that predate life in and around the legislature tend to be the closest. Friends from pre-political days are often deemed the truest—they will be around, it is presumed, after the legislator leaves office and loses power. Kinship does not hurt either. For example, Joe Bell, an Arkansas lobbyist, is the son of Clarence Bell, an Arkansas senator. (It is reported that sometimes the father went along with his son and sometimes he didn't, but there is no doubt as to their relationship.) A friendship that starts out when the legislator first arrives in Tallahassee can also bear fruit. When he began a career as a lobbyist-lawyer in 1972, Jack Skelding also managed an apartment complex in Tallahassee. One tenant was Ralph Haben, then a freshman legislator. Landlord and tenant each had an interest in flying and became friends, eventually sharing apartments and airplanes. When Haben became speaker nine years later, Skelding had a built-in advantage—a long-standing friendship.[3]

Many legislator-lobbyist relationships originated in the legislature itself. In a few states, a number of lobbyists had first served on the legislative staff. About one out of five lobbyists in Sacramento came from the ranks of senate, assembly, or central staffs. Several of the contract lobbyists in Trenton have also had experience on legislative partisan staffs. At least a few Florida committee staff directors or leadership aides followed their legislator bosses who opened up lobbying shops near the capitol. All of them had connections from their previous lives.

Among the closest relationships are those between lobbyists who had once served as legislators and their colleagues who continue in office. The bonding that takes place in the legislature has no substitute: the experiences shared, the favors exchanged, and the debts incurred are without parallel. A Colorado lobbyist reflected on how much of an advantage it was to be a former member of both the house and the senate. "Any way you cut it," he stated, "there is a collegial feeling among members and former members." In North Carolina, for example, among the ten lobbyists named as most effective in 1991 six were former members.[4]

A lobbyist who had served in a leadership position is even better off. As Florida speaker, Ralph Haben had appointed Jon Mills, then in his second term, to an important subcommittee chairmanship; he had also served with T. K. Wetherell and Bolley "Bo" Johnson. After Haben left the legislature and went into lobbying, Mills became speaker, followed a few years later by Wetherell, and then Johnson. They had all gone through legislative wars together and naturally felt a kinship. Having served as a leader, however, may be a doubled-edged sword. As a lobbyist, Haben felt he could not ask speakers to do things another lobbyist might not hesitate to request, because he was especially sensitive to anything that might jeopardize the office of speaker.

As turnover occurs—naturally or because of term limits—and new members replace older ones, these ties obviously loosen. New members do not know the veterans now lobbying. But reputations endure, the respect for former speakers lasts, and someone is invariably around and ready to introduce a former legislator to a current one. In any case, a lobbyist who belongs to a "former members club" is always in a position to call on newer, as well as older, legislators for help (although a number of ex-legislator lobbyists eschew the privilege of being on the floor of the chamber). The mystique lingers. For the lobbyist, therefore, it is better to have been a legislator, even in a distant past, than never to have been one at all.

A lobbyist, of course, cannot establish a relationship with every member. A sorting-out process therefore takes place. Certainly likes tend to attract. Female lobbyists are more likely to develop close relationships with female legislators, African American lobbyists with African American legislators, Hispanics with Hispanics. Public interest lobbyists appear to have especially good relationships with legislative staff. They tend to have similar values. Most lobbyists manage to develop connections on both sides of the aisle because Democrats and Republicans can go either way on many issues of interest.

Not all interactions between lobbyists and legislators are positive. Occasionally, lobbyists make enemies. Sometimes this happens because legislators don't like a lobbyist's client; sometimes it's because they don't like the lobbyist. Whatever the cause, lobbyists still have to try to reach the unfriendly lawmaker. "I cannot get along with ____," notes a Colorado lobbyist, "but I do know someone who can get to him." Even though a personal relationship may be difficult to forge, one's work can still go on.

Forging Bonds

Many relationships between lobbyists and legislators just happen. More often, however, they are cultivated by lobbyists who do not wait for nature to take its course. It is a delicate process—"like courting a woman," said a member of the New Jersey lobby. It takes time. Joe Bell of Little Rock counsels patience: "I wait for the relationship to develop naturally or without trying to make it occur prematurely. Like wine, don't uncork it before its time."[5] Socializing is still important, though different than formerly. Socializing helps develop trust. Then, when the lobbyist argues the merits of an issue, the existence of trust allows the legislator to see the merits of the lobbyist's side more clearly than the merits of the other side. It is not a dinner, or a hunting trip, or a campaign contribution but, rather, a whole string of contacts that forges the link between legislator and lobbyist. Among the many tried and true techniques, the following deserve mention.

1. *Entertaining.* By entertaining legislators, lobbyists get the opportunity to spend time in relaxed settings. The idea is for the two parties to get to know one another. Some think it is easier to get legislators to listen to their case over a meal, but others seldom discuss business. A New Jersey lobbyist explains:

> If I were to take a senator to the Giants game, I wouldn't be inviting him because I want him to vote for my bill. I'd be inviting him because I had an extra ticket, he's a friend of mine, I know him.

Conversation, instead, revolves around sports, families, politics—wherever the lobbyist can gain common ground with the legislator. Entertaining is the means to identifying commonalities. According to one observer, "Entertainment is to a lobbyist as a wrench is to a plumber."

There are more ways to entertain legislators than one can imagine, even today with restrictions on benefit passing. One Louisiana lobbyist, who loves to cook, prepared a crawfish etouffé dinner for the president of the senate and a bunch of his official guests. Lobbyists accompany legislators to football and basketball games and to golf tournaments. They also work close to home. They invite legislators, along with their spouses, to their houses, in the belief that, "if you can get a legislator in your home with his wife, he'll get to trust you." The spouse helps considerably. Today's lobbyists, however, do less entertaining than their predecessors. Growing numbers of legislators will simply not run the risks associated with being wined and dined. More likely, the lobbyists will organize receptions during the legislative session, so that legislators can meet with members of their client groups.

Lobbyists also work further afield. They entertain legislators at the many meetings held around the country by organizations such as the National Conference of State Legislatures, the Council of State Governments, the State Legislative Leaders Foundation, and the American Legislative Exchange Council. Business groups underwrite part of the costs of these meetings and also host receptions and other social events in the evenings. Lobbyists find these to be excellent occasions for entertaining legislators one-on-one or in small groups. In most States restrictions that apply to entertaining in the capital do not apply to meetings out of state.

2. *Trips.* Even further afield are the trips, for purposes of hunting—with deer, quail, and dove as prey—or fishing. These were once favorites for lobbyists and some legislators, particularly in the South. Off in the wilderness lobbyists and legislators could shoot, sit around, spit, and bond. No legislative business was discussed, because, as a Florida lobbyist observed:

> Nobody would ever go with you again. I think you would defeat the real reason for having the trip—to get to know these guys and have them get to know you. If you started talking about legislation, they would be so on guard and everything, nobody would have a good time, and it wouldn't be worthwhile.[6]

According to some lobbyists, a good fishing or hunting trip was remembered long after a political campaign contribution had been forgotten. Today, trips of this sort are relatively rare and for newer members part of the legislative folklore rather than a piece of what they will experience.

3. *Gifts.* For lobbyists, it is better to give than to receive, at least in the process of building relationships. The gifts are small, but they do not go unappreciated. Bruce Bereano, a contract lobbyist in Annapolis, showered

legislators with flowers, candy, and cigars. For years he sent flowers on Valentine's Day to secretaries of each legislative committee and birthday cards to key staffers.[7] Lobbyists range through the legislative office buildings in Tallahassee, leaving in their wake gumdrops, popcorn, peanuts and other tidbits—all of which were consumed mainly by legislators' secretaries. One lobbyist for a national food company would typically leave a can of his company's cashews behind when he visited legislators' offices. One day, a staff member in one of the offices inquired, in jest, whether he was trying to buy votes this way. The lobbyist replied, "If I can buy a vote for a three-dollar can of nuts, it's not worth buying." Gifts, too, are going out of style—even the smallest variety. One California assemblyman had a sign on the door to his suite of offices asking that visitors not bear gifts—under ethics regulations, they would only cause trouble.

Some lobbyists offered special services instead of gifts per se. One baby-sat the small children of legislators. Another even invested in a Chevrolet Suburban (which seats nine, more if passengers are small) so he could haul around legislators. Services extend further. A lobbyist for cable television makes sure that legislators get a quick hook-up from the local company at their summer homes or get invited to appear on a cable interview program. A lobbyist for a telephone company helps legislators when they have trouble with their equipment or when they want a special number for a new phone. The physical therapy association will give legislators massages, the chiropractors will pop their backs, the podiatrists will look after their feet, a pharmaceutical company will screen their eyes—all gratis. In this way, legislators will get to know a lobbyist's clients in a most favorable light. A lobbyist for the acupuncturists has not yet succeeded in interesting many legislators in his client's complimentary services. But he is sticking with it. When the wife of a Florida speaker of the house had a premature baby on a trip to Israel, the lobbyist for the medical school of one of the state's universities made arrangements with Israeli medical authorities for her care. Another category that falls under the rubric of gifts is honoraria. A few legislators once were able to command a fee for addressing association or corporate meetings. In most states now honoraria are banned.

4. *Athletics.* There are probably few better ways for lobbyists to connect to legislators than on a playing field. Jogging, golf, crew, basketball—they all constitute quality time. A Maryland lobbyist got into the habit of going to the Naval Academy gym early in the morning to play basketball with legislators. A Texas lobbyist made it a practice of getting into a basketball game with legislators at Austin's Metropolitan Club. Several California lobbyists play racquetball with legislators at the Capital Athletic

Club. Golf is probably the optimum diversion, as far as lobbyists are concerned, in that it permits leisurely and personal conversation as legislator and lobbyist tramp from tee to tee. There has been a shift from gin mill to athletic field; as was noted by the *New York Times:* "Physical fitness is now an asset for the lobbyist the way tolerance of strong drink once was."[8]

5. *Constituent service.* Lobbyists can be enormously helpful to legislators when it comes to service for their constituents. A contract lobbyist, who represents Blue Cross–Blue Shield, will help a constituent cut through company red tape. A telephone company lobbyist has a note pad at the ready for legislator requests on behalf of constituents who have problems with service or billing. He can take care of a problem almost immediately. The telephone company, with its emphasis on community relations, is unequaled when it comes to service. In Arkansas one legislator had a constituent who wanted compensation for five cows killed by a Union Pacific locomotive, while another had constituents who wanted an old railroad terminal made part of a local cultural center. The contract lobbyist representing the Union Pacific took care of it all.[9] An insurance lobbyist accepted the case of the relative of a receptionist working in the law firm of a legislative leader. The problem was that she was told her insurance did not cover a bone marrow transplant. A lobbyist for a state university estimated that he spent over a third of his time on service to legislators' constituents on matters of admissions, financial aid, and housing. He described the process: "Some people in my position in other schools have an admission or two in their pocket, so if a really key legislator has a constituent who wants to get admitted, he will see to it that the kid gets admitted. . . . I can't do that." What he does instead is to provide legislators with as much information as possible about the constituent's admissions case.

6. *Appreciation and acknowledgment.* There are a host of gestures more subtle than entertainment or gifts. Yet they, too, are effective in relationship building. Respect for members and for the institution is necessary. This comes most naturally to lobbyists who have served in the legislature. Recognition also matters. Groups such as the California Society of Certified Public Accountants honor a "legislator of the year." Just about every group gives, and most legislators receive, a plaque in appreciation of their service, support, or performance. For example, after the Florida legislature appropriated almost one million dollars to the Greater Miami Opera, one of its lobbyists proposed that key legislator supporters be sent a framed poster with a small plaque reading: "BRAVO AND THANK YOU! GREATER MIAMI OPERA." He explained that, "I like members

of the legislature to think about my clients all the time." And the best way for them to do that, he added, "is to put something on their walls."[10] Furthermore, after every battle or even a skirmish, the lobbyist should thank and praise the legislators who were involved. Another form of acknowledgment is promoting the legislator with the public, and preferably constituents. Many companies invite legislators to visit their facilities, take their picture, and put it in a newsletter that is distributed to employees and others.

7. *Understanding.* The lobbyists who, during interim periods, travel to legislators' home districts demonstrate a real understanding of where members live. A Minnesota lobbyist makes good use of the time when the legislature is not in session. He visits members in their homes, drives out to the fields where they may be farming, takes them a cold beer, and inquires as to their concerns. "If you drive two hundred miles, they'll remember that." Before the session begins and after the primaries, one of the leading contract lobbyists in Maryland visits each newly nominated legislator who will not be facing much opposition in the general election. He has breakfast, coffee, lunch, or dinner with almost every new member. (Getting them to go out for a meal cuts out the distractions of secretary, telephone, or office routine.) Seeing them in the context of their districts gives this lobbyist an understanding that few of his colleagues possess. With entertaining and socializing becoming more and more difficult for lobbyists, many are turning to district visits where legislators are more accessible and where the contact is more likely to be remembered.

An aspect of understanding is a sympathetic ear. Lobbyists have to be good listeners, tolerating the most banal or rambling discourse. If lobbyists appear not to care about legislators' interests, legislators are sure not to give a rap about those of the lobbyists. One lobbyist, who knows from the experience of having served in the legislature, prides himself on being an "informed listener." He points out that, "Nothing is as dear to a new member as his recent election. They never tire of talking about it." Therefore, he informs himself about their campaigns and not only listens but also responds to their conversation on the subject.

8. *Advice.* In addition to sympathy, advice is also sought by legislators. Legislators often seek out lobbyists when they need advice on issues on their agendas. "I have an idea, can you help?" Or, "How do I fight this?" To an environmental lobbyist in New Jersey: "Should I put this bill in?" To an environmental lobbyist in Florida: "I want to file an environmental bill; what would you suggest?" One firm in Tallahassee is frequently consulted by legislators and legislative staff for advice on legislative language.

"They know we're proficient in certain areas," said a leading lawyer-lobbyist. On a specific subject, for example, one of the firm's attorneys is so expert that legislative staff will not move before checking with her. Her advice is mainly technical: "This is what will happen if you do this, this is what will happen if you don't." In Colorado, an association lobbyist with particular expertise answers many legislator questions regarding unemployment insurance and workers' compensation. An experienced Texas lobbyist is especially well versed in the parliamentary process. As the session draws to a close and rules and process become critical, more and more members turn to him for advice. A Minnesota lobbyist who has general knowledge but no particular expertise volunteers information from his perspective to friends in leadership—alerting them to incipient issues, who wants what, and what is likely to be going on.

9. *Assistance on legislation.* Years ago, Harmon Zeigler and Michael Baer, in their examination of lobbying in four states, pointed out that legislators used lobbyists to influence other legislators and the public.[11] That is still the case. In Colorado, legislators will check with the education association lobbyist to see whether their bills are consistent with the organization's policy and whether the association will testify and lobby in their behalf. Another lobbyist for an influential Colorado association also receives requests each session from legislators who want to broaden the backing for bills they are sponsoring. If it does not run counter to group policy, she will sign on. Legislators, in fact, seek support from lobbyists more than might be imagined. A 1987 Gallup survey asked New Jersey legislators how frequently they looked to lobbyists for support for their bills. While 7 percent responded "frequently," as many as 44 percent responded "somewhat frequently," and only 11 percent replied that they did not rely on lobbyists "at all." In Minnesota a 1987 survey of lobbyists found that a third of them saw as one of their chief tasks that of helping legislators to build support for their bills. Another study of lobbyists found that 27 percent said they were approached frequently and 54 percent occasionally by legislators seeking help.[12] Sometimes it is a matter of horsetrading. If lobbyists help legislators get their bills passed, legislators will help them. Sometimes it is more subtle. Lobbyists may act as intermediaries for legislators, passing the word to others.

10. *Campaign contributions and involvement.* Relationships thrive in the context of legislators' election campaigns. There is nothing closer to the heart of a politician than the current election, the one coming up, or the one before. Political contributions build relationships. This is not the occasion to enter into the debate over what campaign contributions buy,

independent of other factors.[13] Suffice it to say, lobbyists are never sure of just what is expected and just how a political action committee contribution or a personal contribution will be received. Their operating assumptions are that giving cannot hurt and that it helps to connect lobbyist and legislator. By the same token, they reason that *not* giving (if one has the bucks) *can* hurt and surely will do nothing to strengthen connections.

Further campaign involvement may pay greater dividends as far as relationships are concerned. Teacher associations that endorse candidates and whose members work locally in their behalf help to strengthen the ties between their agents and the preferred legislators. Many contract lobbyists themselves play a significant campaign role, helping to raise money for legislators, particularly for those who have difficulties raising money on their own. These campaigner-lobbyists are extremely helpful to legislative leaders, bundling money from their clients and delivering it to the legislative parties. A few play an even larger role—in gubernatorial campaigns and in legislative races as well.

Trial by Fire

However a relationship between a lobbyist and legislator gets forged, it must undergo trial by fire. And the relationship is tested repeatedly as legislators and lobbyists work together in the legislative process. No matter how effectively lobbyists cultivate the social side, they must also meet the professional standards that legislators have established for them. A number of tests have to be met if relationships are to be maintained.

First, in order to be productive, relationships must be durable. The longer lobbyists have been around, the more likely they will have developed solid ties. There is no substitute for longevity. One legislative leader advised a group of lobbyists to "act like you're around for the long haul." The worst thing is to "hit and run."[14] Lobbyists who have put in time and dealt with legislators on many issues in a variety of circumstances will have proved themselves. A contract lobbyist in New Jersey reflected that legislators trusted him because he had been in Trenton (in various capacities) for twenty years, they had dealt with him, and he had "never let anybody down."

Second, lobbyists must be credible. "When a legislator looks at me," said a Colorado lobbyist, "I want him to see credibility." To be deemed credible, lobbyists will have had to keep their word where their word counts most—on matters of political and legislative business. Lobbyists have to be sure that they give their word to legislators only after they know that they will be able to keep whatever commitment they make. They have to present "the whole truth," not just their client's truth. That means informing the legislator of the other side of the issue, the "down side" from the lobbyist's point of view. That is not difficult to do because, as a Florida lobbyist notes, "I've never seen a position without merit. I just think that I've got more merit to my position." He has met the test; legislators can count on his word and rely on his assessment. "If I go to them and ask them, they won't even question me. They trust me." It takes time and effort to reach such a position. A Colorado cause lobbyist saw the challenge as follows: "You get credibility in teaspoonsful and you lose it in gallons." Any lobbyist can deceive a legislator, but only once.

Third, lobbyists must also be effective. This goes further than credibility. "It's not just that you're an honest guy," according to a public interest group lobbyist in Colorado, "but that you're an effective guy." Legislators will distance themselves from lobbyists who are perceived as losers in the capitol community.

Fourth, there is also the test of reliability. Most important, reliability means eliminating—insofar as possible—the element of surprise. Legislators are on the receiving end of enough surprises and they do not want any more. If a lobbyist intends to work against their bill, they want to know early on. If a lobbyist is planning to introduce an amendment to their bill, they insist on advance notice. A contract lobbyist in Texas explained his modus operandi: "When I find a problem, I call the person I have a problem with. If I'm going to try to amend or kill, I'll go to him and try to work it out." A heavy-hitting contract lobbyist in Florida explains: "If they get blindsided, you're dead." Moreover, lobbyists must keep legislators informed of any changes taking place and what is happening. This will help avert surprises.

Fifth, there is the test of empathy. A lobbyist must be able to put himself or herself in a legislator's shoes. That means the lobbyist must never forget that "the foremost desire of people in power is . . . to stay in power."[15] Lobbyists appreciate this and will not embarrass a legislator nor make him or her look bad. Instead, they tend to be protective. Even if legislators have reneged on a commitment, lobbyists will understand and let them off the hook. A contract lobbyist in New Jersey, who had served on the legislature's staff, met the test of empathy:

> I don't want to hurt them. I don't want to buffalo them. I don't want them
> to vote for a bill they shouldn't vote for. I don't want them to lose an elec-

tion because I get them to vote for some unpopular thing. . . . Then I've lost that person for good.

In other words, lobbyists should think hard about asking legislators to take a position that will get them in trouble—with constituents, legislative leaders, or the governor. Any good lobbyist must know the legislator's district and appreciate the pressures on him or her. A Trenton lobbyist observed that "if the guy has a big organized-labor faction in his district and you are representing a bill that labor is against, you don't ask him to go with you." Instead, the lobbyist goes to others. An Arkansas legislator recounted how, during his second term, he asked a lobbyist about a specific bill. The lobbyist, who was for the bill, gave the legislator the pros and cons, but then added, "Gus, I know the district you represent and you can't vote for this bill." The legislator recalled that he would "always respect him for that."[16] Even when the lobbyist and legislator are on opposite sides of a legislative battle (which, in view of the many issues, happens frequently to people in a close relationship), the lobbyist must be careful not to let the legislator get cut up. The advice of a Texas lobbyist is "Win gently."

Sixth, lobbyists must possess good judgment, which covers a variety of virtues. They must not offend legislators, no matter what. A Florida lobbyist for one of the cities had had words with a legislator. It took several years for their relationship to be repaired. "I'd been righteously indignant," she admits, "when 1 shouldn't have been." Lobbyists must also have the judgment not to be offended, and certainly not to take defeat personally. Stoicism pays dividends. "If someone is doing something to me," indicated a Texas governmental lobbyist, "I want them to feel bad." His hope is that they will feel they owe him one. If they are exercising judgment, lobbyists will also not gossip about members or put any of them down. Nor will they boast of the relationships they have or how they wield influence on issues or members. As a Virginia lobbyist summed up: "There is a new day with every dawning and your strongest adversary today may be your closest ally tomorrow, so when opposing someone's position, be sure you don't oppose the person."[17]

How Relationships Pay Off

When Leon County prosecutors were probing into the undisclosed travel of Florida legislators, lobbyist Willie McCue testified that the purpose of outings such as hunting trips was to help pass bills in the best interest of one's client or to defeat bills that would hurt one's client.[18] It should come as no surprise that lobbyists are representing their clients' interests before the legislature, and that most of their activities are designed to advance those interests. It would be strange were it otherwise.

Assuming that such trips and other social activities help to build relationships between lobbyists and legislators, the question is, what are the payoffs? Lobbyists themselves deny that such relationships (or campaign contributions, for that matter) necessarily lead to votes. They do admit, however, that a relationship with a legislator affords them access. "It is not a question of influence," said a New Jersey lobbyist, "it is a question of access." According to Florida lobbyist Ralph Haben, "You are building natural access, and that is what this game is all about."[19]

What access means is not entirely clear. Nearly everyone can get, or has, access to a legislator, at least in some form and to some extent. At a minimum, access would appear to mean preferential treatment. But "admission," "approach," or "entrance"—the dictionary definitions of "access"—are too weak to convey the benefit to lobbyists of relationships with legislators. A stronger word is "connection," meaning a tie or a bond—one that results from an ongoing relationship. A connection enables lobbyists to advance their positions on issues more effectively.

Connection is especially useful at critical times. Not everyone can get through to a legislator at will, but a good relationship means that a lobbyist has an opportunity for contact at practically any point in the legislative process. If, for example, a senator has thirty pink slips, the connected lobbyist will be one of the five telephone calls that gets returned. At the end of the session, when hundreds of bills have to be dispatched, reaching a legislator can be especially difficult. But if there is trust, understanding, and a track record of successful dealings, the lobbyist will get a legislator's attention. "If we get down to the clutch and I have to see the speaker," says one New Jersey lobbyist, "I'd be able to get an appointment." A lobbyist with a strong tie will get in the door at the critical moment. A strong connection is the result of a relationship that has been built over time. As a result, the lobbyist needs only a few minutes to make his appeal. There would be no need for introductions, explanations of organizational affiliation, or otherwise setting the stage. Relationships, in the view of Dale Florio, a New Jersey lobbyist "allow you to cut through things."

If lobbyists have been properly attentive in building relationships, they have learned as much as possible about the legislators with whom they are dealing. One of the products of such study is that they will know what type of information will work best with a particular individual, and how and when it should be communicated. Some legislators like it written, some like it oral; some prefer words, some prefer numbers. Certain ones are partial to analysis, others need case examples. Some like it hot, others cold.

Relationships make lobbyists not only better dispensers of information but also more likely recipients. In his study of lobbying at the federal level, Robert Salisbury makes the point that lobbyists need access "not so much to apply pressure or even to advocate policy as to be told when something important to them is about to happen."[20] The same applies at the state level. Moreover, legislators who have connections to lobbyists will furnish them with valuable tidbits. A lobbyist may have a problem with a particular legislator but not realize it until a friendly legislator points it out. Only then can the problem be addressed. During the final weeks and last days of a session, when things are moving at a frenetic pace, lobbyists roam the hails of the capitol trying to anticipate events. Who is going to do what to whom is vital information. One can learn from colleagues, and also from friends who are members. They become watchdogs for the lobbyist. They see that "old _____ is going to get screwed." They will pick up the phone and call old _____, the lobbyist, to warn him. Good relationships therefore afford significant tactical advantages.

One thing a legislator can do for a lobbyist friend is to introduce him or her to other members. Opening a door at the right moment can make a big difference. For example, one lobbyist had a problem with the Dade County (Florida) delegation. He sought the assistance of legislator friends from the Panhandle. One of them approached a legislator from Miami on the lobbyist's behalf: "You can trust _____ to shoot straight with you." That got him in, and the problem was worked out.

If lobbyists are well connected, moreover, they are more likely to gain a seat at the table. That means that they are in on critical decision making, as will be discussed further in chapter 9. Whom they represent obviously counts, but who they are counts as well. Depending on their relationships, they may be invited into the back room to participate in the crucial negotiations that take place between opposing sides. And they can be included in the drafting of amendments, which have so much to do with legislation's final shape. If they do not have a chance to participate in the specific details and language of legislation, their influence will be diminished.

A relationship, moreover, makes it more difficult—but by no means impossible—for legislators to oppose lobbyists on issues that they are carrying. "It's harder to vote against someone you know than someone you don't know," concludes a Minnesota association lobbyist. "If you like them," commented a Florida senator, "it's easier to support them."

Personalization helps all lobbyists, especially those with large organizations as clients. A lobbyist in Minnesota believes that personal relationships are extremely important for him because "if they are going to cut someone's throat, they have a picture of me." It is too easy if the target is anonymous. One oil lobbyist is particularly appreciative of the benefit of personal relationships. "They can't disassociate big oil from me, a person," he says. That helps his case.

Even if a legislator cannot vote with a lobbyist, there are other ways to lend a hand. A lobbyist for a Texas association acknowledges that "some of the best relationships I have are with members who never give me a vote." But they will help him in committee or give him information. If a lobbyist approaches a legislator, a friend, with "I need this," drawing on the relationship, then the legislator may vote to get a bill out of committee (although he or she will oppose it on the floor). Or legislators may pass a bill in one house (even if it won't pass in the other) for an old buddy. That permits the lobbyist to move things ahead.

Although a legislator friend may not vote right or even help out, he or she may not hurt the lobbyist as much as might otherwise be the case. There are various degrees of opposition, from a simple nay vote to leading the charge against a bill. Personal relationships work to soften up the opposition from legislators.

If a connection exists, not only will a legislator give a lobbyist the benefit of the doubt, but—depending on the issue—the legislator may well go along with the lobbyist. The legislator will obviously lend support, if that is his or her inclination anyway. The legislator will also be inclined to help, if other things are equal or nearly so, if no major policy issue is involved; if there are no party positions on the matter; if the legislator's constituency is unconcerned or unaffected; if one group has not contributed significantly more to the legislator's campaign than the other; and if the legislator has no real feeling on the subject. A California assemblyman noted that there was a whole range of issues that did not affect one's area of expertise or one's district. When a lobbyist asks for your vote, he says,

> You usually don't have time to weigh the policy. You're faced with a daily agenda of forty bills, and this one hasn't caught your attention, and the person asking for the vote has been nice to you in one way or another . . . you're likely to go with that person.

This could apply to many special-interest issues, discussed in chapter 4 above. When other factors do not come into play and no major issues are involved, if a lobbyist friend asks for support and justifies his or her position in public policy terms, the legislator will probably go along.

Sometimes, however, lawmakers find it impossible to support either the causes or clients of lobbyists they may like. And many legislators inherently want to help and please people. So they feel that they are owing. During recent years legislators have been especially unkind to certain interests, such as tobacco and alcohol. If at all possible, legislators would like to throw a bone to lobbyist friends representing these losing causes. The tobacco industry has been hit by excise taxes and restrictions on smoking in public places, and even the most accommodating legislators have gone against the Tobacco Institute and the industry's contract lobbyists. Therefore, when faced with an industry issue that has some merit and appeal, like prohibiting discrimination by employers against employees who smoke off premises, the attitude of legislators is, "Let's give them one." And a number of legislatures have passed laws designed to protect smokers from discrimination. In these states, tobacco lobbyists had at least something to show for their efforts.

To have a good relationship with legislators confers power on a lobbyist. For one to be close to power is tantamount to possessing it. In the capitol community lobbyists are constantly measured by legislators, statehouse reporters, and other lobbyists, in part, according to whom they know and how well they know them. In addition, relationships with the right people impress the lobbyists' clients—the state relations manager of a company, the board of directors, or maybe the CEO.

All of this is wonderful for the lobbyist, but it is not enough. In lobbying, as in other enterprises, there is a bottom line. A Florida lobbyist, who had previously served in the legislature, had the bottom line in mind when he stated: "I don't care who you are, who you were, or who you know, you have got to win." And to win, lobbyists have to work at more than building relationships.

Effects of Term Limits

The cultivation of relationships is difficult nowadays, because of restrictions on entertaining and the prevailing patterns of contemporary life in the legislature. It is rare for lobbyists to get "quality time" with legislators.

Relationship building also is impeded by the turnover of legislators, since it takes time for lobbyists to earn trust. The key is working together in the legislative arena over a sustained period.

In terms of relationship building and credibility that accrues over time, lobbyists in the nineteen states with term-limited legislatures operate at a disadvantage. Legislators who can look forward to a specified term of six, eight, or perhaps even twelve years have less incentive to develop relationships. They feel that they are passing through the legislature, and are pressured to advance their agendas and worry about their careers. These term-limited legislators are certainly approachable, but probably less open to developing a longer-term relationship. Moreover, many new legislators arrive at the capitol with a built-in suspicion of lobbyists, which takes a while to be overcome.

When anywhere from twenty-five to thirty-five to forty-five legislators are new, as happens with mandatory turnover in term-limited states, the burden on lobbyists is heavy. Developing relationships with a new class in California, Florida, Maine, Ohio, or elsewhere is not at all easy to do. A California lobbyist writes that she used to acquaint herself with the relatively small number of new members during the opening week of the legislative session. But with thirty new members in 1994, she could not meet with them all during the first six to eight weeks of the session. "To my dismay," she continues, "I discovered in mid-summer that the new chair of the highest priority committee for my clients was a first term member whom I had never met." For lobbyists, repeatedly dealing with cadres of new legislators in a destabilized institution is not at all welcome. And lobbyists "lose the pleasure of working with seasoned professionals on difficult issues," she observes.[21]

CHAPTER 7

Playing Politics

In addition to building relationships with legislators, lobbyists also enter into the game of politics itself in order to improve their odds in the legislative arena. One way they do this is through election campaigns, where the stakes have become increasingly high for legislators. With careers in public office becoming more appealing, legislators have a lot riding on winning. By the same token, as Republicans and Democrats become increasingly competitive, each party has a lot riding on gaining (or maintaining) control of the state houses and senates.

Because elections are so important, the role of lobbyists and clients in campaigns has meaning apart from relationship building. In the first place, lobbyists and the groups they represent give—and give generously—to the campaign war chests of legislative parties, incumbents, candidates fighting over an open seat, and even challengers. They do so to help elect friends, create obligations, improve access, and because they are uncertain of the consequences if they do not give. On occasion, their purpose is to defeat enemies. In the second place, lobbyists and their clients play independent roles in the campaign, devoting substantial organizational effort to accomplish their purposes.

Lobbyists engage in politics in yet another way—bypassing the legislature altogether and going right to the people. This is the increasingly popular "initiative game" that enables the electorate to vote on amendments to the state constitution and/or on statutes. It is played to a fare-thee-well in California, Oregon, Washington, Arizona, and Colorado, and from time to time in Florida and Massachusetts. All told, the initiative is an option in twenty-four states. Here, it falls to lobbyists and their campaign consultants to persuade, not the legislators, but the people themselves.

Paying the Freight

The costs of campaigns have been rising (but so have the costs of just about everything else). The population is growing, partisan competition is increasing, and campaigns in a number of districts and states are becoming more professional, with campaign consultants, polls, radio, television, cable, direct mail, and now the Internet.

As far as state legislative races go, however, most campaigns are not outrageously expensive. Raising funds is not an enormous effort for most candidates, and especially incumbents. One study of 1994 legislative campaigns in nineteen states shows the striking variation in spending by district; less than $10,000 per candidate in four states, between $10,000 and $50,000 in eight states, between $50,000 and $100,000 in three states, and over $100,000 in four. Another study of the 1994 elections produces a similar distribution of expenditures per candidate in fourteen states.[1] "For substantially less than the cost of a standard automobile today," writes Gary Moncrief, "one can run a competitive campaign in more than half the states studied."[2] The costs of campaigns in what one Colorado lobbyist calls "small-potatoes states" are modest by big-state standards.

Average spending per candidate in California is about eighty times that of Wyoming or Maine. Illinois spending is about twenty-five times as much and Oregon spending about twelve times as much. California, Illinois, New Jersey, Michigan, Ohio, and Pennsylvania are part of the world that most people think of when the subject is campaign finance for state legislative elections. Where campaign costs are high and where a substantial number of districts are large and competitive, money becomes the focal point for legislative races. In view of the incentives for winning, it is hardly surprising that candidates will try to raise the money necessary to compete. In California, it can cost each side one million dollars or more to win an assembly seat. Even if there is little competition, California's incumbents want to short-circuit a serious contest by amassing a war chest to scare off potential challengers. In Florida, for example, one house incumbent, unchallenged for five years, raised $136,000 by the beginning of the year in which he was running. When asked why, he responded that before every election he presumed he would have an opponent, even if he did not have one before. Not only in California and Florida but in New Jersey and Texas as well, fund-raising by candidates resembles an arms race. It has certainly become one of the principal activities of legislators. The average member of the California legislature, estimate has it, spends almost half his or her time, in one guise or another, raising money.

Someone has to pay. Most candidates cannot afford to, and the public, for the most part, refuses to. Individual citizens, with no business to conduct before the legislative bar, provide some of the dollars simply because they favor one candidate or one party over the other. But the largest share of the tab in most races is picked up by those with deep pockets, the so-called special interests. These are the business, labor, and professional groups that seek "redress of grievances" from the same legislators they endow. One study of interest group contributions in several states found that 53 percent of trade and professional groups and 100 percent of labor unions gave money to candidates for their elections. But only 14 percent of citizen groups did so.[3] Lobbyists and their principals fuel what a Florida lobbyist calls "the giant engine that costs so much."

Lobbyist Giving

Legislative leaders, party caucuses, and legislative rank and file are constantly asking lobbyists and their principals to buy more and more, and higher- and higher-priced, tickets to the fund-raisers they sponsor. Most fund-raisers are in the form of receptions or dinners, but more imaginative ways of separating lobbyists from their money have also been devised. In some states summers are filled with fund-raising golf tournaments—so much so that lobbyists might think they were on the PGA tour.

Lobbyists can easily afford the fund-raiser prices in states like New Hampshire, Vermont, South Dakota, and Wyoming. But in the larger states, where costs are high, fund-raisers are squeezing lobbyists and their principals. In California the average assembly fund-raiser costs lobbyists $775, but to be a host, sponsor, or supporter, a lobbyist has to ante up $50,000, $25,000, and $5,000 respectively. California lobbyists have been expected to fund campaigns for years now, and most now grin and bear it. They see no point in bellyaching about solicitations, for as one said, politicians are simply charging "what the market will bear."[4]

In most places these events take place year-round, but they tend to occur with greatest frequency when the legislature is in session. It is unseemly to have a committee meeting on a bill during an afternoon and the committee chairman's fund-raiser that evening. Today a number of the states prohibit lobbyists from making campaign contributions during the legislative session. An Illinois senator, who sponsored legislation prohibiting fund-raising during the session in the capitol, explained: "It's a matter of appearance. The public doesn't believe that you should be holding a fund-raiser breakfast in a morning and two hours later going over to a capitol building casting votes on legislation."[5] Since the 1980s Minnesota has prohibited legislative fund-raisers while the legislature is in session. Florida followed suit in 1989, banning them during the legislature's sixty-day session. They were all moved up to the months prior to the session, when legislators were in Tallahassee for committee meetings.

Most lobbyists are not averse to attending fund-raisers. As a Minnesota lobbyist said, "To be good at this job, you have to be part of the process." Showing up at legislators' fund-raisers is a way to participate in the process and to signal support. It permits lobbyists to mix and network, and occasionally to enjoy themselves besides. But the number of invitations lobbyists receive and the costs involved have been rising dramatically. One veteran lobbyist in Trenton felt the squeeze: "If I responded to every legislator and candidate . . . who tries to sell me tickets to a cocktail party for fund-raising, it would be easily $50,000 per year." He and his colleagues have to be selective. One of them buys tickets only for fund-raisers given by leaders or committee chairmen or members he knows well. Another makes it a rule never to buy tickets to party events, only to functions put on by individual members. Still another insists on contributing only to the legislators who helped him when he needed their help, and not to those who did not.

The solicitation of funds from lobbyists has become a high-pressure activity. Legislative party leaders, who now have fund-raising as one of their major functions, are particularly difficult to turn down. The house speakers and senate presidents in California, Florida, and New Jersey are especially effective in raising money for their party candidates. Sometimes they host fund-raisers for party members, which lobbyists are sure to attend. They also have their own political action committees (PACs), the monies from which are usually distributed to party candidates in tough races.

The role of legislative leadership and legislative party caucus PACs is substantial in a majority of legislative bodies today. These party mechanisms focus their resources on the competitive races and fund nonincumbents, and thus have an impact on who wins control of the senate or house. Generally, these agencies are legally permitted to raise more than legislative candidates themselves. In Minnesota, for instance, there are no limits on what may be given to parties, including local, regional, or state parties or legislative caucuses. From 1990 to 1996, contributions to the four legislative caucuses increased by 250 percent for the house Democrat-Farm-Labor Party (DFL), 229 percent for the senate DFL, 97 percent for the house Republicans, and 228 percent for the senate Republicans.[6] Minnesota parties are also set up at the senate district level, which allows more money to be raised in a system where public financing limits contributions to, and expenditure by, candidates. The law, however, allows district parties to spend as much as they want, as long as their advertisements involve three or more candidates. (A Minnesota senate district, it should be noted, has one senate seat and two house seats.)

"Leadership funds," according to a Florida lobbyist, "develop the idea that lobbyists have to give—or else." Such a charge was made publicly by a lobbyist for trial lawyers in New Jersey. She alleged that in 1989 four assembly leaders, all Democrats, threatened that if her group did not give $20,000 to the Democratic political action committee, its bills would not get posted by a new speaker. An investigation by the state attorney general did not substantiate the lobbyist's charges. Yet the understanding in Trenton is that lobbyists will help to underwrite campaigns.

No one is precisely certain of what message the legislators are sending through their invitations to fund-raisers, but lobbyists generally interpret it to mean that giving is the better part of valor. Some members, according to a California lobbyist for a professional association, are "outrageous in their behavior." Most are more restrained. Nevertheless, lobbyists have a good idea of what is expected. Every invitation to a fund-raiser, every casual remark about money, carries a "psychological implication," one lobbyist asserts, that you have to pay to play. "You almost feel like you *have to* contribute," says a New Jersey lobbyist. It is hardly surprising, then, that more and more lobbyists get the feeling that they are being shaken down.

Whatever the pressures, lobbyists think that campaign contributions are one important resource in their enterprise. If they or their clients are expected to give—as are business, labor, and professional and occupational interests—they generally fulfill legislators' expectations. There are a number of reasons for doing so.[7]

First, in the large states fund-raisers are becoming the way lobbyists interact with legislators outside of the statehouse. Wining and dining are precluded by benefit-passing regulations, but fund-raisers still offer opportunities for lobbyists to socialize with legislators as well as offer them support. In a term-limited legislature like California's, fund-raisers are the most common way for lobbyists to meet new legislators.

Second, lobbyists and their principals want to help reelect friends—that is, legislators who are like-minded and side with the group on the issues—by contributing to their campaigns. Democratic legislators receive money from labor and Republicans from business, in large part because their philosophies coincide.

Third, by giving, lobbyists and interest groups hope to get more out of friends. Even if legislators are predisposed in a group's direction, their behavior may range from leading the charge to simply casting a vote. The commitments of time and energy on the part of the legislator will vary, as will the possible benefits to the group and its lobbyist.

Fourth, campaign contributions are also given in order to sway the open-minded. On many issues, legislators have no record and their constituencies have no real interest. Many actions occur on issues or specifics that abound in the legislative process but have little currency outside.

Fifth, many groups contribute to legislators on both sides of the aisle, which is known as "playing it safe" or "self-preservation" giving. The motivation here is to hedge one's bets and wind up with friends rather than enemies, even if that does not usually mean a vote. The New Jersey Education Association, for example, has become more bipartisan in its contributions since the Republicans gained control of the legislature in 1986. No longer are the teachers in the camp of the legislative Democrats; today they have a foot in each camp. While money theoretically may also be intended to convert enemies to one's side, this is very unlikely to happen. Few, if any, legislators would consider doing an about-face in gratitude for a campaign contribution. More likely, such a contribution at best can only soften opposition.

To a large extent, campaign contributing is a voluntary activity. But to some extent, it is involuntary. Lobbyists and interest groups give, less to gain influence than to avoid losing influence. Giving cannot hurt and they are not sure what not-giving will cost (if they are among those expected to contribute).

"We didn't make the rules, we just play by them," responds a contract lobbyist in Trenton in justifying his activities. He, along with a number of his politically active colleagues in New Jersey and elsewhere, plays the money game to the hilt. He gathers up contributions from many of his clients, "bundles" them, and presents them to the senate and assembly parties. If his clients were to contribute separately, it would tend, in his opinion, to diffuse what he was trying to put together. Moreover, it would not enhance his own standing with New Jersey legislators, as the larger contribution that he delivers does.

Political Action Committees

Legislators can rely on lobbyists and other individuals as a source of funds. In some places, they can also count on corporations and labor unions. Corporate contributions are either prohibited or regulated in forty-two states. Thirty-eight states prohibit or regulate union contributions. But the primary channels for campaign giving today are the political action committees (PACs) sponsored by labor, business, associations, and other groups. PACs are organizations that collect contributions from particular classes of individuals for the purpose of influencing elections. The rationale is that, by aggregating small donations from a large number of contributors, similarly situated people can maximize the effect of their money.

PACs have grown in numbers, resources, and market share since the 1970s. Nowadays, the percentage of candidates' campaign funds that derive from PACs varies from state to state, but it is not unusual for these committees to account for almost half of the contributions legislators receive. In Massachusetts, for example, the *Boston Globe* (May 23, 1993) analyzed over forty thousand contributions during 1991–92. The newspaper found that three-fourths of the $8.8 million total came from thirty interest groups, with lobbyists and PACs accounting for nearly 30 percent of donations over $50.

PACs proliferate because as one group establishes a PAC, another one feels that it must match the action. "If other people do it, you have to do it," said a New Jersey lobbyist. Within the past few decades, practically every one of them has organized a PAC on the assumption that it is "part of the political program you have to have to be effective." Two-thirds of state chambers of commerce operate PACs.[8] In a survey of fifty-five companies, it was found that forty had PACs that made contributions to state candidates.[9] Since then, a survey of members of the Public Affairs Council (an association of Fortune 500 corporations) found that four out of five had political action committees, which were important to their companies' public affairs strategies.[10]

Not everyone has a well-developed PAC, however. Minnesota law requires that corporations with PACs have individuals contribute to individual accounts and have a say as to where their contributions go. This acts as a deterrent to an effective PAC. Some companies have not gotten around to developing a contributions strategy, so their PACs limp along. Some have decided that they should not tie their influence to spending money. IBM is probably one of the largest business organizations without a PAC. While oil companies, such as ARCO and Texaco in California, make corporate contributions, the American Petroleum Institute decided that none of its state councils could have a PAC. A lobbyist for one such council bemoaned the situation: "We're Big Oil, but we can't even play with nickels and dimes." Associations of municipalities and counties are not permitted PACs and public interest groups and nonprofits either cannot or are not expected to give. Although the money game is not theirs to play, they are not penalized for not playing.

PACs raise money by a variety of means—direct mail, special events, personal contact, payroll deduction, and so forth. Corporations and labor groups often use payroll deductions. Almost half of the state CPA societies use a dues-checkoff system, while the others solicit their members. Large groups who have much at stake and whose members are politically sophisticated can raise the most money for their PACs. Lawyers fit that description. In Minnesota, for instance, about half of them contribute to their association's PAC. Teachers are also excellent providers, and state education associations have devised dues-checkoff systems that facilitate the flow of funds. It is more difficult, in contrast, for companies to raise monies from employees. Their yield is far below that of teachers.

Once money is raised, principal responsibility for decisions regarding contributions is commonly made by a board or committee. A group's lobbyist usually has a role in deciding to whom the funds are to be allocated. Often the lobbyist is the individual running the PAC. Whether or not a board or committee has the final say, the lobbyist will ordinarily have the most to say. Although the process tends to be relatively closed, on occasion it can be quite open. A lobbyist for a major pharmaceutical company expounded his philosophy: "Can you explain it to your mother? That is the ultimate test of anything you do." The company will also have a contribution strategy for determining which legislators affect core issues; ensuring continued support; and indexing legislators' activity. Several company committees, which include executives as members, have responsibility for deciding who would receive money, based on research and advice from staff.

Allocations by the education associations are determined by means of a democratically based endorsement process. For the California Education Association, first-level selections are made by local chapters, and the second-level endorsements are by a state council. Colorado's state education association sends each candidate a questionnaire, and the local chapters interview them. The locals make their recommendations to the association's PAC, which can accept or reject it. But the PAC cannot endorse any other person in the district. In New Jersey, an operating committee (composed of NJEA's officers, members of its government relations and executive committees, and the county association presidents) endorses candidates on the basis of their responses to a questionnaire and of screening committee reviews. In Texas, teachers make nominations locally, but the state association PAC has to be involved if an endorsement is to be made and a contribution given. If the state PAC rejects a local nomination, a process of fact-finding and negotiations takes place.

PACs, like lobbyists, have various motives for giving money to legislators.[11] The following motives help to determine who gets what and how much is given: to show support for and to help elect friends; to oppose and to help defeat those who are not friends; to support those who are likely to be reelected, especially those who exercise considerable influence; to gain or improve access to members, particularly influential ones; and to attempt to change the odds by affecting the overall outcome of an election. For the most part, lobbyists and the PACs they influence pursue the objectives noted in the first, third, and fourth items on the above list. Different types of PACs have different patterns of giving. Ideological PACs give almost exclusively to their friends, as do labor PACs. Corporations and trade associations give to their friends, but also to nonfriends if in the majority. Their giving depends more on who the winners are.

Studies consistently have found that PACs favor incumbents over challengers, since they are interested in maintaining access. Given their high reelection rates, incumbents are most likely to win, so they are the best bets for access-motivated giving. In a study of contributions in seventeen states, Cassie and Thompson found that in every case incumbents got a larger percentage of their funds from PACs than did challengers. In most cases they received about twice as much of their total in PAC campaign contributions. In absolute amounts, incumbents in California got five times as much as challengers, ten times as much in New Jersey, seven times as much in Pennsylvania , and five times as much in Kansas. Candidates for open seats, however, did far better in PAC contributions than did ordinary challengers. As might be expected, business PACs are larger contributors than labor and professional trade PACs. The only exceptions among the seventeen states were in Minnesota (for both parties) and Wyoming (for Democrats only) where professional/trade PACs were the largest contributors. As might also be expected, business PACs favored Republican candidates in almost all the states (all but Illinois and Minnesota), and labor favored Democrats (in all but New Jersey).[12]

The rationale for favoring incumbents, according to a California lobbyist, is "We make campaign contributions to all members of the legislature since all of them have a vote."[13] Another Californian, who lobbies for an association of professionals, explained that in a typical election his group contributed to seventy-five out of the eighty incumbent assemblymen and to ten to fifteen of the forty incumbent senators. Its PAC operates on the principle that "if the individual hasn't hurt the profession, we'll support the campaign." The only ones eliminated, therefore, are out-and-out enemies.

Sometimes, one's friends tend to be in the Democratic rather than the Republican party, as in the case of teachers' unions and organized labor. Sometimes, one's friends tend to be in the Republican party, as in the case of most business groups. But partisan friendship usually is tempered by which party is in the majority. Thus, New Jersey business was kind to Democrats, who had control of both houses of the legislature for most of the 1970s and into the 1980s. Similarly, Colorado teachers could give one-third of their endorsements to Republicans, who had a lock on the two houses.

One thing is certain in fund-raising. Leaders and key members of the legislature pull in more contributions than rank and file. The amount a PAC contributes usually depends on the leadership position, chairmanship, and committee assignment of the recipient. Whether an incumbent sits on a committee overseeing the group's affairs may be as important as anything else. Thus, the members of committees with jurisdiction over economic matters usually fare well. In California, for example, the work of the Assembly Finance and Insurance Committee affects insurance companies, banks, savings and loans, thrifts, credit unions, and doctors and lawyers. Its members receive more in campaign contributions than any other legislators.[14] The state-relations director of one national association explained that his group generally gave to people in key positions, but "not to those [in key positions] who consistently screw us."

Speakers, presidents, and majority and sometimes minority leaders naturally hold the most key positions. Through leadership or caucus PACs, they solicit funds, which they then allocate to incumbents and challengers in their parties, with preference given to those in competitive races where money can make the greatest difference to party fortunes. Lobbyists find it difficult to resist such leadership appeals. A few actually welcome them. A New Jersey contract lobbyist, with a record of service to his party, would rather give to leadership committees than get involved in individual races. Leaders represent the membership and, in his opinion, should be entrusted with the bulk of funds lobbyists raise. They, in turn, can disburse the money themselves to whoever they feel is most deserving. Most lobbyists, however, would rather make their own choices and receive direct credit than let the leaders take matters out of their hands. Some association and company PACs, in fact, have a policy of contributing only to individual members and not to leadership committees.

Finally, some groups in some places target key races where they have friends or enemies. Money can have considerable impact in these contests and the outcome can affect the success of a group's program in the legislature. The teachers and trial lawyers and, from time to time, business interests put themselves at risk here. We shall examine such engagements below.

Whatever the allocation process or the amount contributed, the way it is presented also counts. Contract lobbyists benefit from making the presentation themselves, although their clients get less credit this way. The consensus among state government relations professionals is that a member of the group should hand the contributed checks to the legislator in his or her own district. The presentation is best made by a key contact or constituent at a special breakfast or in the legislator's office. The idea, according to an association lobbyist in Minnesota, is to "get them where they live."

Regulating Campaign Finance

During recent decades, reform efforts have focused more on campaign finance than on any other matter. Changes in campaign finance law throughout the states have been marked. By the late 1990s, thirty-four states limited individual contributions; thirty-nine banned or regulated direct contributions by labor unions; forty-two banned or restricted contributions from corporations; thirty-three limited PAC contributions; nineteen restricted contributions from political parties; eight regulated "bundling" individual contributions; and all states required disclosure of contributors.[15]

The most radical reform, people agree, is public funding of legislative campaigns. Wisconsin and Minnesota have had public funding for a number of years, with little success in the former state and greater success in the latter state. Hawaii also provides for public funding but allocates very little money. Nebraska also has a system that tries to limit spending. Most recently Maine, Arizona, Vermont, and Massachusetts—by initiative or legislation—have adopted schemes in which campaigns are paid for almost entirely with public money. In Maine, for example, the Clean Election option was adopted by referendum in 1996. It was challenged and upheld in a federal court. The new law offers a theoretical maximum of $12,000 for a house candidate and $40,000 for a senate candidate. Previously budgets for house and senate races averaged $5,000 and $22,000 respectively. The 2000 election was the first election to test public funding in Maine, and about one-third of the candidates for the legislature are choosing that option. It is likely also that public finance schemes will be adopted in a few other states in the 2000–2001 period.

Lobbyists and interest group contributors to legislative campaigns have to manage in an increasingly complex campaign finance environment. Those who want to restrict their contributions, feeling that the requests have become excessive, can now use contribution caps as the reason for not giving more. Those who want to contribute beyond the limits established for candidates can usually find alternative ways to channel money into legislative campaigns—through party PACs, independent expenditures, or otherwise.

What Does Money Buy?

Public interest groups and the press have no doubt that money talks and that legislators listen. Admitting that well-heeled groups have a constitutional right to lobby the legislature, the executive director of New Jersey Common Cause articulated a widely held view: "What distorts it is the volume with which the special interests speak, and the amplifier is campaign contributions."[16] Along these lines, environmental and consumer groups complain specifically about the monetary advantages of business. Many critics of the campaign-finance system in the states argue that contributions tend to buy particular votes, even if they do not buy particular legislators. There is little evidence to support such contentions, even though those groups and organizations that make the biggest contributions are also likely to wield substantial influence. The influence, however, may have preceded the money rather than derived from it.

Considerable research has been conducted on the impact of campaign contributions at the congressional level. Most of the studies have tried to relate money to roll-call votes, with very mixed results. A few have found a relationship; others have found a weak relationship, with party, ideology, and constituency more important; and still others have found little or no relationship whatsoever. But studies that focus on floor votes fail to take into account many key actions that take place elsewhere, or more subtle ones, which are difficult to discern and impossible to quantify.[17] A few congressional studies, though, have gone further. One examined contributions to members of the House Ways and Means Committee and found indirect influence. Money tended to "facilitate access and amplify lobbying messages," rather than serve as a direct exchange for favors.[18] Another study, which also looked at the politics of committee decision making, concluded that the participation of members was more important than their votes, especially in the case of representatives who were sympathetic anyway. Money mainly bought the marginal time, energy, and legislative resources that committee participation required.[19]

There is widespread agreement among lobbyists that campaign contributions facilitate access.[20] But nearly every constituent has, or can have, access. "Access," in this sense means more than the dictionary definition of "admission," "approach," or "entrance." It means, to some extent, preferential treatment. If legislators have a pile of telephone (or e-mail) messages awaiting them at the end of the day, they will likely put at the top of the pile—along with other priority messages—those from the angels who back them. If legislators are overwhelmed during the end-of-the-session crunch, their big contributors have a somewhat better chance than others of reaching them.

It is unlikely that campaign contributions buy votes and such, except perhaps in very isolated cases. Most contributions tend to follow, rather than precede, the vote. That is to say, people and PACs alike mostly give to candidates and parties with whom they have a policy affinity. They may not be soul mates, but they share general views, such as Republicans share with business and Democrats share with labor. Contributions, however, may affect not the vote, but other aspects of legislators' behavior. Steady financial support may impel legislators to take leadership roles on an issue that a group endorses. Or, if legislators oppose a measure backed by one of their core contributors, they may vote against it but not lead the charge to defeat it. John Vasconcellos, a veteran member of the California assembly, described the softening effects of money: "When you know that the next day you've got to ask for a thousand dollars or five thousand dollars for your campaign from some group, it is more difficult to explicitly 'anti' their position. You may speak against them, but you speak more softly rather than rant and rave."[21] If a legislator speaks out forcefully, he may persuade several colleagues and bring over some votes that otherwise might have supported the measure. If a campaign contribution can help prevent that, it would have served the contributor's purpose.

Interest groups can cover their bases by contributing to key legislators in both parties. And they may choose to do so. That is because it is difficult for legislators not to notice support or lack thereof when it comes to something as important as their electoral survival. Bill Lockyer, former president pro tem of the California senate, is unusually candid in commenting on the "indelible impressions of who supported you and who opposed you," especially the first time a legislator runs. "It sometimes takes years to be able to sever that sense of connectedness, responsibility, obligation, whatever you might call it." Conversely, Lockyer remembered that the largest contributor against him in his first race was the realtors. "It took a while for me to look at a bill sponsored by the realtors fairly," he recalled. "I'd try, but I'd have this little feeling that they were my enemies."[22]

On broad, visible issues, campaign contributions from lobbyists and interest groups probably have the least effect. The lines, for the most part, are already drawn. Constituency, conscience, colleagues, and consistency with one's past record all play major roles. On narrower, less visible issues, which nonetheless may be of substantial interest to contributing groups, money probably has greater effect. Legislators tend to be inclined to listen a little more attentively to a group's substantive arguments if that group has contributed to their campaign. Much of the policy that is proposed or opposed by various groups affords considerable leeway for legislative decision making. If legislators attend sympathetically to a group's arguments, they will see the merits. For usually there are merits to practically any case made in the legislative process. When the opposing cases are reasonably balanced and other factors—such as one's principles, record, constituency, or party—do not intervene, the legislator is free to decide whom to go with and how far to go. The nudge of generous campaign support can cause legislators, almost unconsciously, to look at the information furnished by the donor group more positively than that furnished by the opposition.

The absence of contributions, where they are expected, may be more harmful than their presence is helpful. A Minnesota lobbyist and former member of the legislature maintains that while a business group might not need to make a contribution, legislators may be waiting for it. Therefore, in his view, "it's better to give than explain why you didn't." A contribution, moreover, highlights a lobbyist's presence; and a lobbyist cannot be successful without one. Another Minnesota lobbyist, who must do his work without benefit of a PAC, observes that "what a PAC gets you is that you're not noticeable by its absence." If money talks, then no money also talks—and lobbyists cannot afford the latter conversation. Moreover, once a lobbyist gives, it is difficult to stop—or even to cut down. A New Jersey lobbyist described what happened when he reduced the size of his contribution to a member who had not been very friendly to his issues. The member got annoyed and complained to him. The lobbyist had no way of knowing whether or how that annoyance would affect whatever case he would make in the future.

Another lobbyist, from Colorado, makes it a policy of not contributing to campaigns. The reaction of one senator was: "Why should I listen to you? You've never donated to my campaign." But, according to the lobbyist's recollection, that type of reaction occurred only four or five times in the last half-dozen years. "It wouldn't hurt anybody, if they refused to give if they had the balls to say no." Still, Colorado's political environment is less high-pressured than that in many other places. Lobbyists in California, Florida, New Jersey, and Texas are uncertain of the consequences of saying "no" very often. Given the uncertainty, it makes sense for them to ante up. Otherwise they risk the perception that they are not players, or even worse.

Contributions serve not only to keep lobbyists and their clients in the game but also to make them competitive with other players. In an environment where interests engage in continuous and keen rivalries, no lobbyist wants today's actual opponents, or tomorrow's possible opponents, to get ahead. One New Jersey lobbyist sees the role of campaign money in this way: "It's just keeping even with everyone else." "You can't name a lobbyist who has won with money," declared a representative of a New Jersey association. "All I want money to do is keep me even." The state governmental relations director of a national association with substantial interests in a number of places agreed as to what money buys. "It keeps us in the pack, although it doesn't give us more than anybody else."

Much like relationships, campaign contributions matter at the margins. One New Jersey legislator is said to have accepted regular contributions from the business community and then done everything the environmentalists wanted. On the major issues that were involved for this particular legislator, other factors outweighed the influence of money. Generally, money may play the deciding role only on issues that do not affect a legislator's district and do not become visible and highly controversial. There are many such minor matters, and on these money can make a difference.

Campaign contributions matter much less than the current public discussion leads people to believe. But lobbyists always want whatever edge they can get. In the case of campaign expenditures, a candidate is never entirely sure what the right amount is and whether more spending makes much of a difference at all. In the case of campaign contributions, a lobbyist is never entirely sure of the consequences of giving or of not giving. Political contributions certainly do not hurt, and they probably help at least somewhat.

But nobody is happy with the campaign finance system. Reformers and the media declare it to be corrupt, or at least corrupting. Legislators do not like to raise money. Lobbyists and other contributors get the feeling that they are being shaken down. Those who do not give feel that they are at a disadvantage. But fixing the system, so that multiple objectives are met, has proved to be an almost impossible task.

Engaging in Battle

In the case of some interest groups, political involvement goes further than contributions to friendly or important legislators. Their involvement can be intense and targeted to key races. In these instances, a group's objectives are to punish enemies, reward friends, and alter the lineup of proponents and opponents in senate and house ranks.

Influential groups that experience defeat on a vital issue may respond by seeking to change the odds in the legislature. They may also want to restore their reputations as powers by taking reprisals. New Jersey's dentists, for example, went after three incumbents whom they deemed hostile to their interests. Two of them were defeated, and the dentists claimed credit. Colorado's optometrists and ophthalmologists fought it out in the legislative arena and in campaigns. After failing to match the optometrists for some years, the ophthalmologists finally helped to defeat an incumbent legislator who had favored their opponents during the session. They felt much better as a result.

Major battles between powerful groups occur in many places. In Texas, for example, the trial lawyers and business interests have fought vigorously against one another's candidates in campaigns in order to get the upper hand in the legislature. For many years, the Texas Trial Lawyers Association appeared to have control of the Texas senate. But opposition to the group grew, as business and other groups coalesced in an association named the Texas Civil Justice League. Having suffered some setbacks in the legislature, the trial lawyers targeted five key senate districts in the 1988 elections. But in all five races their candidates lost. One consequence was that the trial lawyers changed their strategy from one of belligerence to one of making friends in the legislature.[23] Since then, they have regained some ground, and they continue to pursue the political game. Their opposition, however, has been less politically astute. One Texas lobbyist criticized the business community for pouring money into lobbyists when it should have been pouring it into campaigns in order to change the composition of the senate.

Business groups elsewhere in the South have focused their energies on supporting friendly candidates in legislative elections. In Louisiana the business association actually recruits candidates. In North Carolina, it provides analyses and endorsements. In Alabama and Mississippi business is also active. Associated Industries of Florida is a model for electoral involvement. Its political operations department sends candidate profile and issue questionnaires to all incumbents and challengers. It compiles responses and adds on key votes for incumbents. And it holds personal interviews with many of the candidates. In 1995, for example, AIF's political arm, Florida Business United, contributed in sixteen of twenty senate races, and in forty of eighty house races, winning most of them.

Legislators can be intimidated by a group's threat to support a challenger. The lawmaker's attitude toward the group may undergo a subtle, or not-so-subtle, change. If a group *almost* succeeds in unseating an incumbent, that legislator is likely to make a greater effort to see eye-to-eye with it. Accommodation may not be entirely possible, but the effort will be made. And if a legislator is defeated, the message to the capitol community is heard loud and clear. One participant in the electoral struggle acknowledges that, "if your opponents defeat a legislator on your side, it has tremendous impact. . . . We [then] have to defeat one of theirs to get on track."

Groups willing to target close races, oppose incumbents, take dramatic action, and commit people as well as other resources to the fray can be formidable. As the director of one such group declared: "When we win, we win big. When we lose, we lose big." In some state campaigns environmental groups are effective. For example, New Jersey's environmentalists get into races where they can make more of a difference. Their contributions to candidates are in kind—a canvass, media work, radio ads, literature drops—and they operate according to their own campaign plan. Their "resource endorsements" have had considerable effect. One year, for instance, they campaigned for a Democratic challenger who won in a marginal district. Although he had not been an environmentalist when he declared his candidacy, he ended his campaign as one. Then, serving in the legislature, he became a leading spokesman for environmental interests.

Labor traditionally takes on a role in elections. New Jersey provides an example of its involvement. The Communications Workers of America (CWA), the major union for state employees, threatened to back its own independent candidates in the 1991 election in nine of forty legislative districts. This threat was announced when the Florio administration proposed layoffs and demanded salary and benefit givebacks from state government employees as a means toward reducing a huge projected deficit in the 1992 budget. CWA's independent candidates would have taken votes away from incumbents and could have cost Democrats control of both houses. (As it turned out, the Democrats did lose both houses, but mainly because of an antitax vote by the electorate.) After the budget had been settled by the Democratic governor and legislature without the deferral of raises or sacrifice of benefits, CWA dropped its threat. But organized labor in New Jersey continued to be critical of the weak Democratic support of priority labor initiatives, particularly on health care. In July 1991 AFL-CIO leaders put a moratorium on all financial contributions to candidates for the legislature. At its fall convention, to evidence its displeasure, the union decided to restrict official endorsements to only a handful of "proven friends." Finally, the New Jersey Industrial Union Council limited its endorsements to 50 of the 120 legislative races, the fewest since the labor group began operating more than twenty years before.

Few groups become as involved in legislative campaigns as teachers and therefore few have comparable clout. Teachers' groups are the ideal political organization because they are locally based and widely dispersed. There are one or more schools in every legislator's district; and where there is a school, there are teachers. Teachers are educated; and they have high voting rates and time after school hours to participate in politics. Moreover, they are politically motivated and their organizations are skillfully managed.

Teachers' associations are unlike other organizations in having such an array of resources that can be devoted to politics. The Texas State Teachers Association, for example, has gotten involved in campaigns at the grassroots level. The Colorado Education Association (CEA) has provided volunteers for two out of three candidates it endorsed. In addition to furnishing funds, CEA provided analysis, established phone banks, and even hired political consultants (for a few priority races). The association's posture is "We want a piece of your campaign."

The New Jersey Education Association (NJEA) has an integrated campaign support system. The combination of money, association effort, and volunteers makes a real impression. NJEA does not usually give funds directly to candidates. Instead, its PAC approves the expenses of committees of educators who are campaigning on behalf of endorsed candidates. Each committee works with a minimum amount of money, which it spends on mailings, door-to-door canvassing, mobilizing members to vote, and get-out-the-vote activities on election day. Given the strength of its organization and its contribution to legislative elections, NJEA has been especially helpful to legislators—primarily Democratic ones—in New Jersey. But the teachers refuse to be taken for granted. In 1991, after Democratic majorities in the senate and assembly had taken away $360 million from the just-enacted Quality Education Act in order to ease property taxes (having also imposed spending caps on the schools), NJEA reversed its traditional endorsement preferences. Instead of favoring the Democratic candidates, it endorsed only three of them, espousing forty-six Republicans, with thirty-four of the total endorsements going to incumbents. NJEA also targeted the Democratic senate president, John Lynch, for defeat. New Jersey's teachers were playing politics with no holds barred.

At the state as well as the national level, interest groups recently have not only been contributing funds to candidates and parties, but in many places they have been running their own communications campaigns for candidates. Independent expenditures is probably the most rapidly growing form of reported direct action, according to a study of campaign finance in the states. Most independent expenditures are made by a small number of groups, sometimes as few as one or two. The main users of this campaign technique are major business associations, teacher associations, unions, and active trade groups. Independent expenditures—whether for mail, radio spots, phone banks, or television advertisements—are costly and therefore discourage all but the best-heeled groups. Many groups are reluctant to go this route, in part because of the resources required, but also because they do not want to risk making enemies with the other side. They would rather maintain good relations with both parties.[24]

Issue advocacy advertising is another technique, and one that does not require disclosure as does independent expenditures. Issue ads are restricted only in that they cannot explicitly advocate the election or defeat of a named candidate. As a technique, issue advocacy is now being heavily used in national campaigns, both by political parties and interest groups. It is also beginning to be used more widely at the state level. As described by Alan Ehrenhalt, issue advertising came on the Wisconsin scene in 1998 in a campaign for control of the senate.[25] Before that time, candidates raised most of the money for their campaigns and made the critical decisions. Now major interest group clusters—one cluster the Wisconsin Manufacturers and Commerce, along with the Farm Bureau, realtors, and builders, and the other the Wisconsin Education Association Council, along with trial lawyers and the state AFL-CIO—run campaigns in targeted districts. Thus, "most of the funds are raised and spent, and decisions made, without the candidate knowing about it." What the ads do in such campaigns is set the agenda and shape the debate, taking control away from legislative candidates and legislative parties.

Some groups also organize political grass roots for candidates. Teacher organizations and labor unions have been mobilizing members politically for years. But lately other groups have also been engaged in political grass roots or direct political action. The electoral clout of groups of sportsmen, senior citizens, and even teachers is not so much their campaign contributions, but their ability to mobilize members to support or defeat legislators running for reelection. These groups do not threaten many incumbents, but they will take on a few. A study of interest group activity in three states shows that 82 percent of labor unions, 29 percent of trade professional associations, and 22 percent of citizens groups work on campaigns, whereas 100 percent, 53 percent, and 14 percent make financial contributions.[26]

Going for Votes

Lobbyists do not necessarily confine their activities to the legislative arena. In those states where the constitutional or statutory initiative exists, they and those they represent have the option of taking a proposal directly to the voters. Twenty-six states allow some form of direct legislation,[27] whereby the electorate, rather than the legislature, has ultimate authority to amend the constitution or enact a law. The initiative comes in two forms. The direct initiative permits an individual or group to draft a proposition and collect a specified number of voter signatures to get it on the ballot for a vote. The indirect initiative permits an individual or group to submit its measure to the legislature for consideration. If the legislature does not pass the measure, it is placed on the ballot for the voters to decide. The referendum also comes in two forms. The submitted referendum is one in which the legislature places a measure on the ballot. The popular referendum is one in which a measure that has already passed the legislature is placed on the ballot by an opposing individual or group with the aim of defeating it and overruling the legislature.

The direct initiative is the principal technique of interest groups that want to bypass the legislature. In California, Arizona, Oregon, Washington, and Colorado, it is frequently used on issues such as taxation, education, welfare, health, immigration, gay rights, nuclear energy, abortion, campaign finance, and government organization. In 1998 there were 236 measures on state ballots, of which almost three-quarters passed.

An interest group, of course, can take its chances in the legislative process. But if a group has the necessary resources to go directly to the ballot, it may choose that route. Groups whose members are companies and associations can usually mobilize monetary resources, whereas groups whose members are primarily individuals can usually mobilize personnel resources.

In California more than anywhere else, the initiative has been used increasingly in the past forty years. The number of initiatives filed has nearly doubled each decade since the 1950s, with many of them filed by single-issue groups, other interests, and even state elective officeholders. The 1980s and 1990s saw initiative campaigns for no-fault insurance, handgun regulation, the regulation of insurance rates, the regulation of lawyer fees, bottle deposits, cigarette taxes, protecting water resources, toxic-waste issues, antismoking regulations, and establishing English as the official language. The California Teachers Association has made effective use of the initiative. One of its objectives was to make the education budget inviolate. But it would have been impossible to persuade the legislature to earmark a special fund for education. So CTA spent three years preparing an initiative, which it sponsored as Proposition 98 in 1988. Requiring 40 percent of state tax revenues be devoted to elementary and secondary education, the proposition passed.

If lobbyists and the groups they represent lose in the California legislature, or if they think they cannot win, they will turn to the initiative. Environmentalists attribute their frequent resort to the initiative to their lack of success in the legislative process. Even if they have a chance in the legislature, groups may decide on the initiative campaign, anyway. It is a good way to publicize an organization's issue (or an individual's candidacy for statewide office), and it offers the opportunity for an organization to achieve greater strength. Moreover, the initiative may serve to prod the governor and the legislature to take action. As a lobbyist for an environmental group said, "Now we have a viable threat that we'll do an initiative if the bill does not pass." The pressure on the legislature can be considerable.

The interests of business groups, in particular, have been assaulted by initiatives—mainly by those on automobile insurance and the environment. In 1988 the insurance industry spent $80 million fighting Proposition 103, which passed nonetheless. Business adopted a different strategy for the 1990 ballot, on which an environmental initiative called Big Green and a number of other initiatives were to appear. Its strategy was to load the ballot with counterinitiatives or "stealth" initiatives in an effort to confuse the political situation and confound the electorate. This strategy apparently worked, for only a few initiatives (including Proposition 140, which established term limits for members of the legislature) passed.

Colorado has also made use of the initiative to bypass and change the legislature. For years the state chapter of Common Cause had tried unsuccessfully to weaken caucus control of legislation. The organization was perceived, particularly by majority-party Republicans, to be "nagging and ineffectual." But Common Cause had the last laugh. It used its campaign for the Give-a-Vote-to-Every-Legislator (GAVEL) initiative to change that perception. The campaign, supported by the Colorado League of Women Voters and the press, overwhelmed the opposition. GAVEL was approved by the electorate, and the legislature had to live with new restrictions. Common Cause had demonstrated that it could play hardball politics. "While it lost the affection of legislators," observes one lobbyist, "it won their respect."

Citizen groups, which have no financial wherewithal and feel excluded from the state's power structure, make use of the initiative to accomplish governmental reform or limit taxes. For such groups, moreover, the initiative provides the kind of organizing tactic that helps maintain the environmental base of both liberal and conservative citizen groups. Organized interests also compete by means of the initiative. In Massachusetts big retail chains fought against smaller competitors. In Washington chiropractors backed a measure to require insurance to cover their services. In Wyoming denturists, who make and repair false teeth, squared off against dentists. The denturists did not think that they could prevail in the legislature since every legislator had a dentist and few even knew what a denturist was.[28]

It is usually up to a group's lobbyist to help determine whether the initiative is the most appropriate strategy. Normally, it is not. But even the threat of an initiative can cause the legislature to alter its behavior. So, from time to time lobbyists will counsel employers or clients to end run the legislature in the hope of achieving the group's objectives—in uncompromised, unamended form rather than in the customary modified form that is produced by the legislative process.

CHAPTER 8

Generating Support

If direct lobbying refers to what gets done in the legislature itself, with lobbyists and members interacting with one another, indirect lobbying refers to what takes place on the outside to support the efforts inside. Support can be furnished by groups that coalesce to form a coalition. It can also come from the grassroots level—local association members, company employees, plant managers, clients, suppliers, and so forth. Finally, support—or *perceived* support—can come from the public itself, and is generated through the media, public relations campaigns, and advertising.

Coalition Building

Nowadays, organizations seldom act in isolation from one another. Usually several groups will form a loose confederation on either side of an issue. Coalitions of groups, and particularly ad hoc issue coalitions, are practically a requirement for engagement on major issues. Small organizations cannot go it alone on many issues, so they have little choice but to join with others in common cause. Groups that have the same objectives are normally allies anyway. But coalitions can be either traditional allies who take organizational shape or traditional adversaries who get together in an ad hoc coalition on a specific issue. Matters of tort reform or health, for example, encourage the formation of coalitions as few other issues do. The word "coalition" has thus become one of the buzzwords of contemporary lobbying, and coalition building has become one of the major tasks of contemporary lobbyists. "Whenever you can put a coalition together, you do it," counsels one Colorado lobbyist. The more groups on one's side and the fewer on the other, the more effective the effort. As a Florida lobbyist put it, "The more people who hit 'em [the legislators], the better off you'll be."

Coalition building is not easy, but it is well worth the effort. From a lobbyist's perspective, its value is clear. The greater and more broad-based the support, the more likely that legislators will see the wisdom of a particular policy direction. At the very least, they will have the rationale of widespread support to justify their position and a higher level of comfort than otherwise. The downside of a coalition is that each individual member forgoes control. A minority view argues that "you should just go out and do it, and other groups will follow you." Do not spend valuable time, this argument goes, trying to keep a diverse organization in tow. But most organizations today are willing to run the risks associated with coalitions in order to cash in on the likely benefits.

For our purposes, a coalition is a loose collection of organizations that cooperates to accomplish common objectives. It is different from a single-industry association, such as the soft-drink manufacturers, or a multi-industry association, such as the chamber of commerce. A coalition may be ad hoc or relatively stable, made up of like-minded groups or strange bedfellows, and with or without formal organization.[1] Coalitions vary from issue to issue, time to time, and state to state depending on the groups and the lobbyists involved.

Identification and Recruitment of Members

"The first thing I do," reported a California lobbyist, "is to figure out if there's anyone else out there to help." Thus, the initial task of the lobbyist is to identify potential members of a coalition. The question is what other ox is being—or would be—gored by an issue or measure or what other interest might be served. In California a bill was being pushed to ban tax deductibility with regard to advertising tobacco and alcohol products. A lobbyist for a beer company quickly calculated all the different parties that would be harmed by this move. Newspapers were among those who would feel the effects. The lobbyist had no trouble putting a coalition together. In Colorado the issue was a bill to ban cigarettes from vending machines. The tobacco companies naturally formed the core of an opposing coalition, but vending machine and candy companies also joined.

In New Jersey, dental assistants opposed the dental association's plan to create a category titled "limited registered dental assistant." The dental assistants' lobbyist recruited the dental hygienists, the State Nurses Association, and the University of Medicine and Dentistry of New Jersey into the coalition. Another New Jersey lobbyist, representing business clients on the issue of product liability, identified for his coalition—the Federation of Advocates for Insurance Reform (FAIR)—more than fifty groups that faced liability problems. These groups included the Policemen's Benevolent Association, the Hospital Association, the School Boards Association, the Society of Certified Public Accountants, Squibb, Johnson & Johnson, the Restaurant Association, and the Food Council.

A New Jersey lobbyist, whose client opposed a curb on generic drugs, which was proposed by major pharmaceutical companies, started off by identifying those groups that would also be against prohibiting the substitution of bio-equivalent generics for branded drugs. They included the New Jersey Council of Chain Drug Stores, the National Pharmaceutical Alliance (whose members are generic drug companies), the Health Insurance Association of America, and the New Jersey Association of Retail Druggists. These organizations then banded together under the title Coalition for Affordable Pharmaceuticals.[2]

Once potential members are identified, it is up to the lobbyist to recruit them to the cause. That means framing an issue in appealing terms and motivating others to take certain action. Success in this regard depends on a host of factors, not least among them being the issue itself, the relationship among the groups, and the lobbyist's persuasiveness. Those groups with a history of supporting others on issues that are marginal for them have a better chance of forming a successful coalition than groups that have traditionally acted alone. Coalitions generally come hard to organizations whose issues are low on other groups' agendas. Yet those that are willing to trade support on issues are in a better position. They have something tangible to offer one another. One pharmaceuticals lobbyist suggested, for instance, that: "It's a good quid pro quo to tell the docs that you'll help them in return for their help on Medicaid."

More subtle is the lobbyist's job of taking out potential opponents. Lobbyists cultivate relationships with various groups. Such relationships make it less likely that the cultivated group will join a coalition in opposition to the lobbyist's objectives. For example, bridge building is one of the principal lobbying strategies of the trial lawyers in Texas. They hold a joint retreat with doctors every year, work with senior citizens and the AARP, and have reached a modus vivendi with the automobile dealers in the state. The aim has been to deter such groups from joining the opposition.

The Nature of Coalitions

There are coalitions of natural partners and coalitions of strange bedfellows. They may include any combination. One thing is clear, however: even groups that appear to have similar interests and aims are not easy to bring together. Many associations and organizations suffer from internal disunity. Yet an organization must usually develop a consensus within before it can be part of an effective coalition.

Achieving unity is no simple matter for many groups. Business is particularly fragmented, even Balkanized. "It is rare," observed one lobbyist in Austin, "to find business in this state unified against anybody." Instead, tax issues split the service and manufacturing sectors, and other issues divide businesses according to size or product. In Texas perhaps the only big issues on which business has been united in recent years are tort reform and product liability.[3] Environmentalists, even within the same organization, also encounter difficulties. Purists disagree with pragmatists, and it is not easy for them to resolve their differences. "There are more environmentalists per square foot," observes one public interest lobbyist from Colorado, "but they are the least effective group for their numbers." Another public interest lobbyist, from New Jersey, described coalition work as extremely challenging mainly because everybody has different interests. Although various environmental groups all agree in general on issues, "individual interests and individual tactics and strategies tend to vary among groups."

Still, certain groups are easier for a lobbyist to bring together than others. Some already have membership in a formal organization, such as the New Jersey Environmental Federation. This group has been in operation for over ten years as a coalition of about forty-five environmental, labor, and civic member groups. When the Clean Water Enforcement Act was at the top of the New Jersey Public Interest Research Group (NJPIRG) agenda, more than one hundred environmental organizations signed on and worked in the coalition. On the regulation of smoking, the coalitions on each side are also natural ones: physicians and heart, lung, and cancer societies versus the tobacco industry, retail merchants, the restaurant association, and others with an economic interest in tobacco. In Minnesota a group of six major utilities—two electric, two gas, and two combination—work hand in hand on most issues that affect them. The pharmaceutical industry's main allies are state medical associations, which also want maximum flexibility for the use of drugs financed by Medicaid.

Then there are coalitions that cross "family" lines.[4] Perhaps the most visible of these strange bedfellows are business and labor. In many places, these groups have formed the core of the coalition opposing the bottle bill, an environmental measure imposing a refundable deposit on cans and bottles. Indeed, they needed one another if they were to prevail on this issue. In Minnesota, where labor exercises substantial power, business makes a special effort, according to one of its lobbyists, to "get connections whenever we can." The motivation for business to link up with labor is somewhat less in other states. Business and labor united in New Jersey to end the diversion of the state Unemployment Insurance Fund to finance charity care. The coalition worked for a while, but the united front was broken when the legislature lured labor with an offer of a one-time thirteen-week unemployment insurance extension to workers who had exhausted their benefits.[5]

Some companies manage to recruit as allies both environmental and industry or consumer groups, as unlikely as that may seem. Ordinarily, beer and environmental groups are at loggerheads. But in Florida the environmentalists supported beer's opposition to a seven-ounce packaging bill. The environmentalists did not want additional types of containers; neither did the beer wholesalers. Drug companies make their case in terms of "patient care," so their optimal coalition is one that includes doctors, pharmacists, and, whenever possible, patient groups.

Given the right circumstances, skillful lobbyists can recruit groups that will give a big boost to their client's cause. In one state, builders were pushing a bill to allow them to dispose of waste materials on the construction site by digging a hole and burying them—a way for the industry to reduce costs. The lobbyist's client, a solid-waste-management group, would have been adversely affected. Because an environmental argument wielded by the solid-waste group would not have been heeded (the self-interest being too obvious), the lobbyist contacted the environmental groups and got them steamed up. He also appealed to the counties and municipalities that would have been responsible for regulating the builders under the proposed legislation. Although it had been moving through the legislature smoothly, the bill came to a screeching halt when this coalition was activated.

In another state, the natural gas industry, once an ally of the utilities, has lately become an adversary. In seeking additional markets, it sought legislation that would require utilities to use natural gas. The utilities naturally were opposed. Their lobbyist contacted consumer groups. "Have you looked at this?" he asked them. The coalition came together, with the consumer groups opposing the measure on the grounds that it would drive up prices, and the utilities happily going along. On an issue affecting the sale of electricity in New Jersey, the interest of retailers squared more with that of consumers than with that of big business. As a result, New Jersey Retail Merchants Association entered a coalition with NJPIRG, which on other issues it had opposed.[6]

Not only does business turn to consumers and environmentalists for help, but it can also work the other way. The Colorado Public Interest Research Group (COPIRG) took the lead in entering nontraditional coalitions. Some years ago, the big question at COPIRG was "Should you have lunch with an industry lobbyist?" Since then, COPIRG has gotten involved in a coalition with ten businesses (including AT&T) to oppose reduction in the regulation of U.S. West Communications. Nontraditional coalitions such as this are very useful for public interest groups. One benefit is that they open doors in the Republican-controlled legislature. COPIRG's lobbyist met the speaker of the Colorado house by working in such a coalition, achieving access that he might not otherwise have gotten.

Working Together

Cooperative action is frequently essential. But holding a coalition together is as tough as creating it in the first place. A Minnesota lobbyist for insurance interests described the tricks of his trade. His objective was to modify Minnesota's Superfund statute, which had made the cost of liability insurance for environmental impairment prohibitively high. But business groups and the insurance industry were divided, with "bickering, mistrust, suspicion, and dislike" among them. Their lobbyists agreed, however, that the St. Paul Area Chamber of Commerce would act as a facilitator of a coalition seeking to amend the Superfund law. In response to efforts by the insurance lobbyist, the governor established a task force composed of business leaders, insurance representatives, governmental agencies, and environmentalists to look into amending the statute. The business coalition was able to work with the task force as well as with legislative leaders. Near the end of the debate, however, the environmentalists balked. They would not support the coalition's amendment of the Superfund statute unless a victims' compensation fund was established. The business community could have fragmented at this point, but the coalition stood fast. Finally, their efforts succeeded because chief executive officers were involved in the debate and because lobbying, media, and internal business communications held together.[7]

The danger is that coalition members will pull away toward the end of the process. Even though they may agree on the general case, they can diverge on specifics. Some will drop out because their particular interests are being compromised or traded off. Some will make end runs to change an agreement or to cut their own deals. The moderates will be willing to make concessions while the militants will insist on holding firm. An example of a coalition that fell apart occurred in California over oil-spill legislation. The oil industry supported the legislation proposed, but ARCO's position diverged because its crude oil came from Alaska by ship and the bill imposed a fee on oil imported by water. When ARCO's lobbyist succeeded in having the bill amended in the Senate Appropriations Committee, Shell and other companies attempted to restore the bill to its original form. The coalition disintegrated.

Lobbyists are responsible for leading and orchestrating their coalition's campaign. They have to keep members up to date, involve them in planning, assign tasks, and coordinate activities. Take as an example New Jersey's FAIR coalition, which was seeking changes in product liability and tort law. One of Trenton's major contract lobbyists played the lead role. He assigned coalition members tasks on the basis of who knew whom, who had greatest credibility and friendships, where facilities and plants were located, what types of experience the groups had with legislators, and the expertise of various coalition lobbyists. He set up a task force of corporate CEOs, organized a grassroots effort, and arranged for a public-information campaign. He also coordinated the direct lobbying activities of a platoon of professionals under contract to the coalition's member groups.

Grassroots Mobilization

Grassroots lobbying can be defined as "the identification, recruitment, and mobilization of constituent-based political strength capable of influencing political decisions."[8]

Grassroots constitute one element of an increasingly important "outside game" or indirect lobbying that now supplements (but has not replaced) the old-fashioned "inside game" or direct lobbying. On some issues it is no longer sufficient for interest groups to communicate with legislators. Interest groups and their lobbyists now try to mobilize citizens to contact or pressure legislators on behalf of or against a measure. They have to demonstrate muscle by showing that a legislator's constituency or the public in general is on their side.[9]

Those who resort to the grass roots are following examples set years ago by the civil rights and antiwar movements and by environmental and consumer groups. These groups used outside strategies with telling effect. But grassroots efforts are also encouraged by the changes taking place within legislatures themselves. Restrictive ethics laws and high turnover as a result of term limits make it more difficult for lobbyists to establish relationships with legislators, so they often turn outside the legislature for help. A former staff director of the Iowa legislature, who is now a lobbyist, describes how the situation has changed:

> We use those techniques [phone banks and grass roots] because many legislators don't necessarily want to see us at the statehouse. It's partly an ethics issue. . . . There's really very little we can do except talk to legislators at the capitol. We don't go out to lunch and we don't do a lot of things we used to do to gain access. We have about 40 new members in the legislature this year, and we don't know them very well. They are being taught not to trust us, which makes lobbying extremely difficult.[10]

In the words of a Maryland lobbyist, "The old politics don't work anymore, you have to get back home where it really hurts." According to this line of reasoning, the legislator's district is where political power resides, and grassroots lobbying puts legislators into contact with constituents who hold that power. It demonstrates vocal and tangible support (or opposition) for a measure. In a grassroots campaign, constituents tell legislators how the measure will affect them instead of the lobbyist doing it. "Don't believe me," the lobbyist can say to the legislator, "just ask Charlie," a "key contact" from back home.

Currently, nearly every group with a legislative program has to consider mobilizing whatever grass roots it may have, whether to mount a substantial campaign or only to have a few members pay visits to key legislators. Interest groups opt for outside campaigns if they have the capability—and then only on high-stakes matters. Such campaigns are the exception, not the rule. Outside lobbying, at the state level even more than the national level, tends to be targeted at undecided legislators. "As every lobbyist . . . knows," writes Ken Kollman, "persuasion is a subtle business, and careless lobbying strategies can backfire."[11]

Grassroots lobbying is an outside game, but it cannot occur independently of the inside one. The lobbyist therefore has to be involved in planning and coordinating a client's grassroots effort.

Grassroots Capacity

Most groups engage in one form of grassroots activity or another. In a study of organizations and lobbyists in California, South Carolina, and Wisconsin, 92 percent of the organizations and 94 percent of the lobbyists reported that they had influential constituents contact legislators' offices and 83 percent of the former and 82 percent of the latter had inspired letter-writing campaigns. In addition, 86 percent of the organizations and 88 percent of lobbyists reported that they mounted grassroots lobbying campaigns. Corporate lobbyists are less likely, according to this analysis, than lobbyists with unions, trade/professional associations, and citizen groups to engage in these activities, but the differences are not substantial.[12] Indeed, nine out of ten corporations have some grassroots capability,[13] although they may encounter obstacles in bringing it to bear. Another piece of evidence—albeit indirect—that grassroots activity is on the rise was produced by a study of citizen participation in the United States. It found that 25 percent of people sampled reported that they had had contact with a state or local elected official (or staff) during the previous twelve months, with one out of five of them having had most recent contact with a member of the state legislature.[14] Some of these people may have initiated contact on their own, but it is likely that many contacted legislators as part of group and organizational efforts.

Not every group is able to develop an effective grassroots campaign. A group's potential in this regard depends on a number of factors.

First, a group must have the resources to develop a field operation. Some cause groups operate on a shoestring. Grassroots lobbying needs some money to launch a vigorous effort; it is resource intensive. Resources are needed to identify individuals active in an association or company at the local level, to educate these members about the organization's message, to train them to communicate effectively, and to develop their political skills for a grassroots campaign.[15]

Technological advances these last twenty-five years have also made the development of grassroots capacity possible, but at a cost. Computer databases, direct mail, telemarketing, fax, and the Internet speed up and target communications. Grassroots Web sites now number about 6,700.[16] Advances in district-matching software allow interest groups to identify the legislative districts in which their members live. At the corporate level, electronic networks can link employees, retirees, and even suppliers.[17]

Someone has to organize grassroots efforts and keep them organized. Volunteers cannot do it; money is required to pay staff. Common Cause tried with volunteers. It established phone networks in one state; members agreed to call one another. But without someone to ride herd, the network atrophied. People were involved for a little while; then they walked away. Their lobbyist explained: "I would not hold a Common Cause day in [the state capital] because I don't think anybody would be impressed with thirty people." In Florida a lobbyist who represented farm workers had to obtain a grant to pay for the gas to bring some of her members to Tallahassee to meet with legislators. A more extended grassroots campaign was completely out of her financial reach. When it comes to the legislature, local people do have power, but some money is required to mobilize it.

Moreover, if a group wants to bring on consultants to run a grassroots campaign or even build the group's capacity, the cost narrows the field. Today, many public relations firms and campaign consultants are selling "grassroots recruitment and mobilization" and "grass-tops lobbying" as a method of persuading both members and ordinary citizens to serve as front-line advocates.

Second, a group's potential depends on its membership base. For instance, a Minnesota company downsized, going from thirty to ten local offices with correspondingly fewer employees. Although it became more economically efficient, it lost much of its political salience. It was without a grassroots base. Oil companies in Florida, for example, have no plants, no refineries, and no employees. They are not even residents of Florida. They have no base there. In contrast, the jobbers are well distributed and strong throughout the state. They even have the potential to get a candidate to challenge an incumbent legislator. The Wine Institute has a base in California and New York, where wine is an important product, but elsewhere wine interests are weak. In contrast, beer has a wholesaling network throughout the nation. Not only the size but also the distribution of members throughout a state play a role. Retailers reside in all the legislative districts, and that is a source of the beer industry's strength. By way of contrast, ophthalmologists tend to congregate in a few urban and suburban areas; that limits them politically.

Labor unions and public interest groups are well suited for grassroots efforts, because they have large membership lists. Corporations normally reach beyond their employees per se to former employees, vendors, stockholders, and sometimes third parties.[18]

Third, a group's potential depends on its membership and/or product. Politics turns off many citizens, so it is extremely difficult to get them to participate in a grassroots campaign. "Asking people to get involved in politics," says consultant Michael Dunn, "is like asking them to perform an unnatural act."

Particular groups vary in their political dispositions. Some people take to grass roots more than others. At one extreme are local elected government officials, who are already committed to politics. The Texas Municipal League, for instance, has its Grass-Roots Involvement Program (GRIP), the theme of which is "Get a grip on your legislature." Also politically oriented and available for grassroots activity are trial lawyers. Not many teachers are natural political activists, yet large numbers can be galvanized by issues of salary and working conditions that demonstrably affect them. The typical accountant is not at all political; but some of them are, and do get involved in the political work of a state society. A challenge for any lobbyist is Florida farmworkers, many of whom speak only Spanish or Creole, or the homeless, who are difficult to mobilize no matter how loud an action alert.

The best grassroots personnel, in the opinions of lobbyists, are people who have the closest contact with legislators and in whom legislators repose trust, although in a different domain. An auto mechanic who services a legislator's car is an ideal constituent. So is the local pharmacist, and particularly one in a rural area, who often is part of a legislator's district network.

But organizations must obviously make do with the individuals affiliated with them. Corporations have to rely on employees, stockholders, retirees, suppliers or vendors, and customers or clients. From time to time they can get their top executives involved, but one state-relations director cautioned: "You can't play the big chips too often." J. C. Penney's grassroots system is based on a network of about two thousand store managers. American Cyanamid has business councils in six states, which comprise all plant managers and other employees. Industrial Paper is organized under regional managers, but the plant managers at the company's 150 facilities are key.[19] Power and telephone utilities, as well as other companies, use line management from plants in the district.[20] Most companies, and particularly manufacturing companies, depend on operating managers to play leading roles in grassroots endeavors. Johnson & Johnson's grassroots program illustrates one variation. Government task-force meetings are held in each of J&J's target states—California, Texas, Illinois, New Jersey, Georgia, and Florida. Members of these task forces include plant managers, human resource personnel, and finance personnel. Those teams, with the support of headquarters, are responsible for grassroots operations in particular jurisdictions. In all of these cases, however, "calls to action" have to be limited to a few each year, nor is it reasonable to expect a high percentage of members or employees to respond.

Organizations may recruit beyond their own memberships in order to expand their grassroots strength. Dayton Hudson is an example. One of the principal corporations in Minnesota, it awards grants through its foundation and calls on its grant recipients for help when major issues arise that affect the company. On legislation designed to avert a takeover, the message from the foundation was: "You have to save Dayton Hudson." All the grantees, including a troupe of ballet dancers, signed on to help the company.

Public interest groups in some states canvass door-to-door. New Jersey PIRG is an example of a group with impressive grassroots capacity. It has two hundred members canvassing out of five offices around the state. They sign up members, get contributions, and push the issues PIRG is lobbying in Trenton. They circulate petitions or ask people to sign post-cards (and to add a personal touch to the form card), and then PIRG delivers petitions or postcards to the legislators whose districts have been canvassed. On one campaign, to promote clean-water legislation, PIRG had six organizers in eighteen targeted districts setting up local committees to have people get in touch with their legislators. PIRG's grassroots organization can reach far and wide and generate a lot of activity.

Grassroots Organization

One of the outstanding grassroots organizations is that of Anheuser-Busch, the manufacturer of Budweiser and Michelob beers, among other products. The structure and nature of the beer industry facilitate lobbying in general and grassroots lobbying in particular. The industry projects an image of conviviality, having fun, and making friends. That goes with lobbying. It has a large customer base, which helps in grassroots campaigns. Wine, by contrast, has an image of being more upscale and formal—even a little snobbish. It has a smaller customer base. Thus, with regard to grassroots lobbying effects, beer is a natural, wine is not. The difference in products also gives beer an advantage over wine. Beer has a short shelf life, so its wholesalers visit retailers more frequently. The beer-distribution system consists of many people with small territories to serve—the ideal situation for grassroots organizing. In wine, there are fewer people serving larger territories—and communicating less often.

Anheuser-Busch employs more than twenty-four thousand individuals, who can be activated at almost any time. They are assigned to legislative districts through a computer matching system. The company's strength is greatest in those states where it has plants—Virginia, Texas, Ohio, California, New Jersey, Florida, Colorado, Georgia, and New York.

In addition to its immediate employees, A-B can call on its family of wholesalers, about 750 across the country, including 26 in Texas and 49 in California. These wholesalers have solid small businesses, employ a total of more than thirty thousand people, and are well-positioned in their communities. Day-to-day they make contacts throughout their states since they are dealing with a total of almost five hundred thousand outlets in the nation. Every two weeks each person who holds a liquor license is visited by an A-B wholesaler, and these wholesalers receive the company's action alerts with support and briefing materials, as well as notification on the phone. A-B relies not only on employees and wholesalers (and, indirectly, retailers) but also on its suppliers. Barley growers in Montana and hops growers in Oregon can be mobilized, in addition to can companies and paperboard manufacturers.

The strength of the Anheuser-Busch grassroots organization does not guarantee success, however. Even with instantaneous communication, it takes three to four weeks for A-B to mobilize its troops for an effort in any state. If A-B is on the offense, it can plan ahead. But, in most instances, the company is defending against regulations or taxes and the lead time is less. For example, the governor of Illinois at the last minute advanced a proposal to increase the beer tax, and A-B was taken by surprise. The legislative session was almost over, and maximum grassroots pressure could hardly be brought into play. Thus, one tactic for countering a grassroots system is for an adversary to wait until the last two weeks of a legislative session before making a move.

On issues like bottle bills, which were on many state agendas in the 1980s, its grass roots came in handy for A-B. But the recycling movement took steam out of bills requiring deposits on bottles, so mobilization has not been necessary of late. On other issues, such as the regulation of marketing practices, grass roots is not the most appropriate type of lobbying for A-B.

Another example of effective grassroots organization is that of teachers. Education associations are apt to have a government relations committee or the like, with teacher representatives from around the state and local legislative-action teams. The latter may be chaired by a member of the government relations committee, charged with grassroots work, and staffed by headquarters professionals. In New Jersey these legislative-action teams promote attendance at the New Jersey Education Association (NJEA) Legislative Conference, at teacher lobby days in Trenton, at special rallies, and at legislative and political training seminars. Members of these teams are trained by NJEA's lobbying staff, and summer workshops educate an additional twelve hundred teachers in political action techniques.

Teachers' associations also possess excellent communications systems whereby they can inform and alert members. In both Colorado and Minnesota, for example, the associations have "action lines." Teachers can call in on a toll-free number and receive up-to-the-minute information, messages, and campaign instructions. The Texas State Teachers Association has more than thirty field offices linked by computer and a phone bank at its main office in Austin. Newsletters and legislative bulletins are also employed. At budget-writing time, it is not unusual for NJEA to send out a bulletin to its membership, noting a crisis in state aid, asking for an increase in school funding, and suggesting that members reach out to legislators; local and county presidents organize letter writing and telephone calls to legislators, and local legislative-action teams begin letter-writing campaigns to the chairpersons of the senate and assembly appropriations committees. NJEA considers that its major political strength is its ability to mobilize, not only its own members, but also twenty-five thousand retired educators in an affiliated organization.

Grassroots Techniques

Interest groups have the option of hiring a consultant to conduct a campaign on their behalf. Many "boiler room" operations will try to manufacture grassroots opinion and stimulate an outpouring of certain messages. Referred to as "Astroturf" lobbying, the effort here is to create the appearance of a popular ground swell for the client's position.

Michael Dunn's advice, as a consultant in the field, is that organizations should develop their own ongoing grassroots program rather than employ outsiders to run campaigns on an ad hoc basis. Another consultant, Charles Mack, details the important elements of such a program, which include a network and a call to action that tells voters whom to write or call, the issue and bill number, the position to be expressed, and talking points (backed up whenever possible with personal experience). He stresses the importance of individual involvement, including dropping in on legislators, annual legislative dinners and receptions, and facility visits.[21]

Consultants in this field believe lobbyists ought to be intimately involved in the grassroots enterprise. It is up to them to determine a strategy, select the most appropriate techniques, plan and coordinate activities, and see that things do not get out of hand. Involvement does not necessarily mean prominence, however. Lobbyists can work behind the scenes, with members and other constituents out front. "When I am doing my job best, I am invisible," is the way one professional saw his grassroots role.

Grass roots can be broad-based, whereby members and others are mobilized to contact legislators with a group's message. Or it can be more narrowly based, where only a few members are called on to present the group's position. The two kinds of approach can, of course, be combined.[22] The broader the campaign and the more one's troops are stirred up, the greater the noise level and the more intense the conflict. A show of force tends to give friendly legislators political cover. It also tends to increase the pressure on legislators who might go either way and raises the costs for legislators who are in the adversary's camp.

Among the variety of techniques in grassroots campaigns, writing letters and making telephone calls have been the most common. Some legislators question the efficacy of mass letter-writing efforts, saying they are unimpressed by postcards, preprinted letters, and letters drafted on the computer. Lobbyists, however, try to stay ahead of the legislators on the matter of mail. One contract lobbyist in New Jersey, for example, used different grades of paper, various type styles, and computer letters with words misspelled in order to make the messages seem spontaneous rather than stimulated.

Lobbyists generally have confidence in the efficacy of letters and telephone calls. A cause lobbyist in California activates groups and members of his coalition, who in turn write and call. "It doesn't take many letters to get their attention," he pointed out. A legislative leader from Maine agreed: "Ten phone calls to a legislator is a groundswell." The sheer weight of communications matters; the more, the better. A lobbyist for a professional association in California confessed that "when we decided not to use mail, they stuck it in our ear." Now his group errs on the side of writing. If a member warrants it, "blitz him" is that lobbyist's rule of thumb. It works: "When you blitz them, it's overwhelming."

Many organizations therefore devote substantial resources to phone and/or letter-writing activities. The Texas Civil Justice League, a coalition whose focus is product liability and tort reform, has forty phone-bank operators in a special facility in Austin to support its grassroots operation. During one of its major campaigns, the league's staff went through every phone book in the state, identified businesses that would be interested, and made calls to thirty-five thousand of them. These businesses were sent materials and sample letters and asked to write to the legislature. Associated Industries of Florida has its own computer staff and software to send out action requests to which members will respond. The association claims that it can put a thousand letters or telegrams from constituents on a legislator's desk with a twenty-four-hour turnaround.

E-mail makes communications cheaper, more convenient, and more immediate. It is easier, in a grassroots effort to get members to e-mail their legislators than to write, fax, or call them. Most legislators in most states can now be reached electronically. Groups can bypass their office staff (if they have any) and communicate directly. Nor is printing or postage required.[23]

It is generally agreed that one of the most effective techniques is the use of key contacts, in what now are called "grass-tops" programs. These are people who are members of the group who have some tie to a legislator in whose district they live. They know legislators, according to a Colorado lobbyist, "in settings other than asking them for something during the session." It might be someone from a manufacturing plant or facility. It might be an insurance broker who has the legislator as a client. The Colorado Association of Commerce and Industry relies on its 150-member board of directors, which includes 35 CEOs. All told, the association has at least ten people in each district who serve as key contacts. The trial lawyers are diligent in this regard. In Texas they try to get members who have worked in a legislator's campaign. In Minnesota they have key contacts in every legislative district. Each one, of course, cannot ask for a legislator's help on every bill of concern to the group, but each may make an appeal once or twice during the session.

State societies of certified public accountants have developed key-contact networks and are trying to increase the number of members involved. The subject is a delicate one, however: some CPAs will not use their client relationship to try to advance the profession's goals. However, a number of them know legislators through a business or civic club or on some basis other than a client relationship. They are willing to use their relationships as long as the effort does not seem heavy-handed. Some state societies mail questionnaires out after each election to every CPA whom they know in the legislature. The staff takes it from there in recruiting new key contacts.

Associations of municipal and county officials comprise practically nothing but key contacts. Their members are elected public officials who are distributed geographically among the legislative districts of the state. They are people who know politics, possess political skill, and are likely to be well acquainted with the legislators in their districts. They are easily mobilized on issues affecting local government's interests. The Texas Municipal League is particularly impressive when it comes to key contacts in grassroots campaigns. It begins by sending questionnaires to all elected officials (and department heads, too) asking how well they know senators and representatives. That becomes part of the league's database. Texas local officials do not often seek state legislative office, so they are not viewed as rivals or threats by legislators. That makes for a much smoother key-contact system.

Visiting with legislators in the capitol or in the district is also an effective technique, especially if the right people are involved. The "right people" are those who are connected in the legislature or affected by proposed legislation. They may testify, or simply make a cameo appearance, before a legislative committee. One lobbyist got the mother of a committee member to testify in favor of a particular bill. The member signed on as a sponsor as his mother was addressing him. In the Delaware legislature, a bill relating to crabbing on Sundays was at issue. On the day of the public hearing, the lobbyist appeared with a number of commercial crabbers wearing their work clothes—rubber boots, worn tee-shirts, and rough pants. These hulking men made a dramatic presence.[24] A lobbyist in the employ of the tobacco industry, to flesh out his argument against banning the sale of cigarettes in vending machines, brought fifty vending-machine truckers to the committee.

Many groups sponsor what are often called "lobby days" or "a day at the legislature." A few hundred business people visit their senators and representatives in the state capitol in St. Paul. Thirty or forty teachers roam through the halls of the capitol building in Austin. More than one hundred people, wearing stickers saying "Make Polluters Pay," seek out legislators in the statehouse in Trenton.

A Florida lobbyist for farmworkers has made a special effort to have her clients and legislators meet face-to-face. She arranged for them to make a trip to the capitol to meet with legislators. They left their homes at 4 a.m. and drove in trucks and vans (some of which broke down) to Tallahassee. They visited legislators, presenting them with oranges and bell peppers as gifts. Then they had a soup-line lunch, with several legislators serving. That night they slept on the floors of local churches before returning home the following day. It was a moving event, one the lobbyist hoped would grab the legislature by its conscience.

On occasion, groups mobilize a large number of members in an effort to intimidate legislators. Florida's doctors turned out in the thousands for a visit to the capitol on tort reform. The New Jersey Education Association, in an attempt to get broad-based bargaining on non-wage-related issues, turned out twelve thousand teachers for a march on Trenton. When the New Jersey legislature debated a bill to restrict assault firearms, almost a thousand members of the Coalition of New Jersey Sportsmen and the National Rifle Association held an aggressive demonstration in Trenton. One assemblywoman reacted: "Never in my life have I been subjected to the abuse, the verbal abuse, the vandalism of my office that occurred just this morning." A senator had a similar reaction: "I've never seen that kind of intimidation in sixteen years."[25] But the gun enthusiasts had certainly made their point and many legislators—like it or not—got the message.

Using tactics closer to home, the New Jersey Education Association hosts annual legislative dinners in each of the state's twenty-one counties, both to honor the legislators and to demonstrate organizational strength. It also arranges for small-group meetings between members of the legislative-action team and legislators in order to discuss one or two key issues. Colorado's teachers have receptions for legislators in their districts at least once or twice a year and in at least one locality breakfasts are held regularly throughout the session.

Business operates in a similar fashion. The New Jersey Business and Industry Association's employer-legislative committees in each county hold a monthly meeting to discuss issues of concern. Legislators from the area are invited and several show up. Companies in New Jersey bring legislators to their facilities to have lunch with workers, thus giving legislators a chance to meet with constituents and simultaneously building rapport for the company. Johnson & Johnson invites legislators to tour company plants and to meet with the chief executive officer; those on a health committee are brought in to meet with company researchers.

In New York, fourteen Democratic members of the state assembly visited Kodak in Rochester. At the outset of the two-day visit one of the legislators described Kodak as the biggest polluter in New York. When he left, his mind was changed and he said, "I'd like to help spread their gospel." His colleagues, who had spent much of their time chatting with workers on the line, left Rochester expressing concern about Kodak's problems.[26]

New Jersey PIRG also works along these lines. It organizes meetings of constituents and asks the delegation of legislators from the district to attend. When constituents, who have been chosen by PIRG, express their concerns, legislators feel the pressure. Sometimes, in fact, they commit publicly then and there. Other times, they agree to consider the PIRG position. If they do not attend at all, it can be considered a slap in the face to those constituents who care about the issue.

One way to convince legislators that their constituencies favor a certain measure is to make use of public-opinion polls. Statewide polls tell members very little about their own districts, but they still have an overall impact. If the results are unambiguous, they may serve to push fence-sitters to one side or the other. For example, poll results made a difference in an effort to get full funding for abortions for low-income women in California. Choice had become a hot issue in the elections, and the California Poll had found that 67 percent of Californians were pro-choice and 59 percent supported abortion funding for poor women. Florida's soft-drink and bottling industries, in opposing a "pop tax" in the legislature, took a statewide poll. Their poll showed that consumers disliked the idea of a tax on soft drinks by a margin of 62 to 36 percent. Minnesota's leading corporation, Dayton Hudson, in its campaign to promote antitakeover legislation, hired a pollster to find out if Minnesotans from all over the state favored saving the company. They did.

It costs a lot of money to conduct polls in the districts of undecided legislators (that is, those whose votes are still up for grabs). As a result, very few polls are taken in individual districts. But some are. On a bill regarding pensions for police officers in New Jersey, the knee-jerk reaction of a number of legislators was, "My constituents don't like this." So the lobbyist handling the issue commissioned a poll in several legislative districts and went to the skeptical legislators with the results. He explained the data to them and concluded: "You can believe what you want to believe, but here is as factual information as we can possibly provide."

Polls were central to a campaign launched by the Casino Association of New Jersey to permit wagers on athletic contests at Atlantic City casinos. It would have required a change in the state constitution, and therefore the association's initial objective was to persuade the legislature to place it on the ballot so that the electorate could decide. Some legislators favored sports betting, some simply favored putting it up for referendum, some were opposed to doing anything. After the constitutional amendment to legalize sports betting had been approved by the senate, the Casino Association's lobbyist and consultants targeted thirteen members of the assembly, who were possible swing votes. Telephone surveys in these districts drew the response of over 27,000 voters, 80 percent of whom supported putting the question to the people. Of these respondents, 55.8 percent were in favor of legalizing sports betting. Nine out of ten of them (about 11,000 voters), when asked, authorized the association to send a letter on their behalf to their legislators urging them to vote for the constitutional amendments.[27]

On big issues, polls and focus groups are being used more frequently by lobbyists nowadays. Some results are conveyed to legislators, as part of a group's grassroots effort, but most of these studies and analyses are primarily intended to help lobbyists shape their campaign strategies.

Does It Work?

Grassroots campaigns are effective if they are applied to appropriate issues, employed with sensitivity, and kept under control. These conditions, however, are not always met. If the inside-lobbyist game works, there may be no need for outside strategies. Some contract lobbyists are completely sold on direct lobbying and apparently need little external support. They certainly prefer working their contacts. Bruce Bereano of Maryland, for example, is a one-man operation who depends on energy, knowledge of the process, and close relationships. A New Jersey lobbyist focuses primarily on leadership and sees little need for pressuring the rank and file with grass roots. "If the speaker puts the bill up," he concludes, "it's going to pass."

Certain issues, moreover, can be handled within the institution without stirring up the waters outside. A Minnesota association lobbyist pointed to one bill of importance to his industry. The public had little interest in the issue; the legislature did not have much more. On this issue, one-on-one lobbying was most appropriate. His association has not had "life-or-death" issues, or ones of much interest even to its members, during recent years. It has thus focused on the inside game and never considered a grassroots effort.

On some issues, grassroots campaigns simply will not work, not because members are uninterested, but because they are skittish. In New Jersey, when the legislature was deciding on an ethics bill for local government officials, the New Jersey League of Municipalities opposed it on the ground that, if enacted, such legislation would discourage talented and successful individuals from running for local office. But because mayors and city council members could hardly speak out against an ethics bill, the league could not generate grassroots support. Elected officials could not run the political risk of taking a public position against a "motherhood" issue like this one.

There is no guarantee, however, that organizations will always be able to rely on an inside strategy. Issues change, as does the composition of the legislature. In earlier years Anheuser-Busch was able to prevail on tax issues by working within the legislatures. Taxes are still the major issue for the company, but nowadays grassroots constituencies play a greater and more frequent role in the process. Fact sheets and white papers are prepared. Letters are sent out to wholesalers. Employees, retailers, and suppliers are alerted; displays are placed in bars; and delegations are advised to visit the capitol and talk taxes with legislators.

Grassroots campaigns are not without risk. As a lobbyist for a Colorado governmental association summed up: "Grass roots can be great or it can be a disaster." This is particularly applicable in Colorado, where members of the general assembly are adverse to outside pressure stimulated by interest groups. In the words of one lobbyist, "They don't like to see the pot stirred," especially if it does not have to be. One veteran legislator from Colorado warned a group of lobbyists: "You're attempting to intimidate me and overwhelm me when it may not even be an issue." His view was supported by a legislative leader from Maine, who admonished organizers of grassroots campaigns: "If you don't do it right, you will be taken to the cleaners." For these legislators, grassroots campaigns are a last resort; they prefer direct-lobbying campaigns first.

One danger in grassroots efforts is that the wrong legislators will be pressured. Appeals can be misdirected, having little effect on die-hard opponents and a boomerang effect on friends. Proper targeting is necessary. But rarely can individual participants throughout a state be adequately informed or carefully supervised. A teachers' association lobbyist recalled instances in which teachers (as part of a campaign) accused senators of being enemies of education when the senators were actually friends. Even if such mistakes are not made, there is the danger that certain legislators will always be hearing from the same people. Those who run campaigns must be selective; otherwise legislators will come to regard key contacts as the little boy who cried wolf.

Having the right members helps. According to a lobbyist for an association of local government officials, "If you have good, strong commissioners with knowledge, experience, and personality, it works well." But such people are hard to find, beyond perhaps the ranks of elected public officials. Few groups can manage to let their members loose in the capitol without some negative consequences. (It is true that the negatives might be outweighed by the positives.) Lawyers are politically attuned but "too damned smart," according to a lobbyist who works for them. His job, he says, is to ratchet them down to what a rural member of the legislature wants to know. Members of a Police Benevolent Association (PBA) may also know too much and go too far, according to a contract lobbyist who represented them: "Cops are great amateur lawyers. . . . They know their legislator. They have no fear and sometimes go right over the line. Tact is not something that they learned in the police academy." Many legislators regard the lobbying style of doctors as arrogant. They had their day at Florida's capitol, fighting for tort reform, declaring a doctors' holiday, and traveling to Tallahassee in chartered jets and buses. A legislator recalled a delegation's visit to her office. "Let me give you some education about the medical field," was the way one of the doctors opened up the conversation with her. The legislator replied that she did not need the education he could give; she had been chairing the health committee of the house for years.

"If it isn't carefully orchestrated, it can be dangerous," said a Colorado state government relations professional. Grass roots must be tightly managed to be effective and avoid embarrassment. But lobbyists cannot be certain of maintaining control when many people are involved. Just one loose cannon in a campaign can cost an organization dearly, as when a beer wholesaler called up a senator, told him he had given him a contribution, and declared: "Now, this is what I want you to do."

Not only are there the problems of maintaining control and the possibility that a campaign may veer off course. Those managing the campaign can also make mistakes. Trial lawyers brought handicapped children to the New Jersey Legislature to demonstrate against tort reform. Some legislators resented this. New Hampshire legislators received postcards with pictures of dead fetuses. Such mail, apparently, does not predispose them to support the cause advocated by the writers. In Florida, one organization tried to make its point on a bill by overwhelming legislators with phone calls. It managed to tie up all the capitol's lines, getting the sponsor of the bill so angry that he slipped in an adverse amendment over the group's opposition during the final hours of the session.

When properly planned and executed, however, grassroots campaigns can be a potent force. There are numerous examples, but a few will suffice. The New Jersey Cable Television Association (NJCTA), representing an industry that was under criticism for scrambled signals, poor service, and rising rates, was confronted by the prospect of a new telecommunications tax.[28] Within weeks after the release of the governor's budget message proposing the tax, Nancy Becker, the association's contract lobbyist, who also served as executive director, got a grassroots campaign under way. She took a proposal to her board of cable-company operators, the majority of whom wanted to flex their muscles. Becker sent a packet to each NJCTA company, including sample letters, press releases, a position paper, a copy of the bill, and a list of legislators.

Also included were instructions as follows:

1. Order a thirty-second public-service announcement on the issue from NJCTA and air it often.

2. Write a letter to the editor of your local newspaper (sample enclosed).

3. Ask your employees to write their legislators (letter and list of legislators enclosed).

4. Distribute media release (sample enclosed).

5. Write letter from general manager to all legislators representing your franchise areas (sample enclosed).

6. Provide antitax postcards to your subscribers, employees, and walk-in customers (mechanical enclosed).

7. Record an antitax on-hold telephone message.

8. If your system has a news department, do commentary on the issue or interview your general manager (samples enclosed).

Each company determined for itself what it would do. Becker received 150,000 postcards that she then had sorted and delivered to legislators. After holding a press conference, she informed legislative leaders that the NJCTA grassroots campaign was under way. Within a short time, the issue had been decided. Funds were found that would replace the $39 million in the budget from the tax on cable.

Public interest groups have also used grassroots campaigns with telling effect. Such groups cannot afford to rely on inside strategies, although they engage in direct lobbying along with everyone else. Their strength is pressure from outside the legislature, so public interest groups work with the press and continuously recruit members and supporters. Take COPIRG in Colorado, for example. It canvasses out of Boulder in the winter and out of Boulder, Denver, and Colorado Springs in the summer (when the days are longer and more students are available). The board of directors, composed of students, decides at the beginning of the year what bills to get involved with. Then the canvassers raise their issues at people's doors, by way of soliciting members and stimulating involvement. One session the COPIRG canvass was put to use in support of a safe-drinking-water bill. People were activated district by district, and hundreds of contacts were made with legislators. COPIRG won on this issue because legislators were sensitive to what their constituents thought. The operation was not as efficient as it might have been, however, so the organization resolved to spend additional energy on improving its grassroots efforts.

The significance of grass roots extends beyond any single issue on which it may be decisive. An organization's ability to weigh in on critical issues is the important matter. Legislators may downplay the effectiveness of grassroots tactics, but a lobbyist for a large association in California demurred: "Member contact really shakes them up." Hence we can conclude that legislators will develop greater sympathy for the goals of groups employing outside-pressure tactics. As one contract lobbyist in New Jersey puts it: "PIRG can have a thousand kids going door to door in a legislator's district. Those politics will carry the day."

Most legislators and lobbyists agree that hearing from constituents makes a difference in how legislators deal with an issue. The effort to influence legislators does not have to be massive. As a lobbyist in Delaware explained, "If somebody gets five calls on an issue they think they are being flooded." A former legislative aide commented that letters from 25 to 50 constituents easily outweigh visits from a lobbyist.[29] Beyond a few constituents here and a few there, there is the organized grassroots campaign which has substantial impact if it is conducted well.

The conventional wisdom holds that legislators pay more attention to the spontaneous communications they receive than they do to communications that are stimulated by an interest group. Similar letters, identically worded postcards, and filled-out forms inserted into envelopes are considered by some to be manufactured grass roots, and probably not worthy of attention. But today's technology provides a means by which just about any communication can appear "handwritten" and spontaneous. Moreover, most legislators—like their congressional brethren—take stimulated messages as seriously as spontaneous ones. Such communications carry weight because they convey to the legislator an idea of the group's intense concerns on an issue and its organizational ability to spur constituents to action. Any group that can organize people to contact their representative between elections can probably organize an impressive number of voters to support or oppose an incumbent on election day. Grassroots campaigns thus send the message: "Don't mess with us, or do so at your own electoral peril."[30]

In signaling to lawmakers that group members care about an issue or in expanding beyond the group to a mass public, an interest group exerts pressure that is different than the persuasion used in direct lobbying.[31] The consequence is a more adversarial climate, in which the threat of electoral opposition, albeit tacit, is never far from the surface.

The latest development in the outside game, the Internet, offers a powerful tool to lobbyists and groups with a membership base. It allows virtually instantaneous access to lawmakers. As of 1999, members in thirty-nine of the ninety-nine state legislative bodies had computers at their desks in the chambers and could send and receive e-mail while in session. The potential for members to be hit by organized campaigns after standing committees have made their recommendations, but before a vote is taken on the floor, can have significant impact on the deliberative process.

The Media, Public Relations, and Advertising

One way to generate support is to place an emphasis on communications. The lobbyists' objective in managing the media and conducting public relations is to project their client's issues and image favorably to the public and public officials. The media and public relations approaches, like grassroots mobilization, are designed to impress lawmakers with the power of a cause. But these approaches target not only members and related groups, but also the public at large. Their objective is to mold and mobilize public opinion generally, or at least to give legislators the distinct impression that such is being done. The techniques that fall within this domain include newsletters, position papers, brochures, news releases, press conferences, television and radio interviews, editorial board meetings, advertisements, community relations, and so forth.[32] Reaching the public and thereby affecting the legislature through the media have become particularly critical for groups that are not equipped or disposed to play an inside game. Citizen groups and their lobbyists have considerable advantages with the media, while other groups are trying to counter them or catch up. A study of lobbying in three states found that three out of four lobbyists and the same proportion of groups reported that they regularly talked to representatives of the media.[33]

Citizen groups rely on the media more than trade, professional, corporate, and labor groups. And they seem to have greater success in getting their message reported. Common Cause lobbyists tend to be very adept with the media. They know that if legislators read about something in the press (or see it on television), they regard it as important. One Common Cause lobbyist cultivates the press, hangs out with reporters, and gives them information and a point of view. He will start off by sensitizing the press corps to an issue, such as campaign-finance reform. His objective is to supply reporters with both a context and the perception that the issue is appealing. Then, with data and statements—geared to the slower news days—he keeps the story alive. As the press takes hold, legislators cannot help but take notice. Advocacy groups and the media probably have an affinity for one another. An Illinois public welfare coalition, for example, worked mainly through the media, using press conferences in Springfield and Chicago, regular letters to the editor, appearances on radio and television talk shows, and faxed press releases during legislative sessions. The coalition made four hundred or more press contacts each year, and the media began reporting stories of welfare mothers running out of food or being unable to clothe their children.[34]

When issues are featured in the media, they take on greater emotional content; that is the way stories are played. More and more groups are therefore tailoring their message to the media. A leading contract lobbyist in New Jersey recognizes that there is a whole new side to lobbying not previously explored. He now uses videos, cable, talk shows, and other forums to help his client address the community. A communications strategy, he believes, is especially useful on emotional issues like incineration or packaging. "The more communication you have and the earlier communication is," he advises, "the less chance you have of it becoming an issue so dominated by one side versus the other side." In other words, business had better respond to environmentalist and consumer groups in the latter's language, that of the media.

The growing inclination of lobbyists and the organizations they represent is to use consultants to help with both issues and image. Public relations firms are being employed by groups to get into the press (and sometimes to keep out). Some now have a media consultant on retainer. The notion is that a good public relations campaign can soften the public and thus improve the climate for legislation desired by the client.

Dayton Hudson employed a public relations strategy when it pressed the Minnesota legislature to pass a law that would prevent a hostile takeover. With the help of experienced media consultants, Dayton Hudson portrayed its struggle as one between a good corporate citizen of Minnesota and a raider from Washington, D.C. The company's campaign conjured up images of a cherished local employer of thirty thousand people on one side and Darth Vader on the other. "You can't come into my state and pillage" was the theme. Through meetings with capital reporters and editorial boards around the state, the large corporation got its homey message across.

The alcoholic-beverage industry undertook an intense public relations effort designed to improve its image. In creating the Century Council (an independent organization funded by beer, wine, and spirit companies), the industry sought to stem the tide of negative attitudes toward alcohol. The industry had never presented a united front, and the big-three beer companies (Anheuser-Busch, Coors, and Miller) went their own way instead of joining the council. Nevertheless, this three-year, $40-million campaign appeared to have real potential for impressing citizens and, ultimately, legislators.

Although the Century Council campaign helped to improve the image of the alcoholic-beverage industry, another event helped even more. In the late summer of 1991 the study findings of researchers at the Harvard School of Public Health were announced in the national press. This study of 51,000 men found that, apart from its effects on other aspects of health, moderate drinking was actually good for one's heart. Men who consumed from one-half to two drinks a day were shown to have reduced their risk of heart disease by 26 percent compared with men who abstained from alcohol. And the beneficial effects for the heart increased with consumption (that is, two drinks were found to be more beneficial than just half a drink). By confirming the results of several previous studies, the Harvard findings could not help but improve public attitudes toward alcohol, despite the personal health and public problems attributable to drinking. The indirect, longer-term effects on legislator attitudes toward the alcoholic-beverage industry might be substantial. Yet PR consultants, lobbyists, and the industry itself had nothing to do with the study, suggesting that not everything affecting the legislative process happens by plan or design.

Some issues have great appeal for the media, and groups that deal in these areas have special access. The media gives favorable coverage to environmental issues, growth management, consumer issues, and to ethics and campaign-finance reform. Although there obviously are exceptions, reporters in the state capitals generally regard the environmental and public interest lobbyists as wearing the "white hats." Business lobbyists, in general, are not as well received and have a tougher time getting their stories across. In the middle are lobbyists for local government associations, also "white hats" as long as they are not opposing the environmentalists and taking the side of business.

A statehouse correspondent in New Jersey, in characterizing public interest groups, had this to say: "The media perception of these groups is more favorable. They are the first groups we will go to when we want the public's opinion on an issue." Thus, lobbyists for these groups generally have good rapport with the capitol press corps and the editors of the state's newspapers. The press, according to one Florida cause lobbyist, "has been sympathetic to our cause." But her group did not have sufficient resources or as much time to spend on press relations as she would have liked. She expressed disappointment in not being able to take full advantage of the opportunities before her.

It should be noted also that extreme groups—whether on the right or left—also get coverage, because of the newsworthiness of their stories. One lobbyist for conservative groups in Florida believes she gets press attention because no one else carries her message. The print press will always turn to her for a quote and television will invite her to appear on talk shows. All of this has helped make her known throughout the state (although her constituents, she reports, are not inclined to read the liberal press).

It is becoming more common for public interest, governmental, and business groups to arrange meetings with editorial boards seeking support. They contribute op-ed pieces. A Florida lobbyist for an association of local governments has sent a package of memos on a number of issues to twenty editorial boards. His thinking is that they will keep the materials on file. When they get around to an editorial on the subject, they will use what he has supplied and not have to rely on the wire service.

Press briefings and conferences are the preferred technique of cause groups. New Jersey PIRG is an example of a group that knows how to appeal to the press. Its lobbyists have an excellent sense of just what the press needs and when. The release of PIRG's studies naturally gets attention. Beyond that, PIRG lobbyists think in terms of events and "visuals." Press conferences are held at a "dangerous" or "contaminated" site. "Wanda the Fish" was used for clean-water legislation and a Ben Franklin character was used to sign a declaration of independence from toxic wastes. On Halloween, PIRG went to Hoboken with people dressed in costumes as toxic avengers. They went door to door, talking to residents about toxicity in the community. And, of course, PIRG held a press conference on this "scariest day of the year." The judgment of one of the group's lobbyists was that, "people like such an activity, the press reports it, and people read it." Timing is key, and relevant reporters are notified of an event a few days in advance. With a little experience, public interest and environmental lobbyists have learned how to talk in "quotes" for the print media and in "sound bites" for the electronic media.

There is no doubt that the press can be, and is, used by contestants in the process. Staged events and so-called media tours are important. Having the right sorts of issues is paramount. The effective lobbyist has all these in mind and develops the most appropriate bag of tricks for his or her particular needs. A lobbyist for one of Florida's cities knows, for example, that if a reporter attends a legislative committee meeting, it will help her cause. The presence of the press changes the dynamic. "I may even get their vote," she said, "or at least they'll shut up."

A group's public relations efforts reach further than its day-to-day attempts to manage the press. PR is a long-term endeavor and over time should contribute to a group's governmental goals.[35] The idea is to get on the side of the angels, build goodwill, and fashion the most positive image. For example, the dairy industry works on the following image: dairy products are portrayed as inexpensive and nutritionally beneficial; consumers are shown to benefit as a result; and the dairy industry is then depicted as being on the edge of chaos without governmental help.[36]

Community involvement is one means of achieving favorable public relations. For example, a Minnesota bank is involved in inner-city-neighborhood programs. It also sponsors a community home-buyers' program. Community activity proves, in the words of its lobbyist, that "the bank is willing to put its money where its mouth is." The bank thus gains credibility with inner-city legislators who can see things happening in their neighborhoods. There are other community projects as well, such as one in which bank employees adopt a high-rise building or a senior citizens' development and then work with the residents. In the lobbyist's opinion, community involvement pays off politically—as much as or more than financing political campaigns.

In part because of initiative battles, California probably has more experience than other states in using public relations experts for legislative ends. Firms that once specialized in corporate public relations have turned toward political PR, and corporations have found that they need both lobbyists and PR experts. According to a consultant in a corporate and political public relations firm, there is a growing realization that "you just can't sell your issue to the legislature, you have to generate public acceptance for it." In more and more situations, the California legislature feels it needs public support for its position. "What used to be done in back rooms is now done by public consensus building," the PR specialist noted.[37]

An organization's image and standing can benefit from any number of public relations approaches. The institutional advertising of telephone companies has an impact. So do the television spots designed to enhance the image of teachers as caring and competent professionals. The athletic tournaments and other events sponsored by Avon, Pepsico, and Philip Morris also work. They help these companies maintain an effective network of friends. And full-page advertisements describe an industry's contribution to employment in the state.

"Advocacy advertising" or "issue advocacy" is probably the greatest growth area in lobbying at the national level. This strategy differs from grassroots and public relations strategies, but has similar objectives—to shape public opinion and influence lawmakers. Sometimes issue advocacy (in contrast to express advocacy) is conducted as part of a campaign to defeat or elect a candidate for office. Sometimes it is conducted as part of a campaign, the purpose of which is to promote a policy. In 1997 and 1998, at least seventy-seven groups sponsored issue ads, spending about $300 million.[38] Health organizations spent about $60 million in 1993–1994 in the battle over Clinton's health proposals. Although the most common forms of outside lobbying are still low-cost, like talking to the press and urging members to contact members of Congress, 52 percent of the groups surveyed in a recent study fund or help fund advertisements on policy issues.[39]

Issue advocacy is practiced less at the state level, but its use as a lobbying tool is on the rise. In the three-state survey cited earlier, about one out of five lobbyists and the same proportion of groups reported that they ran advocacy advertisements.[40] New York is a state that regularly sees issue advertising used in campaigns to win over the legislature. In opposing Governor George Pataki's 1995–1996 budget, unions of hospital workers, teachers, and state employees waged a multimillion-dollar advertising campaign that included TV and radio commercials, as well as direct mailings.[41] More recently, with the regulation of the entertaining of legislators in New York, more money is being spent on ads, as well as telephone banks and marketing research. Expenditures by the lobbying industry in 1999 were $12.2 million for advertising and only $1.4 million for social events. As the president of the health workers' union summed up: "It's not about what happens in the halls of Albany, it's about what happens in people's living rooms, that resonates in a far stronger way."[42]

Teachers in a number of states—including Connecticut, Washington, and Wisconsin—are into advocacy advertising, not only in the context of specific campaigns to win over legislators but also in the context of longer-term campaigns to change how both the public and legislators think about teachers and the public schools. The New Jersey Education Association, for instance, has been engaged in a "Pride in Public Education" advertising campaign since 1994. The campaign was undertaken to counter the criticism of public education leveled by national and state media. In order to undertake its campaigns, NJEA changed its membership dues structure in order to raise $10 million for its campaign. The overall campaign included not only TV ads but also grassroots efforts at county and local levels. With the assistance of a pollster, NJEA decided that it had to promote New Jersey as a suburban state and to target woman over forty-five. The ads focused on real teachers who talked about the values of personal responsibility and work that they tried to inculcate in students. NJEA believes that its efforts are bearing fruit, and advertising has become a regular feature of its operations. The association tracks its campaign's effectiveness with periodic polls and focus groups and claims that the increasing frequency with which local school budgets have been approved by the public is testimony to the effectiveness of "Pride in Public Education" advertising.

If lobbyists tend to the business of coalition building, grassroots mobilization, and the care and feeding of the electorate through media relations and advertising, they will be in position to engage directly on legislative terrain. Having laid the groundwork, they now have to make the case, agree on specifics, and reach a settlement on the issue in dispute.

CHAPTER 9

Making the Case

The outside game of building coalitions, mobilizing grassroots support, and conducting media and PR campaigns is not only useful. For groups whose abilities to directly lobby the legislature are limited, the outside game is essential. These "outsider" tactics can be very effective. This is especially true for cause lobbyists, who are temperamentally and philosophically less disposed to compromise. As a lobbyist for a public interest group in Texas notes, "As an outsider, you can stand up for principle and say what's right."

Many special-interest issues (such as those relating to taxes and jurisdiction and pertaining principally to business) require little outside action; an inside strategy normally suffices. An outside strategy, however, rarely stands alone. The public interest lobbyist who noted that outsiders are freer to adhere to principle also observed that his outsider status was now being threatened. At the previous session of the Texas legislature, he had been invited to "sit at more tables to negotiate more deals." Admitting he may have been a bit uncomfortable, he nevertheless realized he and his client were better off. He could now play *both* games.

At some point, direct lobbying techniques have to be employed if an organization is to make its case for or against a particular piece of legislation. By "direct lobbying," we mean forms of personal persuasion and involvement in the legislative process itself. Federal lobbyists surveyed in Washington, D.C., for example, said that among their direct lobbying techniques they testified at hearings (99 percent of respondents), contacted officials to present their point of view (98 percent), engaged in informal contact with officials (95 percent), and presented research results or technical information (92 percent).[1] Nearly everyone in Washington seems to engage in direct lobbying. The same is true in the states, as the study of lobbyists and groups in California, South Carolina, and Wisconsin shows.[2] Six inside techniques and the percentages of lobbyists using each are: testifying at legislative hearings, 98; contacting government officials directly to present their point of view, 98; helping to draft legislation, 96; alerting state legislators to the effects of a bill on their districts, 96; consulting with government officials to plan legislative strategy, 88; and engaging in informed contacts with officials, 83. Just about every lobby-ist engages in several of the activities mentioned.

Direct lobbying involves numerous strategies and tactics. We shall explore below (1) the principles of direct lobbying; (2) the elements of defense and offense; (3) the targets in the process; (4) the role of information; and (5) the art of compromise. Strategies and tactics differ from issue to issue and group to group. "It depends," said a Colorado lobbyist, "there are no general rules." A Florida lobbyist agreed: "The strategy and tactics have to be tailored to each individual case." Two New Jersey lobbyists offered the following observations: "It's like a dance. You have to feel your way," and "You have to take advantage of the opportunities as they arise." Everyone involved seems to agree that generalizations do not apply to specific situations, but they do help clarify what effective lobbying requires.

The Principles of Direct Lobbying

When asked, "How do you lobby them?" an association lobbyist in Minnesota responded, "Carefully." The notion that lobbyists have to exercise care when dealing with legislators means different things to different people. It requires, as we have explored earlier, forging and maintaining relationships. It also requires personal qualities such as credibility. Moreover, it requires having respect for both legislators and the legislative process. All of these are by way of background characteristics. More in the foreground are several principles that many lobbyists observe:

1. *Be there.* Nothing can substitute for the lobbyist's presence. That is why contract lobbyists, who usually reside in or near the capital and belong to the capitol community, are believed to have an advantage over other lobbyists insofar as the legislative process is concerned. To be around all the time means being first to know about what is happening and who is up to what. A lobbyist cannot afford to go home early or get there late, particularly as the session nears its close. During the final week or so, something buried in committee can emerge or an amendment can pop up. If a lobbyist is on guard, with Patriot missiles armed and ready to go, the chances of an assault will diminish (at least somewhat). One of Tallahassee's leading contract lobbyists said that legislators have to know that a lobbyist is around—in committee, outside the chamber, or wherever. "You have to be there so they see you," he maintained.

2. *Stay with it.* Showing up may be 90 percent (or is it 80 percent?) of life for Woody Allen, but it is only the first step in effective lobbying. The persistent, single-minded lobbyist has the best chance of winning. "Keep it up and keep it up and keep it up," advises one Florida lobbyist. "Keep on going, but don't become a pest." Another Florida lobbyist may have crossed the line; she bothers legislators constantly until she gets them. Does she go too far? She doesn't think so: "If I were a man, I would have been punched by now—but as a woman I can get away with more stuff." Guy Spearman of Florida exemplifies persistence. His intention was to get an amendment that would allow Sea World to import exotic snakes for a new display on dangerous sea animals. He got it on a house agriculture bill, but lost three separate attempts to get senate approval. Still, he continued looking for another vehicle to accomplish his client's ends, and his efforts finally bore fruit.

3. *Be brief.* Although lobbyists should be persistent, they must be respectful of a legislator's time. One consultant follows the thirty-second rule; the message must be conveyed quickly. A lobbyist in Maryland echoes this advice: "You can't take up a lot of their time. Get right to the point," she cautions, adding that lobbyists need to explain succinctly what a bill does and doesn't do. An Arkansas lobbyist recommends the following pitch to a legislator: "I have a client who is interested in this bill. The client's problem is this. The way to solve the client's problem is this. Here is the up side and the down side of it as far as you're concerned."[3] A Colorado lobbyist describes how he often spends more time discussing the down side, giving the legislator answers to questions opponents might have. For some clients, he prepares a one-page summary of the strengths and weaknesses of their case and leaves it in the legislator's office. He then returns, and the legislators, who have yet to look at the summary, read it in front of him. This gives him further—if brief—opportunity to make his case.

4. *Take nothing for granted.* If there is no organized opposition, a lobbyist's bill will pass—except when it doesn't. It needs to be shepherded, or else it may simply be neglected in a very busy process where many bills compete for attention. Furthermore, something unexpected can happen. A Colorado lobbyist found this out when he was carrying a bill for a professional association. He had gotten an influential legislator to sponsor the bill. The association's key-contact network had been activated. The chairman of the house committee having jurisdiction was on board. The state regulatory agency had announced its support. There was no organized opposition. All his ducks were in a row. But, unexpectedly, several house

committee members voiced objections, adopting the attitude, "Let's make them fight for it." The lobbyist and his client had to redouble their efforts. Although they finally won, it was not without a struggle.

Legislators can be extraordinarily independent. A lobbyist and former legislative leader in Colorado pointed out how quickly the scenario can change. "You think you're in control, and then 'boom.' " In the words of a Colorado lobbyist, " *Nothing* is a slam dunk." It can all fall apart at any moment because of the most trivial things. And because a lobbyist beats back a bill or amendment one time does not mean the opposition cannot resurrect it. With Florida's legislative session advancing to the second half, one veteran lobbyist uttered the pronouncement: "It's never safe, until they leave."

5. *It is necessary to choose.* Lobbyists and organizations cannot pursue everything on their agendas. They therefore need to set priorities. A contract lobbyist from Utah told the Pharmaceutical Research and Manufacturers of America: "You can only go to the well so many times in one session." A contract lobbyist from Maryland gave similar counsel to PRMA with respect to the issue of using animals in testing: "If we want other things to fall in line, we have to back off on that one." The problem for an association, in particular, is that because it has many members with different interests, it may take on too many issues. Similarly, contract lobbyists, who typically have multiple clients (each with its own issues), tend to present legislators with a large portfolio. Legislators will take on just so much work for any particular interest or any particular lobbyist.

6. *Be prepared to lose.* This principle is not intended to imply that a lobbyist should try to advance an obviously hopeless case. A lobbyist cannot afford to become identified with too many defeats. But both lobbyist and client must be willing, at least on occasion, to take a beating. No one involved in the process can expect to have his or her way all the time. Or even to come out with a satisfactory compromise. Everyone will suffer losses, and how they are suffered is important. In the words of a Texas lobbyist, "You have to be able to lose with style and grace"—but not with frequency.

The Elements of Defense and Offense

Most lobbyists spend most of their time on the defense. A New Jersey contract lobbyist explained: "A great number of our clients, and obviously a great number of everybody's clients, want to be protected from the legislature. And they don't want bills to pass." Princeton Public Affairs is one of New Jersey's principal lobbying firms. Seven in ten of its clients hire the firm to stop a particular legislative course of action.[4] A defensive position, everyone agrees, is easier to play. It is harder to push a bill through the legislative process than to stop one. One chief executive officer, who takes an interest in state government relations, observes that "trying to affect policy is like pushing a rope." To move forward, a bill not only requires greater consensus but it must also overcome a series of obstacles as it moves from committee to caucus to floor in one house and then through the other. It is said that one Colorado lobbyist, "can't pass things, but she can kill them in the senate." Anywhere along the line, the lobbyist has a shot at a bill.

Moreover, if there is doubt on any issue, it is simpler and safer for a legislator to vote no. A coalition can fall apart; the bill can pick up a gutting amendment; all sorts of things can happen to it. There are, in the words of a Colorado lobbyist, "a hundred ways to kill a bill and only one way to pass one." This particular lobbyist is said to have gone further, jokingly claiming that he and his colleague "couldn't pass Mother's Day, but we could defeat it."

In defending, lobbyists may pursue several paths. First, they may try to get the bill they oppose withdrawn or shunted aside. They will talk to the sponsor and ask that the bill not be pushed, or at least not pushed vigorously. Although the sponsor may refuse, there is a good chance that he or she will have been softened up. And perhaps the two sides will be able to get together and discuss a compromise. Indeed, most defensive lobbying does not succeed in killing bills. Rather, it succeeds in rendering the bill less harmful and achieving a compromise. It is preferable, if possible, to leave the bill in the hands of a legislator with whom the lobbyist has close ties. A New Jersey lobbyist detailed his strategy:

> It is better, even if you oppose a bill, to have it in the hopper under a sponsor with whom you are reasonably friendly than to have it withdrawn . . . because he or she will not move that bill. The strategy should be to keep it where I can see it, as opposed to where I don't have control over it.

Second, instead of opposing it head on, lobbyists may formulate an alternative bill. When presented with a problem, legislators usually ask for a solution. If lobbyists oppose a measure, what would they put in its stead? A lobbyist for the chemical industry, which has been under intense pressure from environmental groups in recent years, explained why it was necessary to be proactive: "We get beat every time we say no, particularly on emotional, high-charged issues." Associated Industries of Florida has developed a number of alternatives to proposals that it opposed. It even prepared a transaction tax on business, which would substitute for a sales tax on services were that to be brought up again in the Florida legislature. In a contest over the banning of ultimate fighting in New York, the lobbyist for the entertainment industry sponsored his own legislation requiring regulation. His objective was to give legislators a way to respond without resorting to a ban.

Lobbyists for New Jersey business appreciate the importance of having an alternative when in opposition. For years they turned back public interest groups and environmentalists who were trying to get a bottle-deposit bill enacted. Recycling was their alternative. In contrast, they opposed the "right to know" bill directly and lost a bruising battle. They learned their lesson. Shortly thereafter, New Jersey industry again came under assault, this time by the Hazard Elimination through Local Participation (HELP) bill. HELP would authorize local community- and facility-based groups to conduct environmental and public-health inspections of plants where hazards might exist. The New Jersey Business and Industry Association, along with other groups, opposed the measure and prepared an alternative that would have authorized local emergency planning committees, formed on a county level, to conduct a specified number of on-site inspections. A good lobbyist is often able to have a bill amended so that it is not so injurious to his or her client.

Third, lobbyists may try to amend a bill to death by making it too costly, too encompassing, or too controversial. Frequently attempts are made to "poison pen" or "artificially sweeten" bills through amendments or committee substitutes that arouse the antagonism of other players or entail expenditures that are beyond the realm of political possibility. For many years a proposal to require seat belts in school buses was sidetracked in the New Jersey legislature. The lobbyist for the school bus owners was able to get a substitute bill that was so comprehensive and costly that it could not pass, and if it did the governor would have vetoed it.

Fourth, on occasions where a bill cannot be bottled up or a satisfactory compromise cannot be worked out, the lobbyist must launch an all-out fight on the floor of the house and/or senate, and possibly in the office of the governor.

When on the offense, a lobbyist's initial consideration is to recruit a legislative sponsor. The legislator who introduces the bill and then champions it will frequently play the key role in its enactment. If a lobbyist gets the wrong legislator as sponsor, no matter how good the arguments in its favor, the bill will go down in flames. The "author," as the person who introduces and carries the bill is called in California, is most critical in that state. If the author is seen as credible, he or she can get votes from other California legislators with few questions asked. The sponsor is also important in Colorado, where legislators are limited in the number of bills they can introduce. This makes it more difficult for lobbyists in Colorado to get sponsors. But they begin early, press their clients for a decision, and by the fall have sponsors lined up so that bills can be pre-filed before the December deadlines. If necessary, lobbyists can go to legislative leaders and obtain "late bill" status from them. Where there is a legislature, there is usually a way.

In choosing a sponsor or author, a number of factors are taken into account. The higher up in leadership, the more attractive the sponsor. Occasionally the speaker, president, or majority leader may agree to take on a lobbyist's bill. More frequently, the chairman or a member of the committee with jurisdiction is approached and asked to act as sponsor. A Maryland lobbyist described the process. She went to the committee chairman and asked, "What do you think of this bill?" He responded, "I think I can support it." The lobbyist continued, "Will you be the sponsor?" She then explained that the concept was a good one, there was no opposition, and essentially no down side. "You do the homework," he replied, "I'll put my name on it." The first visit a California association lobbyist makes is to the staff consultants and chairman of the relevant committee. If, after discussion, the chairman says the proposal would be a great committee bill, then the matter is settled—from the lobbyist's point of view, settled in ideal fashion.

The advantages of having leaders sign on as sponsors are obvious. They exercise greater control over scheduling and other aspects of the process. They have status, power, and, usually, respect. Such sponsors are more inclined to stand firm when the going gets tough. If the chairman is unavailable, lobbyists will then seek out the "most powerful person in the business of passing that particular bill"—someone who, at the least, gets along with the chairman and other leaders. That tends to be a member of the majority party, particularly in a partisan legislature such as in California, Colorado, Minnesota, or New Jersey. A Colorado public interest group, for example, routinely seeks Republican sponsors, even if they are conservative and not traditional allies of the group. They are the people with greatest influence there.

Other considerations relating to sponsorship involve whether legislators have shown an interest in the issue, whether they are effective advocates, whether they work hard (and, in some places, have staff that work hard), and whether they are looking for an issue to get publicity for reelection or a run for higher office. Many legislators, of course, take on bills because they believe in the issues. For some groups, such as those advocating a particular stance on abortion rights, potential sponsors are limited to the universe of true believers, maybe a half-dozen members in each house who would be willing to lead the fight.

Legislators frequently initiate an action and then ask interest groups for their help. The leadership may also decide who the sponsor should be. According to a New Jersey public interest group lobbyist: "We may encourage a legislator to introduce a piece of legislation, but when they go in [to the leadership] with the idea, they may not necessarily get that bill. It may go to someone else." Once legislators agree to sponsor a bill, they can exercise as much control as they desire. Or they can delegate the managerial job to the lobbyists. In California the tendency is for authors to take control, steering the bill through each house. They are largely responsible for deciding which amendments to accept and which to reject. And the bill may take on a shape not originally intended by its lobbyist advocates. One Colorado public interest group lobbyist advised:

> You have to act like it's their bill from the moment they put their name on it. The sponsor is the leader of the campaign who may defer to your advice. But you can't take the attitude that the sponsor is rubber-stamping your game plan. If you do, you'll get slapped down.

A public interest group lobbyist in New Jersey had similar feelings. He was taking orders, he said, from the senator whose name was on the bill. The senator had had to make changes with which the lobbyist disagreed; there was no alternative but to go along. The legislator was at the helm.

With a strong sponsor, therefore, the lobbyist takes on a supportive role. If the sponsor has other priorities—such as twenty or thirty bills he or she is pushing—then the lobbyist will have to manage the process. This is often the practice in Florida and New Jersey, where lobbyists negotiate on behalf of the sponsors. On occasion, moreover, "talk sheets" prepared by the lobbyist are used by sponsors when their bills are brought up on the floor. These sponsors are not overly familiar with the legislation that bears their name. More often than not, lobbyists do not rely on legislator sponsors to run the bill for them. They have ultimate responsibility for getting the job done.

Targets in the Process

Once a bill is introduced, the process is formally under way, although informally much may have already been worked out. (Special attention will be given below to negotiating strategies and techniques.) It is not unusual, in fact, for the arguments to have been made and a consensus established by the time a bill is referred to committee. But often a sponsor (and his or her lobbyist allies) will try to rush a bill through—the theory being, says one Florida lobbyist that "the first pig out of the pen is the hardest one to catch." Known as a "ram job" in New Jersey, speedy passage of a bill is, whenever possible, the lobbyist's objective. It should not be done at the risk, however, of annoying legislators of another persuasion.

One lobbyist described the campaign he waged on behalf of a professional association engaged in a turf battle with a rival. His client's bill had been kicking around for a while before he was hired. After spending six months laying the groundwork, he succeeded in getting the bill passed by both houses within two weeks. He had secured the committee chairman's agreement to hear it at the first possible moment and then asked the presiding officer to post it right after the committee reported it out. The same schedule was being followed in the other house. The opposing group could do nothing at this point because the committee chairmen and leadership in both houses had agreed to support the measure. The element of surprise is critical, but "you really have to know what you're doing and with whom," cautioned this lobbyist, "and you must meet with all these people ahead of time."

Often the strategy chosen is intended to divert opponents from a lobbyist's real concern in a bill. A Texas lobbyist proposes that in crafting a bill a tough issue should be injected, if only "to get trouble makers scrapping." Raise the tough issue first, so adversaries will get excited and expend their energy fighting. When they wear themselves out, the initiator can give in on that issue and then turn to the other items, ones that really matter.[5] A Maryland lobbyist also advises that a provision be put in a bill to distract the opposition from more critical provisions. He calls this technique "chasing the rabbit." The opposition will chase the rabbit until it finally thinks it has won, leaving the other provisions of the bill untouched.

Things move fast, but whatever the velocity of the process, lobbyists have a sense of the people with whom they have to deal. Who is in a key position? Who is respected? Where is the opposition? What about the committee? It always depends on the issue, but leaders, committees, rank-and-file members, and staff—in one sequence or another—are the principal targets.

Leadership

Many lobbyists pursue a "top-down" strategy, concentrating on the presiding officers and committee chairmen. Such efforts account for about half of the work of many lobbyists, at least in those states where the legislative parties and leaders are still somewhat strong. The lobbyist for a California association focused her energy on the assembly speaker and the senate president pro tem. "There's no point in putting in a lot of time with a lot of members," she said, "when I can put in focused time with the decision makers." Not only do the leaders have the ability to influence members on issues, but they also exercise procedural control.

A Massachusetts lobbyist, who has privileged access to the leadership, actually consults with the senate president and house speaker before taking a client's case. He wants to find out if the client's case is a persuasive one. In other words, is there a good chance of success?

It is normally up to the presiding officers, with the assistance of staff, to refer a bill to committee. A bill can be drafted so that it comes within the jurisdiction of one committee or another, but leaders still have discretion—if they want to use it. A lobbyist wants his or her bill to go to a friendly committee (and an opponent's bill to be sent to an unfriendly one). It is not unusual for a lobbyist to ask a presiding officer to refer a bill to a particular committee and, according to a New Jersey lobbyist, "he will do it, if it's reasonable." But then, the lobbyist added, "you wouldn't ask him to do anything if it wasn't reasonable." Florida's lobbyists, it has been reported, routinely made recommendations to the senate president's staff regarding committee referrals, not only about which one but also how many. In some cases they asked that their bills be sent to as few committees as possible; in other cases they requested multiple referrals.

The presiding officers can also decide, either directly or through rules committees, when, and if, a bill will be taken up (calendared, posted) on the floor of the chamber. In Florida, for example, many of the bills that were favorably reported by committees and took their places on the house or senate calendars never got considered. A bill had to be placed by the rules committee on the special-order calendar in order for the presiding officer to get around to it. And the speaker's or president's top lieutenant chaired the rules committee. The question every lobbyist asked, therefore, was "How do I get my bill on the special-order calendar?" Since the Republicans took control of the Florida house, several policy councils took on the job of prioritizing bills reported by committee. Though the target may have changed, the job of the lobbyist who was pushing a bill remained substantially the same.

In some instances, lobbyists also attend to executive leaders—the governor and his or her staff and department heads. This can be an important part of lobbying, although we touch on it only briefly here. On environmental issues, the governor and the environmental department usually play a leadership role. For a county or city, support may have to be lined up in the department of community affairs. On taxes or budget issues, the administration is generally out in front. If a lobbyist's client is concerned with finances or an appropriation, the place to start is with the particular governmental agency's budget request. After that, the governor's budget office needs to be lobbied.

Whatever the issue, if lobbyists are attempting to get a bill passed, they will want to make sure that the governor signs it. There is always the possibility of a veto. It is therefore customary for them to check with the governor's office before a bill's introduction, during the legislative process, or after its enactment. And lobbyists who fail to defeat legislation they oppose have as a final resort the veto. There is little to be lost in making a last-ditch effort in the governor's office.

Committees

The standing committee is, perhaps, the lobbyists' principal focus. If a lobbyist is advocating legislation, it has to be reported out of committee favorably in both houses (although in some states, bills do not have to be referred to committee in the second house). When the chair and committee members vote for a bill, they will ordinarily do some work to have it pass on the floor. The committee has acquired a stake in the legislation by virtue of its favorable action, even though in some places the author or sponsor manages the bill. If a lobbyist is opposing legislation, it takes only a few votes, and perhaps only the decision of the chair, to kill it at this stage. If the bill gets to the floor, however, many more votes are required to defeat it; a substantial effort is required to overcome the committee's recommendation. Bills are rarely defeated on the floor, although a number are amended there. One Washington-based lobbyist for an association has made it a practice of developing relationships with committees in a number of states. "If I'm doing my job well," he commented, "I never have to deal with leadership." The issue does not get that far; he has managed to stop things in the committee.

The lobbyist's primary target is the committee chair. If the chair (or even a majority-party member of the committee) is sponsoring the bill, it has a very good chance at the committee level and, thus, a good chance in at least one house. Committee members will ordinarily defer to the chair and to one another, just as house members generally follow the recommendations of their committees. What happens in the other chamber, however, may be a different story. In most states, committee chairs have virtual life-and-death power over bills referred to their committees. So, if a lobbyist wants to stop something, the chair is the one to do it. Except in a few legislatures, such as Colorado's, the chairman may choose not to schedule a bill for consideration. Without his or her assent, that bill is unlikely to be reported out, although it may be reincarnated later in the form of an amendment.

As much as anything else, therefore, a lobbyist wants the chair's support. Sometimes the chair is an old ally. Occasionally he or she has agreed to this one piece of legislation. Frequently the chair is sympathetic, but a compromise still has to be negotiated. The chair may say that he or she cannot vote for the bill unless a change is made. More than likely, the lobbyist will accede to the request. Or the chair may simply refuse to vote for a bill. However, the chair can be helpful in other ways, such as by not showing up the day the bill is on the committee calendar.

Whether the chair is on board or not, lobbyists rarely stop there. Most will also work committee members, one by one. Nothing can be left to chance. A Maryland lobbyist recalls legislation she was promoting. The chair of the committee had introduced the bill. So the lobbyist thought it was a done deal. There was no organized opposition. One member of the committee objected, however. The bill almost died because, as the lobbyist admits, "I read it wrong. I should have worked the bill."

The lobbying of members starts before the bill is heard. This is the time when grassroots key contacts are used and when lobbyists (if there are more than one on a side) divide up members according to who has the closest ties. A Minnesota lobbyist points out that people can change their minds and that no one should be written off. "I don't think you ignore anyone on a committee, even if you know they're on the other side," he observed.

An important aspect of the committee process is the hearing, at which proponents and opponents testify. A committee hearing brings out every lobbyist on the issue. They sit in the audience, often with witnesses for their case. Yet many view such testimony as a "show and tell" exercise. Although a witness may present absolutely compelling testimony on an issue, the position being advocated can still lose overwhelmingly. That is because the other side has been hard at work, having rounded up the votes before the hearing. It is widely believed that testimony at hearings seldom changes votes. But hearings allow a group's position to become part of the record, attract media attention, transmit information to legislators, and—last but not least—impress the group's membership.[6]

Lobbyists and the groups they represent do more at committee hearings than present their specific case. They present themselves, and this matters for longer-term relationships. The Pharmaceutical Research and Manufacturers of America, for instance, takes advantage of hearings to have physicians and scientists make the more general case for the industry. A lobbyist will take great care to instruct his clients on their demeanor before committees. One counseled doctors scheduled to testify: "Don't be condescending. Don't give them the impression that you think you're wasting your time here but should instead be treating patients."

Hearings not only offer groups an opportunity to be seen and heard, they also give legislators a chance to take the measure of lobbyists. How a lobbyist responds to questioning can help to determine his or her future treatment at the hands of those legislators. A Colorado lobbyist described how committee members work new lobbyists over: "The cowboys want to see if you'll run away. They may kill your bill again, but they'll do it with less vigor if you behave well." Good behavior is imperative for the lead lobbyist of a coalition in Texas. After their bill is heard, instead of walking out of the room, as is the prevailing custom, lobbyists on the coalition team remain at the meeting until the entire agenda is completed and the meeting ends. On their part, it is a sign of respect for the committee.

Staff

A former staff member of the California assembly has detailed the decisive role he played in the legislative process. According to his account, staff would frequently meet with lobbyists to obtain support for what staff had already decided on. They would bargain with the lobbyists, offering to include or delete certain provisions of a bill in return for backing from groups with political strength. As group after group signed on, staff would then make use of their lobbyists to influence legislators they knew.[7]

This may not be the normal process, even in California. But there is little question that such influence exists in legislatures with substantial staffs. In states such as California, Florida, New Jersey, and Texas, staffs cannot be circumvented. Lobbyists must work with them. As a New Jersey lobbyist put it, "We need to deal with staff because legislators rely on them."

Although lobbyist-staff interaction depends on the issue, many lobbyists devote considerable time to staff. In California, they may indeed spend more time with professional staff than with legislators themselves. Elsewhere they work with a member's staff and/or with committee consultants, particularly on the details of legislation and amendments to bills. Some staffs will assume responsibility for the work if their member or their committee favors the legislation. Others will let the lobbyist do all the work, according to the preference of the legislator principal. Even where a legislature has relatively little staff support, as in Colorado, staff can play a role. Before a legislator sponsors a lobbyist's bill, he or she may ask a bill drafter on the central staff to work on the bill with a lobbyist.

Florida's staffers—especially the chiefs of staff for the presiding officers and the staff directors of the standing committees (particularly the rules committees)—are seldom bypassed. Their involvement can be critical in shaping compromises that can achieve consensus. In New Jersey it may be someone on the partisan staff or a legislative service agency professional, both of whom are staffing the committee. The lobbyist's contact will vary, but some staffer is likely to be targeted. "My approach," said a Trenton contract lobbyist, "is to not ignore anyone associated with the issue." At the initial stage, this generally means committee members and their staff. The approach is essentially the same in Texas, where lobbyists do a lot of visiting with staff of the leader, the committee, and the individual members.

Members

Even if lobbyists have won in committee and have leadership on their side, they cannot afford to neglect the larger membership. Votes count, especially on controversial issues (lobbyists must be able to count, too). This is not to suggest that lobbyists have to buttonhole every legislator; they may choose to pass over those who are clearly adversaries. "As the saying goes," counsels one experienced professional, "never try to teach a pig how to sing. It wastes your time and annoys the pig."[8] An early study on lobbying confirms this adage: lobbyists rarely attempt to change an opponent's mind, and such efforts constitute a very small part of the lobbying process.[9] Lobbyists concentrate their efforts instead on the fence-sitters—the legislators who can be won over.

On a few issues legislators may be committed to a lobbyist's cause by virtue of conscience, constituency, or consistency (that is, one's previous record). On a few, legislators may belong to a group a lobbyist represents. Trial lawyers who serve in the legislature are apt to carry the trial lawyers' case. Teachers who serve in the legislature tend to sympathize with the teachers' case. In Alabama, many teachers or former teachers are in the legislature. If a vote directly affects education, lobbying them helps but is not vital: "The huge bloc of legislators with teaching backgrounds doesn't need to be told what to do."[10] Legislators may have some other characteristic that will impinge somehow on a client's case. Being a smoker or nonsmoker may matter. One lobbyist who represented tobacco interests complained that in the particular state he was working, only 1 out of 40 members of the senate smoked and only about 10 out of 120 in the house did.

Most members hang loose on many issues that concern interest groups. Neither their fealty nor their enmity can be relied on. Therefore, lobbyists tend to cast a wide net, approaching as many members as they, or their colleagues, can. The case can best be made member to member, but lobbyists nevertheless reach out to whomever they can—with the obvious exception of those leading the charge against them. Although lobbyists will not approach implacable opponents, they will try not to alienate them. "You can't get their votes," said a Florida lobbyist, "but you may be able to keep them from killing you." Another Florida lobbyist said that although he would not "waste his time" with a particular senator, he does send someone else to cover him "so he can't say we didn't come by." No gain can be derived from a legislator who feels ignored, as was the case in California where business associations had neglected personal contact. "I can't actually remember," says one legislator, "when I was personally lobbied on a bill by someone representing the CMA (California Manufacturers Association) or the Chamber."[11] It is important for lobbyists to come by and visit even with those legislators who are not especially friendly to their issue or to their clients. Nothing can be taken for granted on the current issue; moreover, the visit may help a lobbyist on the next issue.

If the lobbyist needs votes to pass or defeat a bill or, more likely, to adopt or stave off an amendment on the floor, then there can be no substitute for working the members. "Work every son of a bitch in the legislature," advises a Florida lobbyist, "Then, go back and see them again. And again. If you get them to commit three times, you have them." Lobbyists spend much of their time trying to discover where legislators stand and asking them to make a commitment. They are constantly taking vote counts, carrying tally sheets or notebooks that list legislators who can then be checked off according to their positions on the issue at hand.

Getting legislators to commit themselves before they actually have to may be among a lobbyist's toughest jobs. Legislators often try to cooperate with both sides because they see merits on one hand and also on the other. They also have regard for lobbyists in both camps and do not want to alienate anyone unless they have no alternative. A legislator may therefore be kind, agreeable, and encouraging. The lobbyist should interpret none of this, however, as a sign of commitment. The lobbyist must therefore not only make the rounds of rank and file, but also identify the solid supporters, the definite nos, and the question marks in between.

The crucial final stages of the persuasion process may be in caucus, on the floor, or later in a conference committee. In New Jersey, if a bill survives the majority-party caucus, there is little chance of its being reversed or revised on the floor. But when legislators are meeting in caucus, events are harder to predict. This is extremely frustrating for lobbyists. In Minnesota and Texas, conference committees settle many issues, so lobbyists make their last-ditch efforts there. It is critical, for example, for Texas lobbyists to have at least one of "their" people on the ten-member conference committee—"someone who will carry your water," says one lobbyist in Austin, "and can get other votes." "Someone on the inside," he explains, "can keep you informed."

Every lobbyist hopes to have things worked out well in advance of floor consideration. Many do, but they cannot be sure that they will. "If you have a floor fight," commented a California lobbyist, "you haven't done your job in the legislature." At least, that is the way it used to be in California. Today, the lobbyist cannot afford to wander far from the floor. Often it is the job of lobbyists to quarterback their side, when the bill is on second or third reading. A Colorado lobbyist had a major bill on the house floor. She and her colleagues stood behind the glass at the rear of the chamber. As amendments were introduced, legislator allies would carry them back to her. She and the others would read the amendments (the last one had not even been printed), make quick decisions, and signal which way to vote to legislators in the chamber.

There are certainly instances where powerful lobbyists sit in the gallery of the chamber, signaling thumbs up or down to members. This is usually the case when amendments are coming fast and furious and members have had little chance to read, let alone make sense of, them. More often, the signals are given by legislative leaders or members who sponsored and are carrying the bills. They are necessary cues for members.

Lobbyists face their greatest tactical challenges during the final days of a session. They still want bills to be enacted that may have died, or even been rejected, in committee. Their bills may have emerged from committee but not been taken off the calendar for action on the floor. This is the last chance, furthermore, for lobbyists to insert words, phrases, or additional language into someone else's bill as a way of getting their own measure enacted into law. What they need is a "vehicle," the title of which is broad enough to encompass their amendment.

Two Texas lobbyists, known as the "Booze Brothers" (one represents whiskey and wine, the other beer), were particularly adept during the session's closing hours. According to one lobbyist, a frequent victim of their successful tactics, "the two would wait until the very last minute, put their entire legislative package in one bill, and then run it through the chamber." The liquor code is so complicated that few legislators understand it or realize what is happening until it is too late.

Lobbyists must also keep amendments off their own bills and prevent hostile bills from slipping through as amendments to other measures. The last few days of the session in Florida are especially hectic. One lobbyist compared it to a basketball game, with the ball going up and down the court. Lobbyists have to ascertain who is in control. Key staff members therefore have to be identified at this stage in order for lobbyists to be able to find out as quickly as possible what is happening and who is planning to do what. Lobbyists will have "watchers" who scan the process for them, pick up amendments filed with the clerk, and just hang out, hoping to pick up bits and pieces of vital information from members and other legislative creatures. Without timely intelligence, it is difficult for lobbyists to figure out how to react. There just isn't enough time to think.

Education and Information

Today's lobbyist will almost invariably have to make an argument on the merits. Personal relationships still count, as do grassroots efforts and political campaigns, but lobbyists also have to present a reasonable case. A Florida lawyer-lobbyist maintained that, before, it was more "who you knew," but, today, it is more "what you know." A lobbyist can no longer rely simply on approaching a legislator friend and saying, "I need this." On most issues today, the weight of the argument is what matters.

A Minnesota lobbyist described how lobbying in his state was "merit and substance based," although some folks still did the job old-style. "Effective lobbying is taking a reasonable position," he explains, "supporting it with facts, selling the idea from legislator to legislator, and being there all the time so that when the decision is about to be made, you're around." Merit and substance may play a slightly larger role in states like Minnesota than in Florida or New Jersey, but everywhere lobbyists have to present legislators with information and educate them as to their clients' positions. Public-interest and other cause lobbyists, in particular, spend considerable energy in this regard. They present their facts, argue the merits, and often put an emotional spin on the whole package.

Providing Information

About twenty-five years ago a study of lobbying in Massachusetts, North Carolina, Oregon, and Utah inquired into how dependent legislators were on lobbyists for information. Forty-one to 83 percent of the legislators in these states replied that they depended on lobbyist information a good deal or some of the time; 55 to 88 percent answered that they had a lot or quite a bit of confidence in the information; and 28 percent to 61 percent replied that they found all or most of the information helpful.[12]

Today, with more staff and other sources of information available and with lobbying under fire from the press, it is unlikely that legislators would respond as positively to questions such as those noted above. Nonetheless, they still seek information from lobbyists and lobbyists still seek to provide it. Legislators tend to be overwhelmed by communications, newsletters, reports, and data of every kind. But they are constantly on the search for information, which is essentially data that have been manipulated, interpreted, and packaged. Lobbyists can furnish such information—processed, understandable, and politically and policy relevant. What a lobbyist does, therefore, is to provide basic information—quickly and intelligibly.[13] Moreover, it reaches legislators about when they need it, not too early and not too late. In the words of a New Jersey contract lobbyist, timing is crucial: "Getting the right information to the right people at the right time. . . . It's a home run to make that combination work." The supply of information ideally should match legislator demand—helping members do what is right; making friends, allies, and constituents happy; and protecting significant interests in their district.

To be sought out by legislators for information, lobbyists themselves must be knowledgeable. Knowledge of an issue is a weapon a lobbyist has to carry into battle. A lawyer-lobbyist, who is an expert on land use, is much in demand by members of the Florida legislature. A lobbyist for the chemical industry has developed the reputation in California of furnishing reliable information, which is especially useful for the record. Trustworthiness is also essential. Legislators must trust the lobbyist in order to rely on his or her information. "People trust us," is a comment many lobbyists offer about why legislators use their information. A Florida lobbyist, for instance, has spent his entire career in the field of alcoholic beverages, including a stint as director of the division of alcoholic law in a previous gubernatorial administration. He is a trusted source of information on such issues. A Minnesota lobbyist is an expert on insurance, and on such issues legislators turn to him.

Lobbyists are indispensable when it comes to providing legislators with what is primarily political, rather than substantive, information. Most important, because they represent their clients, they can communicate what their positions are and how intensely they are held. That is vital information. In addition, they can tell legislators how other actors might be affected by a measure being considered. They also try to give legislators an idea of how their districts would fare if a bill were enacted. A number of lobbyists are in the habit of preparing position papers on issues. They also try to tailor their arguments to individual legislators. A member with strong business ties will be presented one argument; a member with strong union ties will hear another.

Among the information communicated is that which assures lawmakers—assures them not only that the issue is worth paying attention to, but also that their side has substantial support. Legislators who sign on will not be wasting their time.[14]

Lobbyists also provide substantive or technical information. They conduct research and issue reports. California business associations, for instance, are known for the research papers their lobbyists write in their particular areas of responsibility. Common Cause, in New Jersey and Florida among other places, acquires and reports considerable information on the subject of campaign finance. And legislators inevitably use it. Policy and fiscal analyses are in great currency. Some explore the actual effects of ongoing programs and policies. Others challenge policies that are proposed. In Florida, for instance, the governor wanted to increase environmental fees. Lobbyist Wade Hopping responded with an analysis, however, that demonstrated that the fees were excessive. As a result, the increases were scaled back.

In view of their declared rationale, public interest research groups in the states naturally devote substantial energy to research and its dissemination. New Jersey PIRG, for instance, usually leads off a major campaign for legislation with a research report on an environmental or consumer issue. In addition to analysis, the report will make recommendations on legislation, regulation, or enforcement. One such report was entitled "Polluters' Playground—An Investigation of Water Pollution Violations in New Jersey." It focused on permit violations and the government's response. In virtually every area of study, PIRG found "a pattern of corporate and municipal violation" that was "coupled with government action which can best be described as lethargic." PIRG recommended stiffer penalties and less discretionary authority. Reports like these are aimed as much at the press and the public as they are at legislators themselves. In the ensuing battle, legislators sympathetic to environmental causes did not fail to use PIRG's research.

In addition to research and reports, lobbyists and their clients deliver experts, who testify before committees and even speak to members one-on-one. A lobbyist for a government association in Maryland set up a panel of finance and budget experts to explain at two hearings just what a proposed tax-collection bill would do. This resulted in a study group being appointed to explore the matter further. Or take the issue of whether industrial laboratories should be permitted to use animals in their research. This is an emotional issue to the public, and one that the pharmaceutical industry feels strongly about. A lobbyist explained the approach that his company took:

> You try to get people who are involved with that issue in the legislature to meet with people who are involved in your research and have them share all the information as to why we need to have animals—not because it's something that we want to do, but because it's something we think we have to do.

Arguments furnished by experts and technicians can be persuasive.

Arguing the Merits

The fact is that, in many cases, lobbyists represent special interests that are seeking sanction or advantage from government action. The contestants are mainly self-serving in these disputes, although they also believe that what benefits them is also good public policy. And this is the argument they make. Such an argument must be made today; it is practically a requisite for success. One of Tallahassee's major lobbyists (before taking a position with Gov. Lawton Chiles's administration) was not one to besiege the legislature with a bunch of statistics. He nevertheless admitted "you like to know that what you are arguing makes some good policy sense and has some strength to it."

Practically every group argues merits in terms of constituents, the state, the public. Groups believe that their cause benefits the public, as well as themselves. The resolution of many issues depends, in considerable part, on the merits—philosophical, policy, and political.

The public policy rhetoric used by lobbyists varies from issue to issue, but some general examples are in order. Most, but not all of them, are defensive.

1. *"It isn't fair."* The tobacco and alcoholic-beverage industries rely heavily on the "it isn't fair" argument to combat tax increases and stiffer regulations. A Florida bill that would disallow business expenses connected with the promotion of tobacco products is "unfair," according to industry lobbyists. Taxes on tobacco and/or alcohol to fund health care and social programs are also opposed for the same reasons. These programs, the industries maintain, should be funded out of general revenues and not by earmarked monies derived from a tax on a few products. Recently, tobacco has effectively used the fairness issue, enacting legislation in a number of states that prohibits employers from discriminating against job candidates who smoke. The issues involved were hiring practices, smoking in the workplace, and telling employees what they could or could not do. Even though legislators had been in the habit of kicking tobacco around, the fairness argument was telling.

2. *"It won't work."* Frequently lobbyists will argue that, whatever the merits of a proposal, it does not make sense in practice. This is presented as one of several arguments. The pollution of New Jersey's beaches with debris led to a bill that would prohibit the sale of tampon devices that used a disposable applicator made of plastic or other nonbiodegradable materials. Playtex, a manufacturer of tampons, produced a study that showed that plastic applicators represented less than .4 percent of beach debris in the state.[15] What was the point of the ban if debris would not be substantially reduced!

3. *"It can be done in other ways."* Lobbyists try to persuade legislators that there are other, less hurtful, ways to skin the cat. The main line of defense against the bottle bill is that recycling offers a better method of cleaning up. Moreover, now that recycling programs are in operation, lobbyists for beer, soft drinks, glass, retailers, and recyclers argue that a bottle bill would kill recycling by taking the profits out of the solid-waste stream. They have a point. The tobacco industry and restaurant associations oppose legislation requiring restaurants to set up smoking and nonsmoking sections. They argue that restaurants are already providing these sections on a voluntary basis, and the system is working.

4. *"It is too costly."* Especially if the tab has to be picked up by the state, the cost argument can be powerful, and more so in times of budgetary stringency. Business lobbyists usually maintain that environmental measures are too costly and will harm not only business but also consumers

and taxpayers. Lobbyists for municipalities will argue that a particular measure would cost the cities $300 million, and impact heavily on local taxpayers.

5. *"It will help consumers."* Lobbyists and their clients justify many special-interest measures in terms of how they would benefit consumers. When a group seeks to become licensed by the state, for example, its rationale is to protect the public. For example, occupational therapists desire state regulation, maintaining that a law would prevent unqualified individuals from claiming they are professionals. Regulation would serve to protect the elderly people and other populations that need therapists. In the case of the so-called car wars, lobbyists for Hertz and Avis charged that Alamo's collision-damage-waiver practices constituted unfair competition and therefore hurt consumers. Alamo rejected the charge and argued that consumers should have the right to decide. New Jersey is one of only two states where self-service gasoline stations are banned. The oil industry, advocating self-service in addition to full-service, justified its position in terms of consumer choice. The New Jersey Gasoline Retailers Association, supporting the ban, maintained that choice would raise the price of gas for consumers. (It also argued that self-service stations would inconvenience the elderly and disabled and could pose safety problems.)

6. *"It will hurt the public."* Professions that are resisting encroachment on their turf will often argue—and not without some justification—the health and welfare of the public. Ophthalmologists, who have opposed legislation to allow specially trained optometrists to prescribe certain drugs, maintain that it would authorize nonphysicians to practice medicine. They suggest that there might be serious consequences. In their testimony before health committees, ophthalmologists may tell of patients who became blind after optometrists failed to diagnose diabetes. Veterinarians, who resist the efforts of pet groomers to get authorization to brush animals' teeth, use a similar argument. Veterinary dentistry, they maintain, is a medical procedure. Veterinarians, they maintain, have to undergo a licensing procedure and demonstrate clinical competency in an examination in order to protect the public from incompetence. When a veterinarian examines an animal's teeth, he or she will look for a disease of the mouth, malocclusion, cavities, tooth fractures, tumors, wounds, and so forth. By contrast, groomers have a purely cosmetic objective.

7. *"It will hurt the industry."* Before a company moves into a state, it has bargaining power. Chase Manhattan and Citicorp were successful in getting a bill through the Delaware legislature by promising to locate in the state and provide jobs. American Express has also used economic-de-

velopment rhetoric to advance its legislative priorities in a state where it may locate a facility. But once an industry is located within a state, its economic-development argument is much weaker. A California lobbyist for business pointed out that damage to an industry and loss of jobs is no longer the argument it used to be. "We lose a thousand jobs, we'll create another thousand." A New Jersey lobbyist for business went further: "Legislators don't want to hear that you are going to move out of the state. They've heard it too many times in the past, and nothing happened." It is not sufficient, therefore, to base the case on harm to industry. It is preferable to argue other merits, as is done by the pharmaceutical industry. Access to quality health care, patient care, the doctor's ability to prescribe the best drug, cost effectiveness: these are the merits on which pharmaceuticals rest their case. A lobbyist for a major firm describes how he presents things: "This, we believe, is in the best interest of our company, our industry, the health care of individuals, and the whole health-care delivery system." That is a tough combination to beat.

Among the information that counts heavily are two types—(1) what other states are doing and (2) what difference a measure has made. The enactment of a bill authorizing New Jersey's physician assistants to practice was helped considerably by the group's argument that every other state in the nation had already passed similar legislation. And New Jersey optometrists, arguing for their bill, told their legislators that similar laws were in effect in twenty-seven states. No damage had been done, they claimed, as evidenced by the fact that real-practice insurance premiums for optometrists had not gone up.

Statistics, it should be noted, can be extremely helpful to a group's case. They played a key role in legislation to require motorcyclists to wear helmets. Proponents of the legislation, including the insurance industry, showed that 76 percent of those injured and 83 percent of cyclists killed in California motorcycle accidents were not wearing helmets. Based on data from other states, they argued that the toll in California would go down if cyclists wore helmets. The legislature passed the helmet law and Gov. Pete Wilson signed it.

Putting On Spin

Sometimes lobbyists have to do more than simply provide information. They may also have to doctor it or put on some spin. At the least, they have to get legislators' attention. Thus, one of the lobbyist's roles is "illuminating" the issue. For a state government relations professional in

Washington, D.C., this entails "making the light so bright that they are overwhelmed."

For a New Jersey contract lobbyist the challenge was to get the attention of legislators who did not quite grasp the issue. The weekend before his bill was to be considered, he still had not been able to get them to appreciate the significant savings his measure was going to achieve. How could he make the numbers he had for each legislative district look real? The answer was to have checks printed up, on heavy blue paper, with "Pay to the order of Taxpayers in [the number of the legislative district]" and numbers ranging up to $4 million typed out. The idea was that legislators would realize that their districts would get a refund if the measure was enacted. The facsimile checks were put in window envelopes and given by the lobbyist to legislators in the halls of the New Jersey State House annex. Legislators thanked the lobbyist, stuck the checks in their pockets, and walked around the corner, pulled out the envelope, and opened it up. The lobbyist had devised a clever way of getting their attention, although some legislators might have been a trifle disappointed in discovering that the check was a promotional gimmick and not a campaign contribution.

One way lobbyists get their points across is by labeling. What a bill is titled can matter enormously. One contract lobbyist recalled that he could not get occupational therapists the licensing bill they wanted. The title of their bill would have aroused every doctor in the state. "They can have what they want," he explained, "if they just call it something different." That way, there would be little opposition at all. Thus, frequently "the name is the game."

The environmental movement has a distinct advantage in that virtually every legislator wants to be perceived as an environmentalist. Environmentalists maximize their advantage by the most artful labeling. They structure the issue first, label it second, and then release it to the press with fanfare. "The Clean Water Act," "The Safe Drinking Water Act," "The Clean Air Act," "The Right to Know Act," and "HELP." The wording implies that these will all benefit the public. Labeling, of course, works both ways. In the battle over restricting smoking in public places, the proponents of the ban referred to the bill as "The Clean Indoor Air Bill," while the opponents called it "The Smoking Restriction Bill."

Another way that lobbyists seek to get their message across is by personalizing it. "I try to translate it into real people for members—welfare lines, the homeless," is how a lobbyist for one of Florida's cities described her approach. Another Florida lobbyist pointed out the personalization in the outdoor advertising association's campaign to restrict the ability of cities to regulate billboards. The association did not argue the interests of the billboard industry, but rather those of poor old Mom and Pop, who own one sign that Coca Cola rents from them. Regulation would put Mom and Pop out of business.

A New Jersey lobbyist, who opposed a proposed tax on plastic containers, figured out that this would apply to milk cartons and the milk that children buy in school. In testifying before the committee, he brought a haft-pint milk carton (which would have been taxed the same as a one-gallon carton) and asked the assembled legislators if they were going to hurt the children in school by taxing their milk. The legislators responded that they did not intend to do anything like that. The bill died and the children went on drinking their milk at the same prices.

Public interest lobbyists are especially adept at personalizing their issues. They frequently see a tactical advantage in identifying a villain. Often, too, because of ideology and/or strategy, they portray the struggle as one between good and evil.[16] "If you're against us on this bill, you're against the environment" is what they often contend. For most other lobbyists, this might be a high-risk strategy, and therefore unacceptable. Yet it fits the overall posture of those lobbying for a cause.

Related to this personalization of an issue is imbuing it with a lot of emotion. This can be done in practically any fashion. For instance, Colorado dentists opposed a bill authorizing dental hygienists to set up shop independently of dentists. The hygienists were not a real political force, but the bill became a women's issue because hygienists were women, as were many of Colorado legislators.[17] Cause lobbyists have emotionally laden issues to begin with, and they can be made even more so. When that occurs, it is difficult for those on the other side, usually representatives of business, to counter the argument and hold their ground.

One contract lobbyist was resisting a measure advanced by a public interest group requiring dealers to display warnings about hazardous toys. Representing a toy manufacturer, the lobbyist was fighting the odds. All he could do was sit down with legislators and argue that such a requirement would affect only those companies in the state, not companies in other states. So it would not solve the problem. He further maintained it was a federal problem, adding a gentle threat: why should his client, who wants to expand in the state, be penalized and thus not be able to go forward with his expansion plans? At the same time, he explained to legislators that his client did not want to market a toy that children would choke on, because it would quickly put him out of business. Lastly, he tried to convince the legislators to visit with his client and listen to his side of the story. All of this did little good, and he knew it early on. "You take your shot that way and you know you are not going to win," he concluded. He was correct, as demonstrated when the governor signed the bill surrounded by children at a local day-care center.

The Functions of Information

One lobbyist declared that "information is still power in Colorado," adding, "You can win no matter who you're up against." Conversely, another lobbyist observed that "policy arguments have to be made in Minnesota, but they don't necessarily win out." Both lobbyists are right. Information is but one among many sources of influence. If the lobbyist has not only solid information but also a compelling public policy argument and a good delivery system, his case has a marked advantage.

Information makes legislators more knowledgeable on the specific measures under consideration.[18] Without relevant information, on many issues legislators might be entirely in the dark. One lobbyist allows that legislators know something about a lot of things, but so many matters are beyond their ken:

> They have bills to decide on the release of helium balloons. Come on, these guys don't know about helium balloons! All they know about helium balloons is that you have them at your rally. You can't fault them for not knowing. But sooner or later, somebody manages to get the bill in the position where these guys have to make a life-or-death decision on helium balloons.

What legislator would have ever imagined that he or she would be deciding on balloons! Beyond the immediate issue, information can serve to educate the legislator along a variety of more general lines—about a policy area, a segment of the population, or an industry.

As important as anything else is the reassurance that information (provided by a lobbyist) can bring. Legislators need a justification or a rationale for their decisions. Therefore, one of the lobbyist's essential tasks is to make it as easy as possible for legislators to go along with what the lobbyist wants. And even if they are going to vote against a lobbyist, they still want the information he or she can furnish—so there will be no surprises.

The Art of Compromise

Negotiating is one of the most important phases of the legislative process. Negotiations are constantly going on among legislators, among lobbyists, and among members of groups on both sides of an issue. Most of these sessions are informal, occurring in the offices of legislators and lobbyists, in conference rooms, restaurants, and dozens of other locations. In state legislatures, just as in Congress, formal, open committee sessions are being supplemented by informal gatherings. Legislators, like U.S. representatives, now convene in open session—in committee, on the floor, and sometimes in caucus—to ratify what has been worked out in private.

The primary objective of negotiating is to arrive at an agreement on legislation among the concerned parties. This will almost always entail compromise by each side. On most issues handled by a legislature, compromise (sometimes referred to as the "Vaseline" of the legislative process) is critical to moving things along. A lobbyist for an influential association in Minnesota acknowledged that one side or the other can never get all that it wants. "If you pass a bill," she said, "there is always some give and take."

What's in It for Lobbyists

According to Ralph Haben, a Florida lobbyist and former speaker, lobbyists have a choice: they can work with others to smooth out disagreements or try to run them over.[19] Part of what lobbyists do is to try to kill bills, another part of their effort is to work things out, and yet another, perhaps the smallest, part is to try to get their own bill passed in its original and pristine form. Lobbyists, particularly the insiders with many clients, are usually willing to negotiate and compromise. There are a number of reasons for this.

First, they are in business for the long run, so they have adopted a "live and let live" philosophy. The idea is to keep everybody happy and make nobody mad. Furthermore, in the view of a Texas lobbyist, "It goes against human nature to say no all the time."

Second, lobbyists want to be able to show a client something for their efforts. They cannot stand to lose everything or win nothing; the risks of refusing to compromise can be high.

Third, as we shall discuss below, legislators prefer for opposing sides to work it out rather than fight it out. They do not want to be caught in the middle, so they encourage groups to compromise their differences. Lobbyists are more than inclined to go along with what legislators want.

Fourth, if possible, it is better not to vigorously oppose a bill sponsored by legislators. They may hold it against the lobbyist and his or her client in the future. One lobbyist pointed out that his organization had been fighting a particular bill sponsored by a senator and pushed by a public interest group. His organization was also opposed to several other bills before the committee the senator chaired. The lobbyist thought the chairman had stacked the hearings on these bills in favor of proponents. The message, in the lobbyist's opinion, was: "I'm going to make life miserable for you until you support my bill." After a compromise was hammered out on the disputed bill, the lobbyist's organization began to get wonderful treatment at the hearings on the other legislation. "There was never anything said," the lobbyist concluded, "but it was abundantly clear."

Fifth, sometimes lobbyists have to cut their losses. The best they can do on a bill is to reduce the damage to their client. In Minnesota, legislators are in front of the curve in imposing strict environmental standards. Minnesota business, which has the reputation of being progressive and socially responsible, still objects to particular environmental measures. But because of the legislature's orientation, business can seldom win; it has to compromise. Business in New Jersey faced a similar situation when Democratic governor Jim Florio and a Democratic legislature were in control. It could not win in the contest over the clean water enforcement legislation. It proposed amendments, however, ensuring that those innocent of real environmental harm would not be punished, capping legal fees stemming from lawsuits, and delaying implementation of the act to allow a phase-in period. After Republicans won both legislative houses two years later, business interests could breathe easier, and when Christine Todd Whitman replaced Florio as governor, breathing became easier still.

When the votes for one's side are simply not there, a modifying amendment is by far the best that one can get. "If a steamroller is coming down the mountain," a New Jersey lobbyist explained, "why should I stand in front of it and get squashed?" A lobbyist on the liberal side of a cause can count on twenty-five friends in the Florida house and about twelve in the senate—far from a majority. A lobbyist for a conservative cause can count on about the same number. The latter had to deal with a sex-education bill opposed by her organization. She worked out some problems with amendments, improving the bill somewhat from her point of view. She nonetheless continued to oppose the measure.

Sixth, if both sides want something and if the balance of power is equal, they have to compromise if they want to accomplish anything. This was essentially the case in California when George Deukmejian was governor. Environmentalists were not willing to compromise with industry unless they had to; but because Deukmejian backed industry, they were forced to, and several compromises were effected as a result.

Lobbyists are not always disposed to compromise, however, particularly if they have a "slam-dunk" measure and have little reason to negotiate with their opponents. To pass a bill in Colorado, it takes eighteen (of thirty-five) votes in the senate and thirty-three (of sixty-five) votes in the house. One lobbyist commented, "If you have thirty-three and eighteen, let's roll with it; otherwise, let's talk." Even then, if problems arise and the other side is reasonable, a lobbyist will normally try to work things out. If an influential legislator wants something, lobbyists will consider compromise, even when the votes are almost certainly theirs. Rarely do groups have such a lock on the legislature that they do not have to negotiate at all.

On occasion, lobbyists may be forced to go for broke because their clients insist on it. A contract lobbyist can be dealing with an organizational leadership that decides, "Win or lose, we're going to the mat." Especially on an issue that becomes emotional and where a grassroots campaign has been launched, the attitude may be "Even if we go down the tubes, we should not compromise." A lobbyist will usually try to persuade a client to ease up, but he or she does not always succeed.

Groups that rely largely on outside strategies—mobilizing grassroots support, cultivating the press, and engaging in issue advertising—are less inclined to settle out of court. After all, the best way to get on TV is not to negotiate but rather to take an extreme position. "You don't get a lot of coverage from sitting down with people and working out problems," observes a lobbyist for an environmental group. Cause lobbyists often prefer to stand firm rather than compromise their principles. Pro-choice and pro-life groups, for example, tend to be doctrinaire and therefore not very flexible when it comes to negotiating and compromising. In view of the issues involved and their constituencies, however, it may be difficult for them to give. Cause groups also feel that they have to get as much as possible out of legislation they are proposing because they will not get another opportunity for quite a while. Once the legislature has dealt with an issue, it has little desire to revisit such controversial subjects.

If public interest lobbyists choose to play an inside game, they have little choice but to negotiate and compromise. Still there are dangers in sitting down at the table and participating in the drafting of amendments. Moral-principle lobbying becomes tougher and lobbyists risk being co-opted. They have to be especially alert so that they do not go too far. A Colorado public interest lobbyist admits to negotiating but insists that "you cannot compromise beyond a certain point. You must know where to draw the line." A public interest lobbyist in Texas recently started playing an insider role and had a seat at the table. After negotiations, he says there was always the question: "Could we have gotten more if we pushed harder?" That question inevitably arises, but it cannot be answered. Moreover, once public interest lobbyists take a place at the table and become part of the bargaining process, they forfeit their ability to criticize the results later on.

What's in It for Legislators

John Martin, the speaker of the Maine house, counseled a national meeting of lobbyists: "If you want to have a slug-out, you must win. If you don't win, your effectiveness is gone—and you might as well find yourself another legislature to work in."[20] That is because legislators far prefer compromise to conflict. They do not want to be caught between competing special-interest groups, so they will ask the groups' lobbyists to reach a compromise. By insisting that conflicting groups work out their differences, the legislature can minimize the cross pressures it faces.[21] A New Jersey lobbyist described the dilemma:

> One thing the legislator hates is to get caught between two friends on the opposite sides. Instead, he looks for the conciliatory way out. He really does not want to get caught making the hard decision whether to go with, for example, the mortgage bankers rather than the realtors.

Why displease one side when it is possible to satisfy both sides!

If a settlement cannot be reached, the possibility of legislation passing is much diminished. Take the car-rental dispute, which we have mentioned before. In New Jersey, a proposed bill, backed by Hertz and Avis, would have prohibited the selling of collision-damage waivers (CDWs) under certain circumstances. Proponents argued that CDWs caused consumers to pay for unnecessary duplicate protection, because nearly 60 percent of auto insurance policies provide coverage to rental cars. Alamo's lobbyist offered a compromise: no ban, but a requirement that consumers be furnished specific information about their options with respect to CDW (as was required by law in thirteen other states). The proponents balked at the offer. Because the two sides could not get together, the legislature did nothing.

Apart from increasing their own comfort levels, legislators have other incentives for wanting groups to reach an agreement. If everyone can live with a bill, it is, first, more likely to be enacted into law and, second, more likely to work in practice. Parties on both sides of an issue have "bought in"; they now have a stake in a measure's success. Furthermore, sometimes legislators do not realize the down side of a measure until the opposition has begun to lobby. The negatives can be eliminated or reduced if the concerned parties can get together.

Therefore, legislators will usually ask lobbyists if they have worked matters out with groups and lobbyists on the opposite side, and if not, will suggest that they do so. Often, the committee chairman encourages negotiations. The encouragement typically sounds like the following: "This guy wants this. Sit down and figure out what you can live with. If you come to an agreement, fine. If not, you don't get a bill." The lobbyist will then negotiate and return to the chairman with, "Here's the deal." If an influential legislator asks lobbyists to negotiate a compromise, the request will seldom be turned down. The understanding is, compromise or lose.

Negotiations can take place with or without the participation of legislators. If the various parties go off and reach an agreement, the legislative committee and legislature are almost certain to ratify it. Frequently, however, the committee chairman, bill sponsor, and legislative staff will play a major role in negotiations. This has been a practice in Florida, where leaders and committee chairmen over the years have initiated the negotiating process. On a variety of issues they would get everyone into a room and mediate an agreement. Nowhere has this negotiating process been more in evidence than in the area of growth management. Cities, counties, large and small developers, the environmental community, and state officials each year would meet to try to work out legislation. Leadership by legislators in these efforts has been critical.

One of the best examples of a compromise on a major issue, engineered by legislative leaders, was the "Napkin Deal," which was consummated on September 10, 1987, at Frank Fats, a Chinese restaurant in Sacramento, California. Speaker Willie Brown wanted to resolve the ongoing fight over tort reform. Together with California senator Bill Lockyer (who was later senate president pro tem), Brown brought together representatives of the insurance industry, California Trial Lawyers Association, California Medical Association, California Chamber of Commerce, and Association of California Tort Reform to try to work out a compromise agreement. Each side shared a table in a private room at the restaurant and the speaker shuttled from table to table until a deal had been agreed to. Since no writing paper was immediately available, the outline of the peace pact was scrawled in ink on a cloth napkin. It called for a five-year truce and a compromise change in civil liability laws. Legislation drafted and pushed by the leadership was brought to a quick vote on the last night of the session. Willie Brown counted this as one of his major legislative accomplishments.[22]

Working Things Out

An important objective for most lobbyists is getting into the room where the fine points are being negotiated and a deal is being made. Addressing a group of lobbyists representing opposing clients at a legislative committee meeting, the chairman will declare: "We're going to work this out." He will point to three of the lobbyists to whom he will entrust the final negotiations: "You, you, and you." Lobbyists want to be in the position to be chosen for the job of crafting agreed-on language in a bill. "Everyone can play," says one Florida lobbyist, "but not everyone can get invited into the speaker's conference room behind the chamber." The back room is the place to be, because the moment of truth is in the negotiation of details.

Especially when compromises are being fashioned, details can make a difference. To be accomplished as a lobbyist, therefore, one must master more than the substance of the issue at hand. One must also be technically proficient and skilled in negotiating the fine points of legislation. A Minnesota lobbyist warned: "If you don't draft it, watch out." He knows that agreements can be reached in principle, but legislation has to be drafted in detail. The bottom line is how the agreement in principle is resolved in statutory language. If the lobbyist has a seat at the table and helps to draft amendments, he or she has greater control of the process. "You try to control the process as much as you can—by wielding the pen or the word processor," commented a Minnesota lobbyist.

Negotiations go on throughout the process. They may, in fact, have begun even before a bill is introduced. Recognizing that the legislature is likely to go along if they can get together, the two camps will try to agree on a draft. Lobbyists will seek points of agreement, identify disputed areas, and seek solutions acceptable to all parties. Anything that can be negotiated ahead of time brings tremendous relief to lobbyists. But if one party thinks it will have an edge, it may put off negotiations until later when it will be able to get more. As the process proceeds from pre-introduction to introduction to committee to floor and then to the second chamber, things obviously change, and the settlements differ accordingly.

Negotiating processes do not always succeed. The parties involved are too far apart or they are not inclined to give. A Texas lobbyist was blunt: "Sometimes you can't work it out. You just have to kill shit." Sometimes even though several issues can be resolved, others remain, and the parties in dispute wind up in battle. Sometimes, too, one side appears willing to compromise but does so mainly to stall the process so that the proposal dies along the way. No battle is waged openly—the warfare is surreptitious. Frequently, however, the process works. The contestants sign off on a compromise, legislators accept the settlement, and battle is avoided.

CHAPTER 10

Power and Representation

Anyone who pays attention to policy making in the states will acknowledge that lobbyists are integral to the legislative process. One or another of them is involved at just about every stage of most issues addressed by the legislature. Few legislators remain untouched by some lobbyist on any issue at hand. They are out there advocating their clients' positions, forging relationships with legislators, providing political and policy information, establishing coalitions, orchestrating grassroots campaigns, playing electoral politics, and bargaining and negotiating throughout. It is difficult to conceive of a legislature and its processes working without them.

Lobbyists play an important role in the drama of legislation. But how much influence do they actually have, and under what circumstances? Does their influence derive mainly from their own standing or from the power of those whom they represent? Given the activity of lobbyists and their principals, what about those who are not represented? Is the system fair to them? Is it fair overall?

The Influence of Lobbyists

"How good is he?" "Is she doing the job?" "What can we expect?" Clients wonder if their lobbyists are effective. But these questions are not easy to answer. Take an in-house lobbyist. On what basis can top management of a corporation evaluate the performance of its state governmental relations staff? Some companies count the number of bills their lobbyists draft and have introduced and how often they testify at hearings. Some operate their state governmental relations departments as cost centers, calculating the dollars saved (or lost) as a result of bills enacted, defeated, or modified.[1] Much of this, however, would appear to be misleading. The director of state relations for a drug company agrees: "The difficulty is in judging how important your influence was. There are so many imponderables that affect legislative decisions and votes."[2]

211

From a different perspective, two political scientists write about estimating the influence of lobbying. One would have to estimate a baseline of expected behavior for lawmakers using a set of measured variables—such as ideological predisposition, district interests, party, and so forth—and ascribe any deviation in voting to lobbying. Such an approach is virtually impossible, since it requires that all relevant factors be included in a model.[3]

Yet it should be possible to make a judgment. The chief executive officer of one company reflected on how he would evaluate his state relations director. He could not quantify his performance but would, instead, rely in part on what others thought of the lobbyist and in part on his own gut feelings. It would take time, but he felt he could do it.[4] Most in-house lobbyists have a number of issues in their portfolio. So they usually have some accomplishment to show top management. If enough issues are at stake, a lobbyist is unlikely to be shut out. As one Minnesota association lobbyist says, "I'll always get something to bring home." If he fails to get anything, however, his members will undoubtedly express their dissatisfaction.

In the case of contract lobbyists, their clients want to know whether influence is being exercised on their behalf. Because contract lobbyists have multiple clients, one client can never be absolutely certain that his or her interests are being represented most effectively or more effectively than another client's. Many of those who employ contract lobbyists, moreover, know little about legislative politics and are not always able to hold their lobbyists accountable. In such instances, it is possible for lobbyists to create activity and give the impression that their intervention had saved a client from the most baneful legislation. This happens, although it is probably not a common practice.

Most contract lobbyists have to show clients something for their money. In the words of an Ohio lobbyist, "you got to produce." A Maryland lobbyist, for instance, feels he has to succeed at a variety of tasks in order to keep his clients satisfied. Not only does he have to defend and advance their interests, but, when asked, he also must deliver the house speaker or senate president to address their groups. Other lobbyists also have to show results, or their regular clients will surely leave them. Most independent lobbyists are able to do so.

Lobbyists tend to exaggerate their own influence. A New Jersey lobbyist compared the influence of some of the "power" lobbyists to that of legislators. Even those legislators in good standing, he said, "do not have the influence and the clout with the presiding officers that a handful of lobbyists have." Like officeholders, lobbyists cannot afford to be overly modest in public. Their practice, after all, depends largely on their reputation for influence. A survey of lobbyists in Washington, D.C., is illustrative. The survey, which asked about the relative importance of resources at their disposal, showed that lobbyists tended to assign greater importance to their own qualities than to those of their organizations. Four out of five mentioned that a reputation for being credible and trustworthy was most important; one out of four mentioned a wide circle of contacts. In contrast, only one out of five mentioned a large membership, one out of seven an appealing cause, and one out of thirty a large budget.[5]

What counts, as far as influence is concerned, is how people perceive lobbyists. In the words of a former senate president, who is now a lobbyist in Ohio, "The perception of being able to get stuff done is more important than reality."[6] This explains why few lobbyists object to press stories that charge them with dominating the legislative process or wielding too much power. They prefer to be seen in that light than to be considered ineffectual. They know that the *perception* of influence matters as much as anything else; for in the world of lobbying, perception is reality. Jon Shebel of Associated Industries of Florida (who is also president of the Florida League of Professional Lobbyists) had this to say: "Power is actually just the perception of your power on the part of the people you deal with. If they think you have power, then you've got it."[7] It is in the interests of contract lobbyists, therefore, to give legislators, clients, the press, and the public the impression that they are indeed influential. If that means cultivating a myth or two, so be it.

Top lobbyists at the state level are hard to identify, especially in view of the great variety of people who operate. But, again, perception serves to discriminate. How lobbyists are regarded by their colleagues and by legislators is what matters. In each state capital certain lobbyists are reputed to be the most influential, just as certain groups are known as the most powerful. Often lobbyists with the most clients and the highest incomes are thought to be the most influential. Similarly, the groups with the largest memberships and the largest PACs are frequently considered the most powerful. For example, a Gallup survey of ninety-three New Jersey legislators found that thirty-three rated the New Jersey Education Association, as "most effective" in advancing their interests. The New Jersey Business and Industry Association was named by twelve legislators, and contract lobbyist Harold Hodes and his firm, Public Strategies, were mentioned by ten. The associations of dentists, builders, and trial lawyers each received three mentions.[8]

Despite the case that can be made for the services lobbyists render their clients, it is important not to exaggerate their influence. Lobbyists may exaggerate it, and the press does in the interests of presenting a lively story. Yet it should be stressed that whatever the influence of lobbyists, it is only one among a number of factors that play a decisive role in the legislative process.

The lobbyist's client needs to be factored in. Some distinction must be made between the effects of the lobbyist on the one hand and the independent effects of the interest group itself on the other. A state government relations professional for a large pharmaceutical company expressed the view of many of those who work for large corporations:

> The lobbyist would like to think that it's the lobbyist that has the most influence. I believe that that's secondary. I think it's the organization that the lobbyist represents that lends most credibility to an issue. A company such as _____ that has an outstanding record in the quality of its products, in the way it treats its employees, and in its contribution to its community in a social-investment way, speaks much better than any lobbyist could.

It is much easier, he pointed out, to visit a legislator and say that he represented _____ than to say that he represented some chemical company that was polluting the environment. "I don't care how good he (a chemical company lobbyist) is," he added, "that lobbyist has his hands full."

The success of in-house lobbyists, in comparison with contract lobbyists, is far more likely to hinge on their clients' identity and standing. Contract lobbyists have many clients and therefore cannot be identified by legislators with any single client. Nevertheless, even a contract lobbyist is affected by the aura of his or her clients or cause. A North Carolina legislator explained why a top lobbyist in the state was successful:

> He represents those who have power, so he has power. Anybody with his lists of clients, and the resources and the clout they bring with them, would do well in General Assembly.[9]

The nature of the issue is very significant. In writing about organizations, James Q. Wilson observes that effectiveness can be traced, first, to the organization's characteristics and, second, to the issues it has to confront.[10] Similarly, the influence of lobbyists depends on both the individual and the principal, but it also varies with the issues. The legislative process deals with very different arrays of issues.

Governors and legislators commit themselves and their leadership to broad policy initiatives on education, employment, economic development, and taxes. Groups have lesser weight in these arenas. They can furnish leadership, however, where causes are concerned; for example, the environment, homelessness, and abortion rights. These issues tend to have considerable public significance, and they arouse more than a little passion.

The identities of some lobbyists are linked, not so much to a client, but rather to a cause. They do not lack individual skill or resources, but their influence nevertheless derives mostly from the popularity of their cause. Thus, a highly regarded lobbyist in Florida could admit that most of his success in the process derived from his touting the environment and not from any special talents on his own part.

Finally, there are the essentially special-interest issues that are of concern to economic, professional, and occupational groups vying for protection or advantage. Although participants on both sides will argue the public policy and public interest merits of their case, these issues arouse little concern on the part of either the public or its representatives. If neither the public's nor the legislator's interest is aroused, the role and influence of the lobbyist is more apt to be critical.

With lobbyists scurrying here, there, and everywhere, it is easy to overlook the power of legislators. That would be a mistake. The conception that legislators are putty in the hands of lobbyists is way off the mark. Legislators have their own ideas, interests, and intentions. They have agendas that overlap those of lobbyists. They are advocates, exercising leadership and seeking support from groups and lobbyists, not simply responding to pleas and pressures. They initiate. They persuade lobbyists to sign on. In dealings between legislators and lobbyists, the legislator is almost always the dominant party. Each needs the other, but lobbyists are far needier than legislators.

Legislators act in response to many forces, not only those generated by lobbyists and groups. Constituency is one of the more obvious and more potent of them, although constituency often manifests itself through locally organized groups. As Guy Spearman, a Florida contract lobbyist, said: "A legislator is going to listen to his own constituents any day over me."[11] No matter how close the friendship between lobbyist and legislator, the latter will never go against his or her district's interests. A legislator's convictions, principles, or values also matter. They matter not only on broad issues like capital punishment, choice in education, and welfare, but also on the narrower, special-interest issues. The minds of some legislators are practically made up before lobbyists get to work on even the narrowest issue. In Florida, for instance, a number of lawmakers had had an annoying personal experience with boats speeding by them on the St. Johns River near Tallahassee. They had made up their minds on the need for further regulation of pleasure craft, and they proceeded along those lines. Lobbying did not affect them. In states where the "car wars" were fought, some legislators lined up against Alamo because they had been given a hard sell or paid more for a rental than they had expected or thought proper. No matter who the Alamo lobbyist was, they knew Alamo first-hand and were not to be won over.

In a number of instances legislators look at an issue with virtually no preconceptions. They may then decide according to what they regard as the merits. One story that circulates in statehouses is about the lobbyist who asked a legislator (with whom he had a good relationship and to whose campaign his client has contributed) for his support on a bill. "I can't vote for that bill," said the legislator, "It's a bad bill." "Of course, it's a bad bill," the lobbyist replied. "I wouldn't need your help if it were a good bill." However special or specialized, some bills are not deemed worthy of support, and nothing a lobbyist does will turn legislators around. They will not support what they believe to be bad bills.

In addition to the factors mentioned above, there are so many more factors that help to shape the process. These factors are ones over which lobbyists have no control. If the economy is in recession and the state budget is in crisis, legislators, in the words of one lobbyist, tend to "grab at anything and everything." At such a time, it is difficult to fight tax increases on business. A New Jersey lobbyist pointed out that her organization opposed, but did not lobby hard against, an increase in sales taxes proposed by a Democratic governor to a Democratic legislature. To do so would have been fruitless. Lobbyists and their groups were helpless; it was clear to all of them that the higher taxes were going through.

What happens elsewhere also has effects, and the best lobbyist will not be able to control them. If practically every other state adopts a particular measure, the logic for its adoption may become irresistible. One lobbyist, who represented ophthalmologists in their struggle with optometrists, managed to stave off the assault for ten years. But he finally lost the battle because practically every other state had passed legislation giving optometrists the right to apply eyedrops. Legislators came up to him and said, "Come on! No one has gone blind yet in all those other states." The lobbyist had no way to rebut the argument or buck such a trend.

With so many other factors at work, one might conclude that little room exists for lobbyists to exercise influence. Such a conclusion would be amiss. Lobbyists still have ample room to bring their talents to bear. On the many issues that state legislatures handle, such as those where private interests compete, or where only one interest is heard from, or where the public interest is very difficult to discern, or where most of one's constituents are unconcerned, lobbyists can and do play an important role. No matter what the rhetoric employed, these are essentially special-interest issues of narrow scope, with little salience to the broader state community. This is where lobbyists can earn their spurs. Thus, the less important the issue, the more important the lobbyist. Or as Zeigler and Baer observed two decades ago: "In general, the narrower the scope of a piece of legislation, the greater the opportunity for a lobbyist to intervene in the decision-making process."[12]

Narrow issues that concern special interests constitute a large part of the legislative process, albeit not the part most visible to the press and the public. Association, company, and contract lobbyists will almost always be involved in such issues. Lobbyists for county and local governments involve themselves sporadically, and cause lobbyists, by the very nature of their issues, seldom engage in special-interest battles.

On these issues, it is usually not necessary, nor advisable, to go outside. The inside game tends to dominate here. The relationships lobbyists have cultivated, the clients they are representing, and the way they make their cases count heavily. Relationships are the primary vehicle of influence for the contract lobbyist. For the in-house lobbyist, the client's standing is the primary means of influence. On many of these special-interest issues, legislators may take cues from their leaders, committee chairmen, colleagues, and staff. They may also listen to lobbyists and their principals, depending on how much trust they place in them, how credible they appear, and the reputations they bear. As long as there is no real risk, legislators may be willing to go along. On most special-interest issues, lobbyists provide most of the cues. Insofar as they can, they enlist legislators on their side and encourage them to work their colleagues.

A number of issues are not so narrowly focused. Often a government agency, a legislator, or a group espousing a cause seeks a change in law. Changes in the law typically affect someone's interests adversely. Such issues are usually of broader scope. Conventional wisdom suggests that lobbyists exercise less influence here. "When the issue is highly visible, the persuasiveness of the lobbyist does not make much difference."[13] Two political scientists sum up that the impact of lobbyists is "likely to be less substantial on highly visible issues that engage public passions or media coverage and on issues in which there are strong competing ideological, partisan, or constituency pressures."[14]

The outside game is much more important when these kinds of issues are involved. No longer are relationships or connections sufficient.

Teacher organizations, for instance, make extensive use of grassroots techniques and campaign activity. Cause lobbyists rely heavily on the media to transmit their messages both to the public and to public office-holders. To some extent, a group's resource base affects its strategy and tactics. To some extent, too, the issue and the group itself will determine the adoption of an inside or an outside strategy. The latter expands the audience of an issue and raises its salience for legislators.

Given the likely involvement on broad and visible issues of a legislator's values, emotions, constituents, or prior record, the lobbyist's impact may be reduced. Yet even then, it is by no means negligible. Those lobbying on behalf of teachers for example, have something to win or something to lose. Management of the campaign is in the hands not of teachers but of their lobbyists. Cause lobbyists, too, have to prove themselves. However popular their cause and involved the legislators, their achievements depend partly on their skills and efforts. And those who are lobbying for status-quo groups, trying to resist what may appear to be popular tides, can also contribute substantially to the outcomes. They may not be able to win, but just how well they hold the line and to what extent they reduce their losses is largely in their hands.

On major issues the influence of lobbyists may be at the margins. But the margins are where many important outcomes can be located. Seldom, as has been pointed out earlier, does one side win, while the other loses. Outcomes are more mixed than that. The question is, rather, how much does each side win or lose. The answers come from lobbyists, who are engaged in the hard work of negotiation and compromise.

Arriving at settlements with which each side can live is one of the major objectives of legislators. It cannot always be achieved, but when it is, the inside game of lobbyists is much in evidence. Outside strategies and tactics provide groups with a favorable or unfavorable position. But lobbyists, sitting around the table agreeing to amendments and to specific language, are among the players who finally convert advantages or disadvantages into actual outcomes. They are among a handful of people who control the details. And the details are usually quite important. Such influence is not readily observable (partly because few look in this area), but it does exist.

On minor issues, the lobbyist's influence is likely to be central, and may occasionally carry the day. On major issues, other factors play a much greater role, and a lobbyist's influence is likely to be marginal. But in either case, lobbyists can, and often do, make a substantial difference.

Clients and Causes

A lot rides on the lobbyist's doing a good job of making the case. On narrow issues the lobbyist may bear responsibility for whether a client wins or loses. On broader issues the lobbyist may bear responsibility for the precise terms of the settlement. In addition, a lot also rides with the case itself and the client in whose behalf the case is being made. Some clients start out with an advantage.

Those groups that are perceived to be influential have highest standing in the political universe. Political scientists have provided rankings of interest group power for many of the states. To cite several examples, in Pennsylvania the most powerful groups are the education association, the chamber of business and industry, the trial lawyers, AFL-CIO, and insurance. In North Carolina the most powerful are education, banking, business, state employees, lawyers, and local governments. In Texas, trial lawyers, doctors, realtors, teachers, truckers, oil and gas, chemicals, and AFL-CIO rank high. In Maine, environmentalists, teachers, labor unions, paper companies, municipalities, and utilities are at the top.[15] As of 1998, according to the studies of interest groups in fifty states by Clive S. Thomas, Ronald J. Hrebenar, and their colleagues, the two most influential groups are general business organizations and teachers. The former are perceived as very effective in forty states and somewhat effective in twelve. The latter are perceived as very effective in forty-one states and somewhat effective in eight. Business and teachers are followed by utilities, lawyers, bankers, local government, labor, insurance, manufacturers, and doctors.[16]

Reputational analysis, which is based on external assessment by informed observers, responds to the question of who has political clout in a state. Groups that rank high tend to be those with substantial resources of one type or another and ambitious legislative agendas. But some groups—ones that may not rank high in surveys of state influence—might be quite successful in achieving their goals as each group defines them. In other words, groups can manage to get what they want without being considered powerful. A group's goals may be limited, its opposition may be weak, and its issues may be of minor public concern.[17]

Business associations and large companies are among the groups possessing some of the conventional resources that serve as the basis of group power. Business has money, sometimes jobs in a district, PACs, and capable lobbyists. In Texas the chemical industry, which accounts for almost one-third of the state's overall economy, cannot be overlooked when the question is one of influence. It is true, too, that business and industry generally are well positioned in Colorado, where the Colorado Association of Commerce and Industry (CACI) has clout. But it is influential because, according to one veteran legislator, "its values coincide with those of the Republican party."[18] And the Republican party has controlled both houses of the legislature for some time. IBM in Minnesota gets, at the very least, a sympathetic hearing in the legislature because it is a major employer and a leading member of the brain-power industry that Minnesota wants to keep. The company also has star quality. That all helps, as does IBM's network of relationships with legislators. Despite the standing of some companies, however, business in Minnesota is fragmented and has little clout.

The present exploration of lobbying suggests that business is far from monolithic and, overall, its influence is thereby limited. Business rarely speaks with a single voice and, until recently, it has been less than adept at politics. For instance, despite its strength in Colorado, business is often divided. Large banks compete with small banks and savings and loan associations compete with banks.[19] It should also be remembered that business has assumed a defensive posture. When confronted with a number of demands (for example, on taxes, the environment, consumer protection, and occupational safety), business has had to give ground. It would seem that business in many instances has either had to bow to contemporary political movements or at least engage in measured retreat. As one lobbyist put it, "You win when you don't get taxed or get taxed less than expected." If that constitutes victory, then business has certainly had its share of defeats.

No matter how formidable a group may seem, its influence is checked if its issues arouse opposition from another formidable group. Nowadays, the competition among groups is intense. In Washington, D.C., there is the paradox of more interest groups and more lobbyists wielding less influence over policy results. With integrative institutions becoming weaker, demand making is on the rise and single-issue groups are in the ascendency.[20] There are so many interests and so much pressure in the statehouses that only a few demands go unopposed. Policy making in many places is more pluralistic than before, and any single interest is less likely to dominate. If groups are relatively equal in strength, the influence of each will be curtailed in a competitive situation. If one group is weak, and thus presents negligible opposition, the stronger will likely prevail. The possible lineups are numerous.

If instead of trying to measure the relative strength of interest groups, we focus on how well specific interests are served by public policy, a different picture emerges. Take state societies of certified public accountants, for instance. Few legislators would consider them to be at all powerful. CPAs, of course, do not get everything, but they get much of what they want. They do not have the enemies that doctors or trial lawyers have. And nearly every legislator can support them on most issues. If, or when, the profession becomes involved in more contentious matters, legislators will probably be less inclined to endorse the positions the CPAs take. So if the question is "Have the accountants been influential?" the answer has to be "yes." It helps, then, to have little opposition and needs that arouse little controversy.

As opposition to a group widens and intensifies, however, its interests will almost inevitably suffer. The trial lawyers illustrate the point. They are believed to be powerful, and they probably are. But when just about everybody lines up against them, as has been happening, they too can lose. The proof is that in recent years tort reform efforts in half the states have overcome the opposition of trial lawyers and infringed on their practices to some extent. But neither business on the one side nor the trial lawyers on the other have won total victories or suffered utter defeats.

Some groups, in fact, appear powerful, yet their power is like the emperor's new clothes. The insurance industry is embattled practically everywhere, except in Hartford, Connecticut, the insurance capital of the country. Once an issue becomes politicized, as frequently happens today, insurance finds itself at a great disadvantage. It is not well received in state legislatures. On a measure it wants to achieve, insurance will keep a low profile and hide behind other groups. Its identification with an issue can be the kiss of death.

Oil provides another example. It is an industry that is more powerful at the national level than at the state level. The image we have is of Big Oil. Yet, outside of a few states, oil is not a potent force. It has no local refining base and thus no local roots. And when a refinery or two is located in a state, the benefit of one thousand to two thousand employees does not compensate for the liability oil assumes in producing pollutants. Moreover, the industry has little cohesion, and major and minor companies all pursue their separate ways. An oil lobbyist from one state commented, "Breaking even is a victory; if we don't lose ground, it's a win." A lobbyist from another state said: "No one will listen to us because we represent big oil." Public interest groups, environmentalists, and farmers are not reluctant to pick fights with the industry because oil is such an easy target. Industry's response, as indicated by one lobbyist, is "We don't lock horns with these people. We can't win." The industry feels beset even in Louisiana, a large oil producer. Whenever the state needs revenues, it turns to oil for taxes. It is hard to think of oil as being bullied, but that is the way its lobbyists feel.

The tobacco industry has been on the defensive for years now. Despite its wealth, its campaign contributions, and the talents of the power-broker lobbyists it employs, the tobacco industry faces stiff opposition from the American Heart Association, the American Lung Association, the American Cancer Society, and the American Medical Association. Since 1964 when the first surgeon general's report warned of health dangers from smoking and since 1982 when "secondhand smoking" was labeled a risk, the antismoking movement has had the advantage. Just about every state has imposed limitations of some sort on smoking in public places and workplaces. Tobacco interests have naturally been more successful in North Carolina and Virginia, the nation's largest tobacco producers. But even in these states they have had a fight on their hands. In 1989, in resisting an antismoking bill in Virginia, tobacco had thirteen lobbyists arrayed against the executive director of the state's chapter of GASP (Group to Alleviate Smoking in Public), a volunteer, and a part-time paid lobbyist, who worked for the American Heart Association and the American Lung Association. The sides were as unequal as they could be. Moreover, despite the fact that the industry provided thirty-two thousand jobs and the state's economy depended heavily on tobacco, a bill mandating restrictions on smoking in public places almost passed.[21] If tobacco is not safe in Virginia, then it is not safe anywhere.

In 1998 the tobacco industry settled a lawsuit with the states that cost it $246 billion over twenty-five years. Lately tobacco has been losing class-action suits in the courts. While cigarette prices were rising and cigarette sales were falling, state legislatures were raising taxes on tobacco. In December 1999, for example, New York agreed to a $0.55 pack increase, bringing the state tax on cigarettes to $1.11 per pack, the highest in the nation. The governor and the legislature, according to the *New York Times* report (December 18, 1999), wanted to signal that they were not beholden to tobacco interests, which had been wining and dining legislators and failing to report expenditures. Taking on the tobacco industry is not a political problem anymore; not taking it on is.

DuPont is the major industry and the largest employer in Delaware. One might assume that the chemical company would have little trouble in the Delaware legislature. Yet an examination of its legislative record over the past two decades shows that DuPont's successes have been mixed. While it prevailed on details of the state's right-to-know laws governing employee rights to information on workplace hazards, it has lost in trying to set restrictions on insurance liability. It unsuccessfully sought adoption of a state sales tax and repeal of the state's law limiting coastal development. It has had to compromise on a state bottle bill.[22]

One group that nearly always makes the list of the most powerful in a state are the teachers. This group is perceived to have influence, and it does. The New Jersey Education Association has been among the strongest groups in New Jersey for some time, and over the years, NJEA has unquestionably grown stronger. Its grassroots capacity has increased, its PAC has become larger, and its campaign activities have grown more effective. But while the association has grown stronger internally, its overall influence has probably declined. That is because the NJEA now operates in a more pluralistic environment. Given the many competing needs in the state, it is difficult nowadays for NJEA to achieve many of its programmatic goals. Yet it maintains its veto power. The situation, as described by one lobbyist, is that: "NJEA can't get everything it wants, but it can certainly stop what it doesn't want."

Like the New Jersey association, teacher organizations elsewhere may have less influence than earlier, but they still manage to get something of what they want and block much of what they do not want. Their resources continue to be considerable and to be effectively used. Teachers benefit from having a relatively large and well-distributed membership. Teachers are politically aware, cohesive, and can be mobilized for political action. These are substantial advantages. Teachers contribute money and people to political campaigns. They play a critical political role in rural districts and they are key in marginal ones. Their associations are well organized, well led, and staffed by skillful lobbyists, nearly all of whom have classroom experience. The potential of teachers for influence is high; their actual exercise of influence, however, will depend on the issue, the state's economy, the mood, the political alignment, and the circumstances at the time.

Just as reputedly powerful groups may be weaker than they appear, those groups not usually considered powerful may be stronger than most people think. Public interest and environmental groups are seldom cited in the top ranks of influential interests. Yet they have had a substantial impact on policy in many places. Their resource base is different from that of business and professional groups. Entertainment and campaign contributions have never been their stock in trade. Nor do these groups retain contract lobbyists who pride themselves on having close relationships with key legislators. The influence of these cause groups is based on other factors. The popularity of the issues they advocate, the attention and support they receive from the press, their grassroots canvassing, the strategic and tactical skills of their staffs, and the alliances they have with both executive officials and legislators all contribute to their influence. One lobbyist declared, "We have the issues and the press—and, for the most part, the staff."

Most important, these groups are not perceived as advocating special interests. Instead, they are taken at their word and accepted as representatives of the public interest, leading the charge against selfish interests. An environmental lobbyist in Florida observed that "when an executive agency and citizen groups are together, we're practically unbeatable." No lobbyist wants to take on groups like the Sierra Club, the Audubon Society, or Common Cause. And certainly not when they have substantial sympathy in both the executive and legislative branches.

Citizen and other "outsider" groups often have an advantage in numbers of members and usually have advantage in communicating to the broader public through the media. By 1995, according to one political scientist, citizen groups were considered by the media as factual sources of information, while business sources were considered self-serving. He writes:

> Journalists especially like to emphasize conflict, and thus stories about competing interest groups are often framed as good guys versus bad guys. This works to the disadvantage of business groups, who often are portrayed as fighting public spirited citizens who have organized to fight to protect their community.[23]

His study, focusing on citizen groups' influence at the national level, found that they have an impressive voice in the policy-making process in Congress. They manage to get their issues on the agenda and to get legislation passed.[24]

The New Jersey Public Interest Research Group exemplifies the power of a relatively new kid on the block, one who behaves differently from the older kids. PIRG has had a full-time presence in Trenton since 1984. It took the group a while to get on the political map, but by 1990 it had achieved some big wins and was recognized as a major player. One of the group's lobbyists described how legislators were now "checking with PIRG, seeking our approval, wanting us to work on their issues, and siding with us." Legislators, he asserted, were trying to enhance their political images by identifying with a number of PIRG's issues. Whatever their motivations, legislators did not want to be viewed as opponents of PIRG on environmental or consumer issues.

Representing Interests

Whose interests are represented? The public is extremely cynical about interest groups and their lobbyists. Most Americans believe that legislators simply forget about their constituents and do the bidding of the special interests who fuel their campaigns. Yet, the fact is that seven or eight out of every ten citizens are members of some interest group, and one that has a political agenda. Many people belong to more than a single group. Whether members of a group or not, virtually everyone's political and policy views are represented by interest groups and their lobbyists.

But people do not regard the groups to which they belong as "special interests." It is the others, and especially the large and/or powerful ones that are regarded as "special" and self-serving. Citizen groups and cause groups fare better in the public estimation than do business and labor groups, or even many professional and occupational associations.

While all kinds of interests are represented by groups (and, of course, also by legislators), not all are represented equally. Some interest groups are more equal than others. But what about the "public interest," which is more than the cumulative interests of organized groups? How does the system of lobbying and interest group politics affect the public interest? Is the overall public good served or subverted?

On the large, visible issues—those on gubernatorial or legislative agendas—public preferences and interests are definitely taken into account. On the narrower, special-interest issues, legislators assume that, if on the one hand no one objects or on the other hand all parties agree, the public interest will be served, or at least not undermined. The interest group systems that operate in the states, however, do not necessarily safeguard the public interest, even though each special interest maintains that its agenda will promote the public good.

In those instances where a group is pushing a measure to which no other group voices objection and where there are no direct costs to the state, the legislature will usually go along. It has to deal with enough conflict and does not want to encourage conflict where none has to exist. Why not say yes, and make some group of voters and its lobbyists happy! These are the consensual issues that offer concentrated benefits at no cost, or with very dispersed costs. No one gets hurt as a result. A group—say, one seeking licensing for its occupation—may benefit, while no one suffers except for, possibly, a larger, more diffuse public. Legislative staff members have little time to focus on these narrow issues and few incentives to do so; legislators are not apt to dally over staff presentations when they want to settle something peaceably and move on.

On many special-interest issues two sides do come into conflict. Contradictory arguments are expressed, and legislators can choose between them. In these instances unqualified victories are rare, and compromise is the probable outcome. Legislators encourage the disputants to negotiate and resolve their differences. Legislators may even play a role as mediators or contestants; above all, they are motivated to reach a settlement with which everyone can live. Lobbyists are similarly inclined, realizing that they benefit if fewer legislators have to choose sides and fewer line up against them. The issues in dispute may be complex, and it is often difficult to determine which group got the better of a particular compromise. One contestant may win more than the other, but neither ordinarily loses too much; both may actually come out ahead.

Although a settlement is reached in many of the disputes involving special interests, there can be no assurance that the broader public will benefit from the outcome. Conflict and debate do not necessarily promote the public interest. Some legislators will try to examine the issues from the perspective of the general public, but many will align themselves with one group or the other, and most will want things worked out with minimal bloodshed. Furthermore, the legislators' assumption probably is that if they keep interests in a reasonable state of balance, the public interest will be approximated.

In addition, legislators appreciate that whatever the legislative outcome of such special-interest issues, the governor stands as another line of defense. If indeed a particular interest is overreaching or several interests are dividing up the pie to the detriment of the people of the state, the governor can be expected to exercise the veto. The governor has a broader perspective. The governor and the governor's office are more insulated from lobbyists and the interests they represent; they can both afford and are more inclined to say no. If the review done by gubernatorial staff is different from that done by legislative staff, it is because the two have dissimilar roles on these issues.

Public interest groups, along with many members of the statehouse press corps, portray government as being of the special interests, by the special interests, and for the special interests. John Gardner, the founding chairman of Common Cause, expressed the widespread feeling that "in the Special Interest State that we have forged, every well-organized interest 'owns a piece of the rock.' "[25] If special interests seem to dominate, one reason is that although people today vote less, they participate more.

They participate either directly or indirectly through narrow-gauge groups. Some years ago, a state senator in Texas, in responding to an interviewer's question declared: "They accuse me of being a tool of the special interests. And I plead guilty. Every son of a bitch in my district has one special interest or another." Contemporary America is fragmented into racial, ethnic, social, and interest groups. Ours is a truly pluralistic system, with thousands of groups each with a distinct sphere of interest. James Madison in *Federalist 10* wrote about interest groups or factions, as he called them. There was no way to control the "mischiefs of faction," according to Madison. For faction was "sown in the nature of man," and to restrict groups would be to restrict freedom.

When citizens do not hold views on a subject, as on so many issues before the legislature, they must rely for representation on elected public officials. Even when citizens are unconcerned, they have representatives who are disposed to be responsive. But their representatives cannot express views that are not held, so they must decide on other bases. Such bases are provided in part by interest groups, but they are also provided by a lawmaker's convictions, prior record, party affiliations, and relationships, and the merit of the case.

The interest group systems that operate in Washington, D.C., and in the state capitals are taken to task on several grounds. In the first place, it is argued, the proliferation and strength of special interests have led us to lose sight of a more general interest, that is, the public interest. The concept of the "public interest" has been examined and critiqued by pluralists for years. The arguments need not be repeated here. Suffice it to say that the notion of the public interest rests on the assumption that the citizens of this country—and of each of the fifty states—constitute homogeneous bodies with common interests that transcend narrow group concerns. Is there, in fact, such a unitary and discernible public interest beyond the various factional interests that are articulated? Perhaps, but its existence has yet to be persuasively demonstrated.

The public interest is not necessarily what Democrats say or what Republicans say. It does not necessarily agree with the agenda of environmentalists, nor with that of business or labor. The public interest does not necessarily correspond to the opinions uncovered by public opinion polls or focus groups. It is not exactly the cumulative interest of legislative districts.

The idea of the public interest lacks empirical reality. It is a myth, albeit a useful one. It needs to be taken into account by public officials; indeed, it should weigh heavily in the decisions they make. On the big issues, it does, to one degree or another, but it is mediated by other potent factors.

Governors, legislative leaders, and legislators actually believe in the concept "public interest," and they pay more than lip service to it. It is the legislative process itself that usually produces the nearest approximation to the public interest: as long as the process operates in deliberative fashion, involves negotiation and compromise, and is able to build greater consensus than would be possible under an alternative process.

Another criticism is that the interest group systems do not offer everyone equal access to the arena of decision making. Although no one is completely shut out, some citizens and some groups are relatively advantaged while others are relatively disadvantaged. Representation has broadened of late, but upper- and middle-class interests are still better represented. However, it is not easy to get people to agree on which specific groups come out ahead and which come out behind. In a survey of Kansas legislators, for instance, the members were asked to identify underrepresented groups and groups that were overrepresented in the legislative process. Three-quarters of them responded that, yes, some groups were underrepresented. Half of them named the "average citizen," and one out of five mentioned the poor. Three-fifths of the legislators said that, yes, some groups were overrepresented. But there was no agreement, the researchers found, on which specific groups and, hence, "no general perception that any particular interests are disproportionately influential."[26]

It is generally believed that interests with money also have influence. Money, no doubt, gives additional weight to people's preferences. It costs money to employ contract lobbyists with connections. Political campaigns require money. Most important, money is needed to maintain a basic organization and to mobilize grassroots support. Without some semblance of organization, an interest can hardly make its own case, although the case may be made for it.

Those who have money also have an edge, other things being equal. This is more likely to occur on the narrow, special-interest issues. Other things are less likely to be equal on broader issues, where legislators' values and district interests come into play. As a Colorado business lobbyist pointed out: "All the PAC money in the world will not persuade a legislator to go against his own or his district's interests."

Money is certainly an important resource in interest group politics, but it is by no means the only or the most important resource. Some monetary base is requisite, but beyond that it is only one commodity in the marketplace of competing interests. James Q. Wilson discusses the organizational representation and interest-bargaining system of today. This pluralistic system ensures that organized, affected parties will be heard and that their preferences will be taken into account. Unorganized groups were previously neglected by interest group politics, but that is no longer the case. Nowadays, the mobilization of new groups, grassroots appeals, and the role of the media have widened the arena of conflict, placed new issues on the agenda, and challenged traditional institutional arrangements.[27] What we have is neither a closed system nor one in which every participant is equal. Just how participants weigh in depends on who they are. It also depends on the particular issue in contest, the politics of the time, the people in government, and more immediate circumstances. It depends a lot on those who represent constituencies and make laws.

Lobbyists are an integral part of all this. Just as few people would think of appealing to the courts without the benefit of counsel, few people would consider dealing with government without the benefit of a lobbyist. Lobbyists have access and influence that the average citizen lacks because they are experienced, expert, and work full-time at the job. They naturally help the clients and causes they represent. That is what they are paid to do. But they also contribute to the legislative process in the states and to the pluralistic interest group system that prevails in the nation and works better than Americans think.

Notes

Chapter 1 (pages 1–14)

1. James Deakin, *The Lobbyists* (Washington, D.C.: Public Affairs Press, 1966), 54.
2. *Salt Lake Tribune,* July 1, 1990.
3. Deakin, *Lobbyists,* 34.
4. Jonathan Rauch, *Demosclerosis: The Silent Killer of American Government* (New York: Times Books, 1994), 38.
5. Jack L. Walker, "The Origin and Maintenance of Interest Groups in America," *American Political Science Review* 77 (June 1983): 390–406, and *Mobilizing Interest Groups in America* (Ann Arbor: University of Michigan Press, 1991).
6. See Martin Ryan Haley and James M. Kiss, "Larger Stakes in Statehouse Lobbying," *Harvard Business Review* 52 (January–February 1974): 125–135; and Ronald G. Shaiko, "More Bang for the Buck: The New Era of Full-Service Public Interest Organizations," in *Interest Groups Politics,* 3d ed., ed. Allan J. Cigler and Burdett A. Loomis (Washington, D.C.: CQ Press, 1991), 112–114.
7. Jeffrey M. Berry, *The Interest Group Society* (Boston: Little, Brown, 1984), and *The New Liberalism: The Rising Power of Citizen Groups* (Washington, D.C.: Brookings Institution Press, 1999).
8. Frank R. Baumgartner and Beth L. Leech, *Basic Interests: The Importance of Groups in Politics and in Political Science* (Princeton: Princeton University Press, 1998), 103.
9. Clive S. Thomas and Ronald Hrebenar, "Who's Got Clout? Interest Group Power in the States," *State Legislatures,* April 1999, 34.
10. Virginia Gray and David Lowery, "The World of Contract Lobbying," paper presented at the annual meeting of the Midwest Political Science Association, April 6–8, 1995, Chicago.
11. Daniel J. Elazar, Virginia Gray, and Wyman Spano, *Minnesota Politics and Government* (Lincoln: University of Nebraska Press, 1999), 55.
12. *Salt Lake Tribune,* July 1, 1990; Council of State Governments, *The Book of the States 1998–99* (Lexington, Ky.: 1998).
13. *Sacramento Bee,* July 16, 1995.
14. *The Book of the States 1998–99.*
15. Haley and Kiss, "Larger Stakes," 126.
16. Donald G. Herzberg and Jesse Unruh, *Essays on the State Legislative Process* (New York: Holt, Rinehart, and Winston, 1970), 18.

17. Kenneth G. Crawford, *The Pressure Boys: The Inside Story of Lobbying in America* (New York: Arno Press, 1974), 38.

18. Charles G. Bell and Charles M. Price, *California Government Today* (Homewood, Ill.: Dorsey Press, 1980), 132–133, 140–141; *Collier's,* August 18, 1949.

19. *St. Paul Pioneer Press,* special reprint, April 1992.

20. Collins Center for Public policy, transcript of discussion by members of press at session for Florida House of Representatives, December 11, 1995.

21. Pew Center for the People and the Press, "Politics, Morality, Entitlements Sap Confidence," Washington, D.C., 1997.

22. Christopher Schwarz, "Re-Modeling the Lobby," *State Government News,* May 1994, 31.

23. Baumgartner and Leech, *Basic Interests,* 89–90; Sidney Verba, Kay Lehman Schlozman, and Henry E. Brady, *Voice and Equality* (Cambridge: Harvard University Press, 1995): 62, 65–66, 69, 71, 84, 131.

24. Generally speaking, unless a book, journal, periodical, or newspaper is specifically cited, the information (but not my own analysis) comes from the lobbyists I interviewed. This is not the first time that a political scientist, in order to acquire sensitive information, has assured a respondent anonymity. Nor is it the first time that the reader will have to trust in a scholar's integrity to report and use interview information accurately.

25. Remarks to Pharmaceutical Manufacturers Association (currently the Pharmaceutical Research and Manufacturers of America), Washington, D.C., November 4, 1991.

26. Allan J. Cigler and Dwight C. Kiel, *The Changing Nature of Interest Group Politics in Kansas* (Topeka: Capitol Complex Center, University of Kansas, June 1988), 21–23; Anthony J. Nownes and Patricia Freeman, "Interest Group Activity in the States," paper presented at the annual meeting of the American Political Science Association, San Francisco, September 1996.

Chapter 2 (pages 15–40)

1. Sidney Verba, Kay Lehman Schlozman, and Henry E. Brady, *Voice and Equality,* (Cambridge: Harvard University Press, 1995), 56.

2. Jerry B. Briscoe and Charles G. Bell, "California Lobbyists—Preliminary Report," (Davis, Calif.: Institute of Government Affairs, University of California, Davis, n.d.). See also Allan J. Cigler and Dwight C. Kiel, *The Changing Nature of Interest Group Politics in Kansas,* (Topeka: Capitol Complex Center, University of Kansas, June 1988), 21.

3. Clive S. Thomas and Ronald J. Hrebenar, "Interest Groups in the States," in *Politics in the American States,* 5th ed., ed. Virginia Gray, Herbert Jacob, and Robert B. Albritton (Glenview, Ill.: Scott, Foresman/Little, Brown Higher Education, 1990), 148.

4. Lester W. Milbrath, *The Washington Lobbyists* (Chicago: Rand McNally, 1963), 8.

5. Clive S. Thomas and Ronald J. Hrebenar, "Interest Groups in the States,"

in *Politics in the American States: A Comparative Analysis*, 7th ed., ed. Virginia Gray, Russell L. Hanson, and Herbert Jacob (Washington, D.C.: CQ Press, 1999), 127–128.

6. Jeffrey M. Berry, *The New Liberalism: The Rising Power of Citizen Groups* (Washington, D.C.: Brookings Institution Press, 1999), 369, and Ken Kollman, *Outside Lobbying: Public Opinion and Interest Group Strategies* (Princeton: Princeton University Press, 1998), 51.

7. *Miami Herald*, May 19, 1991.

8. Harmon Zeigler and Michael A. Baer, *Lobbying: Interaction and Influence in American State Legislatures* (Belmont, Calif.: Wadsworth, 1969), 46–48.

9. Briscoe and Bell, "California Lobbyists."

10. John A. Straayer, *The Colorado General Assembly* (Niwot, Colo.: University Press of Colorado, 1990), 186. Also see Cigler and Kiel, *Interest Group Politics*, 21.

11. Thomas and Hrebenar, "Interest Groups in the States" (1999), 129.

12. Robert H. Salisbury, "Washington Lobbyists: A Collective Portrait," in *Interest Group Politics*, 2d ed., ed. Allan J. Cigler and Burdett A. Loomis (Washington, D.C.: CQ Press, 1986), 153.

13. Briscoe and Bell, "California Lobbyists."

14. *Baltimore Sun*, December 19, 1994.

15. *Miami Herald*, May 19, 1991.

16. Straayer, *Colorado General Assembly*, 184–185; Don W. Driggs and Leonard E. Goodall, *Nevada Politics and Government* (Lincoln: University of Nebraska Press, 1996), 148.

17. Mary Lynne Vellinga, "Legislating to Lobbying," *California Journal*, August 2000, 46, 50–52.

18. *Arkansas Democrat*, June 24, 1990.

19. Alan Ehrenhalt, "In Alabama Politics, the Teachers Are Sitting at the Head of the Class," *Governing*, December 1988, 22.

20. Seymour Lusterman, *Managing Business–State Government Relations* (New York: The Conference Board, 1983), 27.

21. Zeigler and Baer, *Lobbying*, 61.

22. Robert H. Salisbury et al., "Who You Know Versus What You Know: The Uses of Government Experience for Washington Lobbyists," *American Journal of Political Science* 33 (February 1989): 175–195.

23. Kim Rogers Burdick, "A Folklorist Looks at Lobbyists" (College of Urban Affairs, University of Delaware, May 1990), 22.

24. James Deakin, *The Lobbyists* (Washington, D.C.: Public Affairs Press, 1966), 154.

25. Ginger Gold, "Lobbyists: A Love Story" (New Brunswick, N.J.: Eagleton Institute of Politics, Rutgers University, May 14, 1990). Gold later on worked as a lobbyist for Nancy Becker Associates and is currently a lobbyist with the New Jersey Education Association.

26. *Washington Post*, March 17, 1995.

27. Cited in Zeigler and Baer, *Lobbying*, 77.

28. "Third House Holds Capitol Power," *Gainesville Sun*, December 7, 1987.

29. *New York Times*, February 7, 1997.

30. *The Sun* (Baltimore), March 13, 1983.

31. *Dallas Morning News,* March 29, 1987.

32. James Q. Wilson, *Political Organizations* (New York: Basic Books, 1973), 315.

Chapter 3 (pages 41–59)

1. Clive S. Thomas and Ronald J. Hrebenar, "Interest Groups in the States," in *Politics in the American States: A Comparative Analysis,* 7th ed., ed. Virginia Gray, Russell L. Hanson, and Herbert Jacob (Washington, D.C.: CQ Press, 1999), 127.

2. Public Affairs Council, *State Government Relations: Results of a Survey of Fifty-five Corporations* (Washington, D.C.: The Council, 1986), 16.

3. State Government Relations Institute, New Brunswick, New Jersey, July 12, 1990.

4. Seymour Lusterman, *Managing Business–State Government Relations* (New York: The Conference Board, 1983), 24. The Conference Board has not updated the Lusterman study.

5. Thomas J. Watson, Jr., *Father, Son and Co.* (New York: Bantam Books, 1990), 400.

6. Lusterman, *Managing Business–State Government Relations,* vii.

7. See Richard A. Armstrong, "Corporations and State Government Relations: An Overview," in *Leveraging State Government Relations,* ed. Wesley Pedersen (Washington, D.C.: Public Affairs Council, 1990), 9–12.

8. Lusterman, *Managing Business–State Government Relations,* 4.

9. James E. Post and Jennifer J. Griffin, *The State of Corporate Public Affairs: 1996 Survey* (Foundation for Public Affairs and Boston University School of Management, 1997).

10. H. C. Pittman, *Inside the Third House* (Austin, Texas: Eakin Press, 1992), 219.

11. Jeffrey M. Berry, *The New Liberalism: The Rising Power of Citizen Groups* (Washington, D.C.: Brookings Institution Press, 1999), 2, 3, 73, 369, 371; Ken Kollman, *Outside Lobbying: Public Opinion and Interest Group Strategies* (Princeton: Princeton University Press, 1998), 51.

12. Daniel J. Elazar, Virginia Gray, and Wyman Spano, *Minnesota Politics and Government* (Lincoln: University of Nebraska Press, 1999), 59.

13. John C. Berg, "Massachusetts: Citizen Power and Corporate Power," in *Interest Group Politics in the Northeastern States,* ed. Ronald J. Hrebenar and Clive S. Thomas (University Park: Pennsylvania State University Press, 1993), 187–188.

14. Charles S. Mack, *The Executive's Handbook of Trade and Business Associations* (Westport, Conn.: Quorum Books, 1991), 79–80.

15. Pittman, *Inside the Third House,* 219.

16. Marjorie R. Hershey, "Direct Action and the Abortion Issue: The Political Participation of Single-Issue Groups," in *Interest Group Politics,* 2d ed., ed. Allan J. Cigler and Burdett A. Loomis (Washington, D.C.: CQ Press, 1986), 28.

17. Kathy Beasley, "Low-Budget Lobbyists," *California Journal*, September 1988, 28.

18. Malcolm E. Jewell and Penny M. Miller, *The Kentucky Legislature* (Lexington: University Press of Kentucky, 1988), 264–266.

19. Lusterman, *Managing Business–State Government Relations*, 8.

20. The waivers guarantee that the rental company will not sue customers if a car is damaged and add $12 to $15 a day to the cost of renting a car.

21. See Robert H. Salisbury, "The Paradox of Interest Groups in Washington—More Groups, Less Clout," in *The New American Political System*, 2d ed., ed. Anthony King (Washington, D.C.: American Enterprise Institute Press, 1990), 224.

Chapter 4 (pages 60–78)

1. Robert H. Salisbury, "Putting Interests Back into Interest Groups," in *Interest Group Politics*, 3d ed., ed. Allan J. Cigler and Burdett Loomis (Washington, D.C.: CQ Press, 1991), 383–384.

2. Information provided by the National Conference of State Legislatures, January 27, 2000.

3. Council of State Governments, *Book of the States 1998–99* (Lexington, Kentucky: Council of State Governments, 1998), 105–109.

4. Kathleen Sylvester, "The Tobacco Industry Will Walk a Mile to Stop an Anti-Smoking Law," *Governing*, May 1989, 37.

5. Tom Watson, "Dale Florio: A Lobbyist's Middleman Who Helps Business Navigate State Capitol Halls," *Governing*, February 1989, 32–34, 37–38.

6. It was important to specify all the possible codes, otherwise something would be missed. A lobbyist for a telephone company, for example, would key the word "utilities" because such bills can also be amended to apply to telephone companies.

7. Randy Welch, "Lobbyists, Lobbyists All Over the Lot," *State Legislatures*, February 1989, 21.

8. This section on the Internet is based on Tom Price, *Creating a Digital Democracy: The Impact of the Internet on Public Policy-Making* (Washington, D.C.: Foundation for Public Affairs, 1999), 12–13.

9. A draft was provided to the author by Wade Hopping, a Florida lobbyist.

10. Harmon Zeigler and Michael A. Baer, *Lobbying: Interaction and Influence in American State Legislatures* (Belmont, Calif.: Wadsworth, 1969), 134.

11. Keith E. Hamm, Charles W. Wiggins, and Charles G. Bell. "Interest Group Involvement, Conflict, and Success in State Legislatures," paper delivered at the annual meeting of the American Political Science Association, Chicago, September 1–4, 1983, 16–17.

12. Kathleen Sylvester, "The Chastening of the Trial Lawyers," *Governing*, February 1991, 28.

13. James Q. Wilson, *Political Organizations* (New York: Basic Books, 1973), 333–334.

14. Ibid., 335–336.

15. Welch, "Lobbyists, Lobbyists," 19.

16. Robin Cincotta, internship paper, Eagleton Institute of Politics, Rutgers University, May 3, 1996.

17. Jennifer Getz, internship paper, Eagleton Institute of Politics, Rutgers University, May 8, 1998.

18. *New York Times,* April 8, 1996.

19. One of the reasons for the plight of the massage therapists was that they were listed in the yellow pages of the telephone book along with massage parlor therapists, a profession of a somewhat different order. In Iowa, for example, the former speaker (who was then working as a lobbyist) shepherded a bill through the house that would distinguish legitimate massage therapists from so-called massage parlors, which, the therapists claim, are little more than houses of prostitution. *Des Moines Sunday Register,* March 29, 1992.

Chapter 5 (pages 79–107)

1. Seymour Lusterman, *Managing Business–State Government Relations* (New York: The Conference Board, 1983), 51.

2. John C. Wahlke et al., *The Legislative System* (New York: Wiley, 1962), 331. Also Daniel J. Elazar, *American Federalism: A View from the States,* 2d ed. (New York: Crowell, 1972), and Alan Rosenthal and Maureen Moakley, eds., *The Political Life of the American States* (New York: Praeger, 1984).

3. Clive S. Thomas and Ronald J. Hrebenar, "Interest Groups in the States," in *Politics in the American States,* 7th ed., ed. Virginia Gray, Russell L. Hanson, and Herbert Jacob (Washington, D.C.: CQ Press, 1999), 137. An earlier classification of the strength of pressure groups ran along the same lines, with Florida and Texas "strong," California "moderately strong," and Colorado, Minnesota, and New Jersey "weak." Sarah McCally Morehouse, *State Politics, Parties and Policy* (New York: Holt, Rinehart, and Winston, 1981).

4. See Alan Rosenthal, *The Decline of Representative Democracy* (Washington, D.C.: CQ Press, 1998), 49–84.

5. See Rob Gurwitz, "California, Here We Come: The Professional Legislature and Its Discontents," *Governing,* August 1991, 64–69.

6. "Calendar" days run consecutively, while "legislative" days may exclude Saturdays and Sundays and those days during periods when the legislature is in recess.

7. *New York Times,* September 4, 1995.

8. Kay Lehman Schlozman and John T. Tierney, *Organized Interests and American Democracy* (New York: Harper and Row, 1986), 302–303.

9. Richard A. Armstrong, "Corporations and State Government Relations: An Overview," in *Leveraging State Government Relations,* ed. Wesley Pedersen (Washington, D.C.: Public Affairs Council, 1990), 8.

10. *Dallas Morning News,* March 29, 1987.

11. Bruce C. Wolpe and Bertram J. Levine, *Lobbying Congress: How the System Works,* 2d ed. (Washington, D.C.: Congressional Quarterly, 1996), 11.

12. William R. Bryant, Jr., *Quantum Politics: Greening State Legislatures for the New Millennium* (Kalamazoo: New Issues Press, 1993), 128, 138, 142.

13. Joseph Vitale, "Confessions of a Lobbyist," *New Jersey Monthly*, October 1990, 95.

14. Paul Hollrah, "Lobbying State Capitols: Rules for a New Game," *State Policy*, January 1984, 4.

15. John A. Straayer, *The Colorado General Assembly* (Niwot, Colo.: University Press of Colorado, 1990), 67–68.

16. Karl T. Kurtz, "The Old Statehouse, She Ain't What She Used to Be," National Conference of State Legislatures, July 26, 1993, photocopy, 16.

17. Phil Keisling, "Thrills, Spills and Bills," *Washington Monthly*, October 1990, 11–12.

18. John Powers, "Altered State: It's a New Era on Beacon Hill, with New Players, New Rules and New Attitudes," *Boston Globe Magazine*, June 16, 1996, 19.

19. Jeffrey L. Katz, "Sipping from the Cup of Corruption," *Governing*, November 1991, 27–28.

20. *New York Times*, December 14, 29, 1999, and April 11, 2000.

21. Alan Rosenthal, *Drawing the Line: Legislative Ethics in the States* (Lincoln: University of Nebraska Press, 1996), 125, 128.

22. Correspondence provided author by Representative Phyllis Kahn.

23. Other capitals have also seen a decline in the restaurant business with the increase in ethics regulations.

24. Christopher Schwarz, "Re-Modeling the Lobby," *State Government News*, May 1994, 28, 29.

25. H. C. Pittman, *Inside the Third House* (Austin, Texas: Eakin Press, 1992), 240.

26. Figures provided by New Jersey Election Law Enforcement Commission.

27. The survey, by Ken DeBow, is cited in Ronald J. Hrebenar and Ruth K. Scott, *Interest Group Politics in America*, 2d ed. (Englewood Cliffs, N.J.: Prentice-Hall, 1990), 255.

28. Thomas and Hrebenar, "Interest Groups in the States," 152.

29. Mary Lynn Vellinga, "Legislating to Lobbying," *California Journal*, August 2000, 50.

30. Harmon Zeigler and Michael A. Baer, *Lobbying: Interaction and Influence in American State Legislatures* (Belmont, Calif., Wadsworth, 1969), 67.

31. *Star-Tribune*, April 5, 1998.

32. Testimony of Katherine Burke Moore before the Subcommittee on Ethical Conduct, Minnesota Senate, April 7, 1998.

33. Interview with John Berglund, June 19, 1998.

34. Letter from Minnesota Governmental Relations Council to Senator Ember Junge, March 26, 1998, and April 3, 1998.

Chapter 6 (pages 108–124)

1. *New York Times*, February 7, 1997.

2. William K. Muir, Jr., *Legislature: California's School for Politics* (Chicago: University of Chicago Press, 1982), 21.

3. *Pensacola Journal*, June 26, 1990.

4. Jack D. Fleer, *North Carolina Government and Politics,* (Lincoln: University of Nebraska Press, 1999), p. 184.

5. *Arkansas Democrat,* June 24, 1990.

6. *St. Petersburg Times,* July 18, 1991.

7. Keith F. Girard, "Bruce Bereano," *Regardie's,* June 1987, 33; *The Sun* (Baltimore), March 13, 1983.

8. *New York Times,* July 23, 1989.

9. *Arkansas Democrat,* June 24, 1990.

10. *Miami Herald,* December 11, 1990.

11. Harmon Zeigler and Michael A. Baer, *Lobbying: Interaction and Influence in American State Legislatures* (Belmont, Calif.: Wadsworth, 1969), 102–103.

12. Gallup Organization, "The 1987 Gallup Survey of the New Jersey State Legislature" (Princeton, N.J.: Gallup, 1987), 17; Craig H. Grau, "Minnesota: Labor and Business in an Issue-Oriented State," in *Interest Group Politics in the Midwestern States,* ed. Ronald J. Hrebenar and Clive S. Thomas (Ames: Iowa State University Press, 1993), 145–164; Anthony J. Nownes, "Solicited Advice and Lobbyist Power: Evidence from Three American States," *Legislative Studies Quarterly* 24 (May 1999): 117–118.

13. We shall examine campaign activity and what money buys as separate issues in chapter 7, below.

14. Zeigler and Baer, *Lobbying,* 136.

15. Paul Hollrah, "Lobbying State Capitols: Rules for a New Game," *State Policy,* January 1984, 4.

16. *Arkansas Democrat,* June 24, 1990.

17. Berne Henderson, "Lobbyist's Ten Commandments," *Virginia Capitol Connections,* fall 1996, 17.

18. *St. Petersburg Times,* July 31, 1991.

19. *Pensacola Journal,* June 26, 1991.

20. Robert H. Salisbury, "The Paradox of Interest Groups in Washington—More Groups, Less Clout," in *The New American Political System,* 2d ed., ed. Anthony King (Washington, D.C.: American Enterprise Institute Press, 1990), 203–229.

21. Elizabeth A. Capell, "The Rich Get Richer: Term Limits and Interest Groups in California," undated paper, 4–5, 14.

Chapter 7 (pages 125–146)

1. Robert E. Hogen and Keith E. Hamm, "Variations in District-Level Campaign Spending in State Legislatures," in *Campaign Finance in State Legislative Elections,* ed. Joel A. Thompson and Gary F. Moncrief (Washington, D.C.: CQ Press, 1998), 62–63; Gary F. Moncrief, "Candidate Spending in State Legislative Races," ibid., 37–56.

2. Moncrief, "Candidate Spending," 56.

3. Anthony J. Nownes and Patricia Freeman, "Interest Group Activity in the States," paper presented at the annual meeting of the American Political Science

Association, San Francisco, September 1996, Table 11.

4. Sekhar Padmanabhan, "Calls for Cash: They Keep Coming . . . ," *California Journal,* August 1999, 24, 26.

5. *New York Times,* June 2, 1999.

6. Daniel J. Elazar, Virginia Gray, and Wyman Spano, *Minnesota Politics and Government* (Lincoln: University of Nebraska Press, 1999), 83.

7. Alan Rosenthal, *Drawing the Line: Legislative Ethics in the States* (Lincoln: University of Nebraska Press, 1996), 147–149.

8. Charles S. Mack, *The Executive's Handbook of Trade and Business Associations* (Westport, Conn.: Quorum Books, 1991), 89.

9. Public Affairs Council, *State Government Relations: Results of a Survey of Fifty-five Corporations* (Washington, D.C.: Public Affairs Council, 1986), 26; also Seymour Lusterman, *Managing Business–State Government Relations* (New York: The Conference Board, 1983), 10.

10. James E. Post and Jennifer J. Griffin, *The State of Corporate Public Affairs: 1996 Survey* (Foundation for Public Affairs and Boston University School of Management, 1997).

11. Charles S. Mack, *Lobbying and Government Relations: A Guide for Executives* (Westport, Conn.: Quorum Books, 1989), 155.

12. William E. Cassie and Joel A. Thompson, "Patterns of PAC Contributions to State Legislative Candidates," in Thompson and Moncrief, *State Finance in State Legislative Elections,* 158–184.

13. Daniel Carson, "The Cable TV Tangle: A New Industry Learns the Legislative Ropes," *California Journal,* June 1988, 252.

14. A. G. Block and Stephanie Carviello, "Putting on the Squeeze," *California Journal,* April 1987, 179.

15. See Michael J. Malbin and Thomas L. Gais, *The Day after Reform* (Albany: Rockefeller Institute Press, 1998).

16. Ed McCool, quoted in *Star-Ledger* (Newark, N.J.), June 29, 1990.

17. David B. Magleby and Candice J. Nelson, *The Money Chase: Congressional Campaign Finance Reform* (Washington, D.C.: Brookings Institution Press, 1990), 77–79; Kay Lehman Schlozman and John T. Tierney, *Organized Interests and American Democracy* (New York: Harper and Row, 1986), 256.

18. John R. Wright, "Contributions, Lobbying, and Committee Voting in the U.S. House of Representatives," *American Political Science Review* 84 (June 1990): 434.

19. Richard L. Hall and Frank W. Wayman, "Buying Time: Moneyed Interests and the Mobilization of Bias in Congressional Committees," *American Political Science Review* 84 (September 1990): 798, 814.

20. The following section is based in part on Rosenthal, *Drawing the Line,* 151–158.

21. Daniel M. Weintraub, "California Leaders Look at Limits," *State Legislatures* (July 1994), 41.

22. A. G. Block, "The Ethics Jungle," *California Journal,* April 1990, 177.

23. Kathleen Sylvester, "The Chastening of the Trial Lawyers," *Governing,* February 1991, 30.

24. Malbin and Gais, *The Day after Reform,* 89, 98–99.

25. Alan Ehrenhalt, "Political Pawns," *Governing,* July 2000, 20–24.

26. Nownes and Freeman, "Interest Group Activity in the States."

27. This section draws on Elizabeth Gerber, *The Populist Paradox: Interest Group Influence and the Promise of Direct Legislation* (Princeton: Princeton University Press, 1999).

28. Charles Mahtesian, "Grassroots Charade," *Governing,* November 1998, 41.

Chapter 8 (pages 147–177)

1. James Q. Wilson defines a coalition very differently—as "an enduring arrangement." And for him an alliance is a "temporary arrangement." *Political Organizations* (New York: Basic Books, 1973), 267, 277–278.

2. Jennifer Getz, "The GluckShaw Group: Three Case Studies," internship paper, Eagleton Institute of Politics, Rutgers University, May 8, 1998, 14–15.

3. Kathleen Sylvester, "The Chastening of the Trial Lawyers," *Governing,* February 1991, 29.

4. Charles S. Mack, *Lobbying and Government Relations: A Guide for Executives* (Westport, Conn.: Quorum Books, 1989), 118–119.

5. Christine Stearns, "Coalitions," internship paper, Eagleton Institute of Politics, Rutgers University, May 1996, 7.

6. Ibid., 6.

7. Ralph J. Marlart, "The Art of the Deal—Advanced Association Lobbying," unpublished paper, n.d.

8. Kenneth M. Goldstein, *Interest Groups, Lobbying, and Participation in America* (New York: Cambridge University Press, 1999), 3.

9. See Ken Kollman, *Outside Lobbying: Public Opinion and Interest Group Strategies* (Princeton: Princeton University Press, 1998), 3, 23, 57. Also Clive S. Thomas and Ronald J. Hrebenar, "Interest Groups in the States," in *Politics in the American States: A Comparative Analysis,* 7th ed., ed. Virginia Gray, Russell L. Hanson, and Herbert Jacob (Washington, D.C.: CQ Press, 1999), 125.

10. Quoted in Karl T. Kurtz, "The Old Statehouse, She Ain't What She Used to Be," National Conference of State Legislatures, July 26, 1993, photocopy, 13.

11. Kollman, *Outside Lobbying,* 4, 23.

12. Anthony J. Nownes and Patricia Freeman, "Interest Group Activity in the States," paper presented at the annual meeting of the American Political Science Association, San Francisco, September 1996.

13. James E. Post and Jennifer J. Griffin, *The State of Corporate Public Affairs: 1996 Survey* (Foundation for Public Affairs and Boston University School of Management, 1997).

14. Sidney Verba, Kay Lehman Schlozman, and Henry E. Brady, *Voice and Equality* (Cambridge: Harvard University Press, 1995), 56.

15. Elizabeth A. Capell, "The Rich Get Richer: Term Limits and Interest Groups in California," undated paper, 15.

16. *New York Times,* May 21, 2000.

17. Goldstein, *Interest Groups, Lobbying, and Participation,* 61; Laureen Lazarovici, "The Rise of the Wind-Makers," *California Journal,* June 1995, 17;

Tom Price, *Creating a Digital Democracy: The Impact of the Internet on Public Policy-Making* (Washington, D.C.: Foundation for Public Affairs, 1999), 12.

18. Kollman, *Outside Lobbying*, 52; Goldstein, *Interest Groups, Lobbying, and Participation in America*, 64.

19. Seymour Lusterman, *Managing Business–State Government Relations* (New York: Conference Board, 1983), 24, 28–31.

20. Richard A. Armstrong, "Corporations and State Government Relations: An Overview," in *Leveraging State Government Relations*, ed. Wesley Pedersen (Washington, D.C.: Public Affairs Council, 1990), 10–11.

21. Mack, *Lobbying and Government Relations*, 131–136.

22. Goldstein, *Interest Groups, Lobbying, and Participation*, 62.

23. Price, *Creating a Digital Democracy*, 9.

24. Kim Rogers Burdick, "A Folklorist Looks at Lobbyists," College of Urban Affairs, University of Delaware, unpublished paper, May 1990, 34–35.

25. *Star-Ledger*, May 18, 1990.

26. *New York Times*, May 25, 1997.

27. It should be noted that the questions asked were introduced by the statement: "Estimates are that legalized sports betting would generate an additional 50–150 million dollars in added revenues to fund utility and prescription drug assistance for senior citizens." This might help to explain the telephone survey's positive response rate.

28. See Ginger Gold, "Lobbyists: A Love Story," internship paper, Eagleton Institute of Politics, Rutgers University, May 14, 1990.

29. Janet B. Johnson and Joseph A. Pika, "Delaware: Friends and Neighbors Politics," in *Interest Group Politics in the Northeastern States*, ed. Ronald J. Hrebenar and Clive S. Thomas (University Park: Pennsylvania State University Press, 1993), 67–68.

30. Goldstein, *Interest Groups, Lobbying, and Participation*, 39, 45; Kollman, *Outside Lobbying*, 4; and Buddy Gill, "Credit Unions vs. Banks," *Campaigns and Elections*, July 1998, 42.

31. Kollman, *Outside Lobbying*, 8, 22, 23.

32. Mack, *Lobbying and Government Relations*, 145–150.

33. Nownes and Freeman, "Interest Group Activity in the States."

34. William P. Browne, "Issue Niches and the Limits of Interest Group Influence," in *Interest Group Politics*, 3d ed., ed. Allan J. Cigler and Burdett A. Loomis, (Washington, D.C.: CQ Press, 1991), 359.

35. Ibid.; also Jeffrey Berry, "The Rise of Citizen Groups," in *Civic Engagement in American Democracy*, ed. Theda Skocpol and Morris P. Fiorina (Washington, D.C.: Brookings Institution Press, 1999), 387.

36. Samuel K. Gove and James D. Nowlan, *Illinois Politics and Government* (Lincoln: University of Nebraska Press, 1996), 59.

37. Ann Bancroft, "The Consultant Is In," *California Journal*, September 1991, 411–412.

38. Kathleen Hall Jamieson, *Everything You Think You Know about Politics . . . And Why You're Wrong* (New York: Basic Books, 2000), 125–126, 128, 129.

39. Kollman, *Outside Lobbying*, 36.

40. Nownes and Freeman, "Interest Group Activity in the States."

41. *New York Times,* March 21, 1995.

42. *New York Times,* April 11, 2000.

Chapter 9 (pages 178–210)

1. Kay Lehman Schlozman and John T. Tierney, *Organized Interests and American Democracy* (New York: Harper and Row, 1986), 150. The authors conducted a survey in which they asked federal lobbyists about twenty-seven techniques of exercising influence.

2. Anthony J. Nownes and Patricia Freeman, "Interest Group Activity in the States," paper presented at the annual meeting of the American Political Science Association, San Francisco, September 1996.

3. *Arkansas Democrat,* June 24, 1990.

4. Loren Otis, "The Big Schmooze," *New Jersey Monthly,* August 1998, 69.

5. H. C. Pittman, *Inside the Third House* (Austin: Eakin Press, 1992), 255.

6. Ronald J. Hrebenar and Ruth K. Scott, *Interest Group Politics in America,* 2d ed. (Englewood Cliffs, N.J.: Prentice Hall, 1990), 96; also Harmon Zeigler and Michael A. Baer, *Lobbying: Interaction and Influence in American State Legislatures* (Belmont, Calif.: Wadsworth, 1969), 162.

7. Michael J. BeVier, *Politics Backstage: Inside the California Legislature* (Philadelphia: Temple University Press, 1979), 74–76.

8. Paul Hollrah, "Lobbying State Capitols: Rules for a New Game," *State Policy,* January 1984, 5.

9. Zeigler and Baer, *Lobbying,* 132–133.

10. Alan Ehrenhalt, "In Alabama Politics, the Teachers Are Sitting at the Head of the Class," *Governing,* December 1988, 27.

11. Max Boot, "Business Associations—Big Names, Less Clout," *California Journal,* October 1988, 454.

12. Michael Baer, "Legislative Lobbying: In Washington and the States," *Georgia Political Science Association Journal* 2 (1974): 26.

13. William K. Muir, Jr., *Legislature: California's School for Politics* (Chicago: University of Chicago Press, 1982), 19.

14. Frank R. Baumgartner, *Basic Interests: The Importance of Groups in Politics and Political Science* (Princeton: Princeton University Press, 1998), 140.

15. Ginger Gold, "Lobbyists: A Love Story," Eagleton Institute of Politics, Rutgers University, May 14, 1990.

16. Jeffery M. Berry, *The Interest Group Society* (Boston: Little, Brown, 1984), 121.

17. Alan Ehrenhalt, *The United States of Ambition* (New York: Times Books, 1991), 205.

18. Muir, *Legislature,* 19.

19. Randy Welch, "Lobbyists, Lobbyists All Over the Lot," *State Legislatures,* February 1989, 19.

20. State Government Relations Institute, New Brunswick, N.J., July 9, 1990.

21. Malcolm E. Jewell and Penny M. Miller, *The Kentucky Legislature: Two Decades of Change* (Lexington: University Press of Kentucky, 1988), 276.

22. James Richardson, *Willie Brown: A Biography* (Berkeley: University of California Press, 1996), 347–351. It should be noted that consumers were not satisfied with the "Napkin Deal" and a year later passed Proposition 103, which imposed drastic rollbacks on insurance companies.

Chapter 10 (pages 211–229)

1. Robert E. Wood, "Measuring Performance: The Critical Factors," in *Leveraging State Government Relations,* ed. Wesley Pedersen (Washington, D.C.: Public Affairs Council, 1990), 50–51.

2. Seymour Lusterman, *Managing Business–State Government Relations* (New York: The Conference Board, 1983), 13.

3. Frank R. Baumgartner and Beth L. Leech, *Basic Interest: The Importance of Groups in Politics and Political Science* (Princeton: Princeton University Press, 1998), 36–37.

4. Andrew Baker, MetPath (remarks at the State Government Relations' Institute, New Brunswick, N.J., July 12, 1990).

5. The survey is reported in Kay Lehman Schlozman and John T. Tierney, *Organized Interests and American Democracy* (New York: Harper and Row, 1986), 104.

6. Stanley Arnoff, quoted in *Columbus Dispatch,* February 2, 2000.

7. Rowland Stiteler, "Influence Peddling," *Florida Magazine, Orlando Sentinel,* May 29, 1988.

8. Gallup Organization, "The 1987 Gallup Survey of the New Jersey State Legislature" (Princeton, N.J.: Gallup, 1987).

9. Jack D. Fleer, *North Carolina Government and Politics* (Lincoln: University of Nebraska Press, 1994), 185.

10. James Q. Wilson, *Political Organizations* (New York: Basic Books, 1973), 308.

11. Stiteler, "Influence Peddling."

12. Harmon Zeigler and Michael A. Baer, *Lobbying: Interaction and Influence in American State Legislatures* (Belmont, Calif.: Wadsworth, 1969), 133.

13. W. John Moore, "Have Smarts, Will Travel," *National Journal,* November 28, 1987, 3023.

14. Schlozman and Tierney, *Organized Interests,* 314.

15. William J. Crotty et al., eds., *Representing Interests and Interest Group Representation* (Lanham, Md.: University Press of America, 1994), 29; Fleer, *North Carolina Government,* 183; Keith E. Hamm and Charles Wiggins, "Texas: The Transformation from Personal to Informational Lobbying," in *Interest Group Politics in the Southern States,* ed. Ronald J. Hrebenar and Clive S. Thomas (Tuscaloosa: University of Alabama Press, 1992), 174–175.

16. Clive S. Thomas and Ronald J. Hrebenar, "Interest Groups in the States," in *Politics in the American States: A Comparative Analysis,* 7th ed., ed. Virginia Gray, Russell L. Hanson, and Herbert Jacob (Washington, D.C.: CQ Press, 1999), 134–135.

17. Ibid., 132; also Clive S. Thomas and Ronald J. Hrebenar, "Who's Got Clout? Interest Group Power in the States," *State Legislatures,* April 1999, 31.

18. John A. Straayer, *The Colorado General Assembly* (Niwot: University Press of Colorado, 1990), 179–181.

19. Paul Brace and John A. Straayer, "Colorado: PACs, Political Candidates, and Conservatism," in *Interest Group Politics in the American West,* ed. Ronald J. Hrebenar and Clive S. Thomas (Salt Lake City: University of Utah Press, 1987), 56.

20. Robert H. Salisbury, "The Paradox of Interest Groups in Washington—More Groups, Less Clout," and Aaron Wildavsky, "A World of Difference—The Public Philosophies and Political Behaviors of Rival American Cultures," in *The New American Political System,* 2d ed., ed. Anthony King (Washington, D.C.: American Enterprise Institute 1990), 203–229 and 263–286.

21. Kathleen Sylvester, "The Tobacco Industry Will Walk a Mile to Stop an Anti-Smoking Law," *Governing,* May 1989, 34.

22. Janet B. Johnson and Joseph A. Pika, "Delaware: Friends and Neighbors Politics," in *Interest Group Politics in the Northeastern States,* ed. Ronald J. Hrebenar and Clive S. Thomas (University Park: Pennsylvania State University Press, 1993), 66.

23. Jeffrey M. Berry, *The New Liberalism: The Rising Power of Citizen Groups* (Washington, D.C.: Brookings Institution Press, 1999), 129.

24. Ibid., 391.

25. Quoted in *Common Cause,* "Lobbying Law Reform in the States," unpublished paper, September 1988, 2.

26. Allan J. Cigler and Dwight C. Kiel, *The Changing Nature of Interest Group Politics in Kansas* (Topeka: Capitol Complex Center, University of Kansas, June 1988), 16–18.

27. Wilson, *Political Organizations,* 345.

Selected Bibliography

The following books and articles are among the most informative scholarly and applied work on lobbying and lobbyists, with emphasis on the states.

Ambrosius, Margery M., and Susan Welch. "State Legislators' Perceptions of Business and Labor Interests." *Legislative Studies Quarterly* 13 (May 1988): 199–209.

Baumgartner, Frank R., and Beth L. Leech. *Basic Interests: The Importance of Groups in Politics and in Political Science.* Princeton: Princeton University Press, 1998.

Berg, John C. "Massachusetts Citizen Power and Corporate Power." In Hrebenar and Thomas, *Interest Group Politics in the Northeastern States,* 167–198.

Berman, David R. *Arizona Politics and Government: The Quest for Autonomy, Democracy, and Development.* Lincoln: University of Nebraska Press, 1998.

Berry, Jeffrey M. *The Interest Group Society.* 3d ed. N.Y.: Longman, 1997.

——— "The Rise of Citizen Groups." In Skocpol and Fiorina, 367–393.

——— *The New Liberalism: The Rising Power of Citizen Groups.* Washington, D.C.: Brookings Institution Press, 1999.

BeVier, Michael J. *Politics Backstage: Inside the California Legislature.* Philadelphia: Temple University Press, 1979.

Blair, Diane D. *Arkansas Politics and Government.* Lincoln: University of Nebraska Press, 1988.

Brisbin, Richard A., Jr., Robert Jay Dilger, Allan S. Hammock, and Christopher Z. Mooney. *West Virginia Politics and Government.* Lincoln: University of Nebraska Press, 1996.

Browne, William P. "Organized Interests and Their Issue Niches: A Search for Pluralism in a Policy Domain." *Journal of Politics* 52 (1990): 477–509.

Browne, William P., and Delbert J. Ringquist. "Michigan: Diversity and Professionalism in a Partisan Environment." In Hrebenar and Thomas, *Interest Group Politics in the Midwestern States,* 117–144.

Browne, William P., and Kenneth Verburg. *Michigan Politics and Government: Facing Change in a Complex State.* Lincoln: University of Nebraska Press, 1995.

Cassie, William E., and Joel A. Thompson. "Patterns of PAC Contributions to State Legislative Candidates." In Thompson and Moncrief, 158–184.

Chi, Keon S. "Lobbying in State Legislatures: Optimism for the Future." *State Trends Forecasts* 5 (September 1996): 1–41.

Cigler, Allan J., and Burdett A. Loomis. *Interest Group Politics,* 5th ed. Washington, D.C.: CQ Press, 1998.

Crawford, Kenneth Gale. *The Pressure Boys: The Inside Story of Lobbying in America.* New York: Arno Press, 1974.

Cronin, Thomas E., and Robert D. Loevy. *Colorado Politics and Government.* Lincoln: University of Nebraska Press, 1993.

Crotty, William J., Mildred A. Schwartz, and John C. Green, eds. *Representing Interests and Interest Group Representation.* Lanham, Md.: University Press of America, 1994.

Deakin, James. *The Lobbyists.* Washington, D.C.: Public Affairs Press, 1966.

Driggs, Don W., and Leonard E. Goodall. *Nevada Politics and Government.* Lincoln: University of Nebraska Press, 1996.

Ehrenhalt, Alan. *The United States of Ambition.* New York: Times Books, 1991.

———— "Political Pawns." *Governing,* July 2000, 20–24.

Elazar, Daniel J. *American Federalism: A View from the States,* 2d ed. New York: Crowell, 1972.

Elazar, Daniel J., Virginia Gray, and Wyman Spano. *Minnesota Politics and Government.* Lincoln: University of Nebraska Press, 1999.

Fiorina, Morris P. "A Dark Side of Civic Engagement." In Skocpol and Fiorina, 395–425.

Fleer, Jack D. *North Carolina Government and Politics.* Lincoln: University of Nebraska Press, 1999.

Gerber, Elizabeth. *The Populist Paradox: Interest Group Influence and the Promise of Direct Legislation.* Princeton: Princeton University Press, 1999.

Gierzynski, Anthony, and David A. Breaux. "The Financing Role of Parties." In Thompson and Moncrief, 185–205.

Goldstein, Kenneth M. *Interest Groups, Lobbying, and Participation in America.* New York: Cambridge University Press, 1999.

Gore, Samuel K., and James D. Nowlan. *Illinois Politics and Government.* Lincoln: University of Nebraska Press, 1996.

Graham, Cole Blease, Jr., and William V. Moore. *South Carolina Politics and Government.* Lincoln: University of Nebraska Press, 1994.

Grau, Craig H. "Minnesota: Labor and Business in an Issue-Oriented State." In Hrebenar and Thomas, *Interest Group Politics in the Midwestern States,* 145–164.

Gray, Virginia, and David Lowery. *Population Ecology of Interest Representation.* Ann Arbor: University of Michigan Press, 1996.

Hall, Richard L., and Frank W. Wayman. "Buying Time: Moneyed Interests and the Mobilization of Bias in Congressional Committees." *American Political Science Review* 84 (September 1990): 797–820.

Hayes, Michael T. *Lobbyists and Legislators.* New Brunswick, N.J.: Rutgers University Press, 1981.

Hogan, Robert E., and Keith E. Hamm. "Variations in District-Level Campaign Spending in State Legislatures." In Thompson and Moncrief, 59–79.

Hrebenar, Ronald J., and Clive S. Thomas, eds. *Interest Group Politics in the American West.* Salt Lake City: University of Utah Press, 1987.

———— *Interest Group Politics in the Midwestern States.* Ames: Iowa State University Press, 1993.

———— *Interest Group Politics in the Northeastern States.* University Park: Pennsylvania State University Press, 1993.

Hrebenar, Ronald J., and Ruth K. Scott. *Interest Group Politics in America,* 2d ed. Englewood Cliffs, N.J.: Prentice-Hall, 1990.

Jamieson, Kathleen Hall. *Everything You Think You Know about Politics . . . And Why You're Wrong.* New York: Basic Books, 2000.

Jewell, Malcolm E., and Penny M. Miller. *The Kentucky Legislature: Two Decades of Change.* Lexington: University Press of Kentucky, 1988.

Johnson, Janet B., and Joseph A. Pika. "Delaware: Friends and Neighbors Politics." In Hrebenar and Thomas, *Interest Group Politics in the Northeastern States,* 61–93.

King, Anthony, ed. *The New American Political System,* 2d ed. Washington, D.C.: American Enterprise Institute Press, 1990.

Kollman, Ken. *Outside Lobbying: Public Opinion and Interest Group Strategies.* Princeton: Princeton University Press, 1998.

Lupia, Arthur. "Shortcuts versus Encyclopedias: Inflation and Voting Behavior on California Insurance Reform Elections." *American Political Science Review* 88 (1994): 63–76.

Lusterman, Seymour. *Managing Business–State Government Relations.* New York: The Conference Board, 1983.

Mack, Charles S. *Lobbying and Government Relations: A Guide for Executives.* Westport, Conn.: Quorum Books, 1989.

——— *The Executive's Handbook of Trade and Business Associations.* Westport, Conn.: Quorum Books, 1991.

Magleby, David B., and Candice J. Nelson. *The Money Chase: Congressional Campaign Finance Reform.* Washington, D.C.: Brookings Institution Press, 1990.

Mahtesian, Charles. "Grassroots Charade." *Governing,* November 1998, 38–42.

Malbin, Michael J., and Thomas L. Gais. *The Day after Reform: Sobering Campaign Finance Lessons from the American States.* Albany: Rockefeller Institute Press, 1998.

Milbrath, Lester W. *The Washington Lobbyists.* Chicago: Rand McNally, 1963.

Miller, Penny M. *Kentucky Politics and Government: Do We Stand United?* Lincoln: University of Nebraska Press, 1994.

Moncrief, Gary F. "Candidate Spending in State Legislative Races." In Thompson and Moncrief, 37–58.

Morgan, David R., Robert E. England, and George G. Humphreys. *Oklahoma Politics and Policies: Governing the Sooner State.* Lincoln: University of Nebraska Press, 1991.

Muir, William K., Jr. *Legislature: California's School for Politics.* Chicago: University of Chicago Press, 1982.

Nownes, Anthony J. "Solicited Advice and Lobbyist Power: Evidence from Three American States." *Legislative Studies Quarterly* 24 (May 1999): 113–123.

Palmer, Kenneth T., G. Thomas Taylor, and Marcus A. LiBrizzi. *Maine Politics and Government.* Lincoln: University of Nebraska Press, 1992.

Pedeliski, Theodore B. "North Dakota: Constituency Coupling in a Moralistic Political Culture." In Hrebenar and Thomas, *Interest Group Politics in the Midwestern States,* 216–242.

Pedersen, Wesley, ed. *Leveraging State Government Relations.* Washington, D.C.: Public Affairs Council, 1990.

Pittman, H. C. *Inside the Third House.* Austin, Texas: Eakin Press, 1992.

Post, James E., and Jennifer J. Griffin. *The State of Corporate Public Affairs: 1996 Survey.* Washington, D.C.: Foundation for Public Affairs and Boston University School of Management, 1997.

Price, Tom. *Creating a Digital Democracy: The Impact of the Internet on Public Policy-Making.* Washington, D.C.: Foundation for Public Affairs, 1999.

Rauch, Jonathan. *Demosclerosis: The Silent Killer of American Government.* New York: Times Books, 1994.

Richardson, James. *Willie Brown: A Biography.* Berkeley: University of California Press, 1996.

Rosenthal, Alan. *Drawing the Line: Legislative Ethics in the States.* Lincoln: University of Nebraska Press, 1996.

———— The Decline of Representative Democracy. Washington, D.C.: CQ Press, 1998.

Salisbury, Robert H. "Interest Representation: The Dominance of Institutions." *American Political Science Review* 78 (March 1984): 64–76.

———— "Who Works With Who? Interest Group Alliances and Opposition." *American Political Science Review* 81 (December 1987): 1217–1233.

———— *Interested Institutions.* Pittsburgh: University of Pittsburgh Press, 1994.

Salisbury, Robert H., et al. "Who You Know Versus What You Know: The Uses of Government Experience for Washington Lobbyists." *American Journal of Political Science* 33 (February 1989): 175–195.

Schlozman, Kay Lehman, and John T. Tierney. *Organized Interests and American Democracy.* New York: Harper and Row, 1986.

Skocpol, Theda, and Morris P. Fiorina, eds. *Civic Engagement in American Democracy.* Washington: Brookings Institution Press, 1999.

Skocpol, Theda, and Morris P. Fiorina. "Making Sense of the Civic Engagement Debate." In Skocpol and Fiorina, 1–23.

Straayer, John A. *The Colorado General Assembly.* Niwot: University Press of Colorado, 1990.

Thomas, Clive S., and Ronald J. Hrebenar. "Interest Groups in the States." In *Politics in the American States: A Comparative Analysis,* 7th ed., edited by Virginia Gray, Russell L. Hanson, and Herbert Jacob, 113–143. Washington, D.C.: CQ Press, 1999.

———— "Who's Got Clout? Interest Group Power in the States." *State Legislature,* April 1999: 30–34.

Thompson, Joel A., and Gary F. Moncrief, eds. *Campaign Finance in State Legislative Elections.* Washington, D.C.: CQ Press, 1998.

Verba, Sidney, Kay Lehman Schlozman, and Henry E. Brady. *Voice and Equality.* Cambridge: Harvard University Press, 1995.

Walker, Jack L., Jr. "The Origin and Maintenance of Interest Groups in America." *American Political Science Review* 77 (June 1983): 390–406.

———— *Mobilizing Interest Groups in America.* Ann Arbor: University of Michigan Press, 1991.

Wilson, James Q. *Political Organizations.* New York: Basic Books, 1973.

Wolpe, Bruce C., and Bertram J. Levine. *Lobbying Congress: How the System Works.* Washington, D.C.: Congressional Quarterly, 1996.

Wright, John R. "Contributions, Lobbying, and Committee Voting in the U.S. House of Representatives." *American Political Science Review* 84 (June 1990): 417–438.

———— *Interest Groups in Congress: Lobbying, Contributions and Influence.* Needham, Mass.: Allyn and Bacon, 1996.

Zeigler, Harmon, and Michael A. Baer. *Lobbying: Interaction and Influence in American State Legislatures.* Belmont, Calif.: Wadsworth, 1969.

Index

Abortion, 60, 73, 165
Access, to legislators, 120–123, 137
Accountants, 47–48, 52–54, 63–64, 69, 75, 132, 162, 221
Acknowledgment, and relationship building, 114–115
Adams, Don, 39
Advertising, 23–25, 143–144, 171–177
Advice, and relationship building, 115–116
Advocacy advertising, 143–144, 175–177
Advocacy groups, 4, 32, 171–172
AFL-CIO, 142, 144
Akron Beacon Journal, 8
Alabama Education Association, 31
Alamo Rent A Car, 8–9, 57, 67, 76–77, 199, 216
Alaska, 5
Albertson's, 51–52
Albritton, Robert B., 232n.3
Alcohol, health effects of, 173
Alcoholic-beverage industry, 172–173, 198
    beer, 42, 44, 51, 57, 74–75, 148, 151, 158–159
    distilled spirits, 5, 42, 48, 51, 74–75
    wine, 45, 51, 74–75, 156, 158
Alcohol taxes, 5, 74–75, 148, 198
Allen, Bruce, 30
Allen, Woody, 180
Amendments, 86, 183, 194
American Cancer Society, 222
American Civil Liberties Union (ACLU), 19, 40
American Cyanamid, 157
American Express, 22, 199–200
American Heart Association, 222
American League of Lobbyists, 105
American Legislative Exchange Council, 112
American Lung Association, 222
American Medical Association, 222
American Petroleum Institute, 47, 131
American Society of Association Executives (ASEA), 104, 105
Anderson, Wendell, 31
Anheuser-Busch, 19, 44, 58, 74, 158–159, 166
Animal testing, 181, 197
Ankle injuries, 78
Antismoking legislation, 53, 64
Appreciation, and relationship building, 114–115
Architects, versus engineers, 59
ARCO, 131, 153
Arizona, 15, 98
Arkansas Society of Professional Lobbyists, 104
Armstrong, Richard A., 234n.7, 236n.9, 241n.20
Arnoff, Stanley, 243n.6
Askew, Reuben, 27
Assault firearms, 163–164

Associated Industries of Florida (AIF), 66, 141, 161, 183, 213
Association for Retarded Citizens, 73–74
Association lobbyists, 18
    career path of, 30–31
    styles of, 39
Association of California Tort Reform, 208
Association of Jewish Federations, 19
Association of Metropolitan Municipalities, 4
Associations
    bases of, 47–49
    growth of, 3
    leadership, 50
    membership in, 46
    membership issues, 50–52
    organization of, 46–53
"Astroturf" lobbying, 160
Athletics, and relationship building, 113–114
AT&T, 39, 44, 57, 152
Attitude, of lobbyists, 35
Audubon Society, 19, 25, 224
Austin, Texas, 23
Automobile manufacturers, 57
Avis, 57, 76–77, 199, 207

Babbitt, Bruce, 12
Baer, Michael A., 25–26, 33, 68, 116, 217, 233n.27, 235n.10, 237n.30, 238n.14, 242n.6, 242n.7, 242n.12, 243n.12
Baker, Andrew, 42, 243n.4
Bancroft, Ann, 241n.37
Barnes, Ben, 31, 89
Baumgartner, Frank R., 3, 232n.23, 242n.14, 243n.3, 245
Beare, Nikki, 32–33
Beasley, Kathy, 235n.17
Bechtel Power, 22
Becker, Nancy, 35, 168–169
Beer industry, 42, 44, 51, 57, 74–75, 148, 151, 158–159
Bell, Charles G., 232n.2, 232n.18, 233n.9, 233n.13, 235n.11
Bell, Clarence, 109
Bell, Joe, 109, 111
Bell, Sam, 27–28
Benefit passing, 100
Bentsen, Lloyd, 31
Bereano, Bruce, 29, 30, 39, 112–113, 166
Berg, John C., 234n.13, 245
Berglund, John, 106–107
Berry, Jeffrey M., 231n.7, 233n.6, 234n.11, 241n.35, 242n.16, 244n.23, 244n.24, 245

BeVier, Michael J., 242n.7, 245
Big Green, 146
Billboards, 201–202
Bills
    alternative bills, 182–183
    amendments, 86, 183, 194
    authorship, 184–185
    diversionary tactics, 186
    enactment of, 61
    introduction of, 61, 85, 86
    limitations on introduction, 85, 86
    lobbyist support for, 116
    policy significance of, 61
    posting, 187–188
    process for, 85–86, 186
    referral to committee, 187, 189
    sponsorship, 85, 184–185
    substitute bills, 183
    uncontested, 71–72
    veto of, 188
    withdrawing, 182
    wording of, 201
Bipartisan contributions, 130, 137–138
Block, A. G., 239n.14, 239n.22
"Bluebird" issues, 56
Boot, Max, 242n.11
Boston Globe, 131
Bottle bills, 65, 150, 159, 183, 198
Brace, Paul, 243n.19
Brady, Henry E., 232n.1, 232n.23, 240n.14
Brevity, 180
Briscoe, Jerry B., 232n.2, 233n.9, 233n.13
Brooks, Becky, 31
Brown, Dick, 39
Brown, Willie, 208
Browne, William P., 241n.34, 241n.35, 245
Bruno, Joseph, 98
Bryant, William R., Jr., 236n.12
Budget issues, 73–74
Bulger, William, 36–37
Bundling, 130, 135
Burdick, Kim Rogers, 233n.23, 241n.24
Bureaucracies, 12
Burke, William "Onions," 96
Busch, Augustus, 57
Bush, Jeb, 80
Business associations, 4, 44–45, 46–53
    and careerism of legislators, 82
    defensive position, 68
    electoral involvement, 140–141
    grassroots lobbying, 164
    and initiatives, 145–146
    and labor, 150–151
    offensive positive, 70
    policymaking, 49
    power of, 219–220
    role of lobbyists, 68
    and taxes, 74–75, 216
Buying votes, 137
Byrne, Brendan, 27, 102

Cable television industry, 35, 75, 168–169
California
    bills, 61
    business and trade associations, 46
    campaign costs, 126

car-rental companies, 77
coalition building, 153
county government, 69
ethics legislation, 97, 102, 104–105
fund-raisers, 101, 127
grassroots lobbying, 164–165
ideological groups, 19
initiatives, 145–146, 175
interest group impact, 79
interest group power, 7
legislative staff, 83, 190–191
legislative work schedule, 84
legislators, careerism, 81–82
legislators, lobbying, 12
legislature, power in, 89
legislature, professionalization of, 81
lobbyists, definition of, 15
lobbyists, former legislators as, 28
lobbyists, full-time versus part-time, 16
lobbyists, number registered, 5
lobbyists, women, 26
partisanship, 87
political action committees, 134
political culture, 79
public relations, 175
registration requirements, 104–105
research in, 11
Artie Samish, 7
tort reform, 208
California Association of Counties, 74
California Chamber of Commerce, 47, 208
California Chemical Council, 51
California Children's Lobby, 19, 49
California County Supervisors Association, 48
California Education Association, 132
California Healthcare Association, 22
California Medical Association, 208
California Society of Certified Public Accountants, 114
California Teachers Association, 145
California Trial Lawyers Association, 208
Campaign contributions, 116–117, 127
    absence of, 138–139
    to both parties, 130, 137–138
    impact of, 136–140
    independent expenditures, 143
    by individuals, 10
    by interest groups, 127, 144
    issue advocacy advertising, 143–144
    by lobbyists, 127–130
    role of, 139
    self-preservation contributions, 130
    by trade groups, 127, 144
Campaign finance, 8
    media coverage of, 8
    political action committees, 130–135
    politics and, 125–140
    public funding, 135–136
    reform, 65, 139–140
    regulation of, 135–136
Campaigns, 116–117, 125, 144
    congressional, 136–137
    costs of, 125–127
Capell, Elizabeth A., 238n.21, 240n.15
Capitol Club, Inc., 105
Capitol community, 91–107
    changes in, 94–99

effects of regulation, 94–102
lobbyist ethics, 102–107
social life, 91–94
Career paths, 26–33
Carlson, Arne, 87
Carpenter, Dennis, 10
Car-rental companies, 8–9, 22, 57, 67, 70, 76–77, 199, 207, 216
Carson, Daniel, 239n.13
Carviello, Stephanie, 239n.14
Casino Association of New Jersey, 165
Cassie, William E., 133, 245
Catholic Conference, 19
Cause groups
  initiating issues, 64
  lobbyists, 19–20, 32–33
  and media, 174
  membership issues, 51
  styles of lobbyists, 40
Cemeteries, 62
Century Council, 172–173
Certified public accountants (CPAs), 47–48, 52–54, 63–64, 69, 75, 132, 162, 221
Chase Manhattan, 199
Chemical industry, 220, 222–223
Children's Defense Fund, 48
Chiles, Lawton, 80
Christian Action Council, 19
Christian Coalition, 48
Cigler, Allan J., 231n.6, 232n.2, 232n.26, 233n.10, 234n.16, 235n.1, 241n.34, 241n.35, 244n.26, 246
Cincotta, Robin, 236n.16
Citicorp, 199
Cities
  interest groups for, 4–5
  state aid to, 75
Citizen groups, 2–3, 4, 19–20, 48, 108, 144. See also Public interest groups
  campaign contributions, 127
  and initiatives, 146
  and media, 171–172
  power of, 224
Clean Cable Coalition, 20
Clean Water Action Alliance, 48
Clean Water Enforcement Act (New Jersey), 88, 150
Clients
  and causes, 219–224
  lobbying of, 58–59
  relationships with, 41
Clyde's (Tallahassee), 94
Coalition building, 147–148
  coalition, defined, 148
  identification and recruitment of members, 148–149
  nature of coalitions, 149–152
  working together, 152–153
Coalition for Affordable Pharmaceuticals, 149
Coalition of Greater Minnesota Cities, 4
Coalition of New Jersey Sportsmen, 163–164
Collier's magazine, 7
Collision damage waivers, 57, 76–77, 199, 207
Colorado
  bills, 61, 116
  coalition building, 152
  grassroots lobbying, 167, 169
  initiatives, 146
  interest group impact, 79

legislation, caucus control of, 146
legislation, on education, 63
legislative environment, 82, 90
legislative staff, 83, 191
legislative work schedule, 84
legislators, women, 82
legislature, professionalization of, 81
lobbyists, for causes, 40
lobbyists, former legislators as, 28
lobbyists, influence of, 16
lobbyists, organization of, 104
lobbyists, women, 26
partisanship, 88
political culture, 79
research in, 11
socializing in capitol, 92
Colorado Association of Commerce and Industry, 162, 220
Colorado Common Cause, 32
Colorado Education Association, 31, 73, 93, 132, 142, 159–160, 164
Colorado League of Women Voters, 146
Colorado Open Space Council, 32
Colorado Public Interest Research Group (COPIRG), 32, 152, 169
Columbus Dispatch, 8
Commerce Clearing House, 66
Committee hearings, 189–190
Committees, 188–190
Common Cause, 19, 32, 40, 65, 146, 155, 171, 196, 224, 226
Communication, 17
Communications strategies, 171–177
Communications Workers of America (CWA), 141–142
Community involvement, 175
Company lobbyists. See Corporate lobbyists
Competition, 23–25, 72–73, 75–78
Compromise, 59, 203–210
  advantages for legislators, 207–208
  advantages for lobbyists, 204–207
  "Napkin Deal," 208
  working things out, 209–210
Concerned Women of America, 19
Conference Board, 43, 44–45, 54
Conflict of interests, 103
Congressional campaigns, 136–137
Connecticut
  capitol community, 91
  contracting lobbyists, 56
  public perceptions of lobbyists, 10
Connection, with legislators, 120–123
Consensus, 72
Conservative groups, 48
Constituent service, 114, 215–216
Constitution, U.S., 1
Consultants, 172
Consumer interests, 151, 199
Contract lobbyists, 18, 20
  career paths of, 26–30
  characteristics of, 33–34, 35
  client relationships, 41
  conflict of interests, 103
  defensive position, 68–69
  ethics, 102–103
  influence of, 212, 214
  styles of, 38–39

Contracting, 53–59
  benefits of, 53–55
  managing contract lobbyists, 55–59
Cookies, 73
Corning Inc., 42
Corona, Dolores "Dee," 31
Corporate culture, 42–45
Corporate lobbyists, 18–19, 31–32. *See also* State
    government relations
  characteristics of, 35
  culture of the corporation, 42–45
  grassroots lobbying, 157–158
  number of, 41
  styles of, 39
Council of Churches, 19
Council of State Governments, 65, 112
Council on Governmental Ethics Laws, 102
County associations, 49–50, 52, 162–163
County government lobbyists, 32, 69
County Supervisors Association of California, 63
Courant (Hartford, Connecticut), 10
Crabbing, 163
Crawford, Kenneth G., 7, 246
Credibility, of lobbyists, 117–118
Crematoriums, 62
Criterion (St. Paul), 95
Crotty, William J., 243n.15

Dairy industry, 175
Davidson, JoAnn, 95
Dayton Hudson, 57, 157–158, 165, 172
Deakin, James, 2, 231n.1, 233n.24, 246
DeBow, Ken, 237n.27
Defensive position, 68–69, 70–71, 85–86, 181–185
Delaware, 5, 222–223
Democrat-Farmer Labor Party, 31, 128
Dental assistants, 148, 202
Dentists, 72, 140, 202
Denturists, 146
Deregulation, 3, 56, 62
Deukmejian, George, 205
Devolution, 3
Direct initiative, 144–145
Direct legislation, 144
Direct lobbying, 147, 153, 178–179
  and committees, 188–190
  compromise, 203–210
  defense and offense, 181–185
  education and information, 194–203
  and leadership, 187–188
  and legislative staff, 190–191
  and legislators, 191–194
  principles of, 179–181
  targets of, 186–194
Direct Selling Association, 47
Disclosure requirements, 100, 135
Disney World, 100
Distilled Spirits Council of the U.S., Inc.
    (DISCUS), 75
Distilled spirits industry, 5, 42, 48, 51, 74–75
Doctors, lobbying style of, 167–168
Dog groomers, 78, 199
Doria, Joe, 89
Dow Chemical, 51
Driggs, Don W., 233n.16, 246
Drunken-driving standard, 105–107

Dry-cleaning businesses, 5
Dues-checkoff systems, 132
Dunbar, Pete, 21
Dunn, Michael, 156, 160
DuPont, 222–223
Dvorchak, Robert, 1–2

Eagle Forum, 19–20
Eagleton Poll, 9
Economic development, 199–200
Economy, of states, 79–80
Edgar, Jim, 88
Editorial boards, 174
Education
  as agenda item, 60
  on issues, 194–203
Education associations. *See* Teacher associations
Effectiveness, of lobbyists, 118
Ehrenhalt, Alan, 143, 233n.19, 242n.10, 242n.17,
    246
Elazar, Daniel J., 231n.11, 234n.12, 236n.2,
    239n.6, 246
Elected officials, lobbyist contact with, 15
Electricity deregulation, 56, 62
E-mail, in grassroots lobbying, 161–162, 170–171
Empathy, of lobbyists, 118–119
Encyclopedia of Associations, 3
Engineers, versus architects, 59
Enterprise Rent-A-Car, 22
Entertaining, 94, 99–100, 111–112
Environment, as agenda item, 60
Environmental Defense Fund, 19
Environmental Education League, 25
Environmental groups, 19, 64, 70, 141, 145,
    150–151, 201, 205
Equal Rights Amendment, 33
Ethics
  codes of, 105
  of contract lobbyists, 102–103
  legislation, 93, 96–99, 101
  of lobbyists, 102–107
Executive branch, 11–12
Experience, of lobbyists, 33–34
Experts, 197
Exxon, 22

Factions, 1, 227
Faegre & Benson, 22
Fairness issue, 198
Farm Bureau, 143–144
Farmworkers, 163
Featherstonbaugh, James, 38, 108
Federalist Papers, 1, 227
Federation of Advocates for Insurance Reform
    (FAIR), 148–149, 153
Finan, Richard, 95
Fiorina, Morris P., 241n.35, 246
First Amendment, 1
Fisher, Hank, 31
Fishing trips, 112
Fish Watch, 25
Fleer, Jack D., 238n.4, 243n.9, 243n.15, 246
Florida
  beer companies, 57
  bills, 61
  business and trade associations, 46, 141

campaign costs, 126
capital press corps, 8–9
capitol community, 91
car-rental companies, 8–9, 57, 70, 76–77, 199, 207, 216
fund-raisers, 128
grassroots lobbying, 165
ideological groups, 19–20
insurance legislation, 62–63
interest group impact, 79
legislative procedure, 86
legislative staff, 27, 83, 191
legislature, power in, 89
lobbyists, contracting, 56
lobbyists, former legislators as, 28, 110
lobbyists, legislative staff as, 27
lobbyists, registered, 5
lobbyists, registration requirements, 16
local government, 69
nonprofits, 19
partisanship, 87
political culture, 79
receptions, 92–93
regulation of lobbying, 100
relationship building, 119–120
research in, 11
retail food stores, 51–52
socializing in capitol, 91–92, 94
specialized practice, 25
taxes, 5, 28, 45, 70, 75, 165
Florida Business United, 141
Florida Impact, 19, 32
Florida League of Cities, 32, 48, 69
Florida League of Professional Lobbyists, 104, 213
Florio, Dale, 120
Florio, Jim, 64, 75, 87, 142, 205
Food Council, 149
Frank Fats (Sacramento), 94, 208
Fran O'Brien's (Annapolis), 95
Freeman, Patricia, 232n.26, 238n.3, 239n.26, 240n.12, 241n.33, 241n.40, 242n.2
French, John, 21
Friendships, 109
Fund-raisers, 93, 101, 127–128, 130

Gais, Thomas L., 239n.15, 239n.24
Galleria (Columbus), 95
Gallo, 45
Galvin's (St. Paul), 95
Gamblin, Briggs, 32
Gambling, 25, 76, 165
Gardner, John, 226
General Motors, 2
General Social Survey, 10
Generic drugs, 149
George R. Steffes, Inc., 22
Georgia, 69, 99
Gerber, Elizabeth, 240n.27, 246
Getz, Jennifer, 236n.17, 240n.2
Gifts
limits on, 97–99, 102
and relationship building, 112–113
Gill, Buddy, 241n.30
Girard, Keith F., 238n.7
Give-a-Vote-to-Every-Legislator (GAVEL), 146
Gold, Ginger, 35, 241n.28, 242n.15

Goldstein, Kenneth M., 240n.8, 240n.17, 241n.22, 241n.30, 246
Goodall, Leonard E., 233n.16
Good government. See Public interest groups
"Good ole boys," 38, 82
Gopher Grill (St. Paul), 95
Gove, Samuel K., 241n.36
Government. See also State government relations
as part of special interests, 226–227
petitioning, 1, 61–62
Governmental lobbyists, 19, 39–40
Governors, 11–12
initiating issues, 64
party of, 87
role in lobbying, 226
veto, 226
Grassroots lobbying, 144, 153–154
defined, 153
effectiveness of, 166–171
membership base for, 156
organization of, 158–160
potential of, 154–158
prevalence of, 154–155
techniques of, 160–165
"Grass-tops" programs, 162–163
Grau, Craig H., 238n.12
Gray, Virginia, 3, 231n.11, 232n.3, 233n.5, 234n.1, 234n.12, 236n.3, 239n.6, 240n.9, 243n.16, 243n.17, 246
Greater Miami Opera, 56, 114–115
Griffin, Jennifer J., 234n.9, 239n.10, 240n.13
Group practice, 21–22
Groups
growth of, 3
membership in, 10
power of, 219–224
Group to Alleviate Smoking in Public (GASP), 222
Guns for hire. See Contract lobbyists
Gurwitz, Rob, 236n.5

Haben, Culpepper, Dunbar & French, 21
Haben, Ralph, 21, 72, 109, 110, 120, 204
Hagan, Tom, 31
Haley, Martin Ryan, 231n.6, 231n.15
Hall, Richard L., 239n.19, 246
Hamm, Keith E., 68, 238n.1, 243n.15
Hanson, Russell L., 233n.5, 234n.1, 236n.3, 240n.9, 243n.16, 243n.17
Harrington, Kevin, 36–37
Harvard School of Public Health, 173
Hawaii, 5
Hays, Frank, Jr., 25
Hays, Frank, Sr., 25
Hazard Elimination through Local Participation (HELP) bill, 183
Health, as agenda item, 60
Health Care Industry Manufacturers' Association, 45
Health insurance, 75
Health Insurance Association of America, 149
Health organizations, 176
Hearings, 189–190
Helmet laws, 200
Henderson, Berne, 238n.17
Hershey, Marjorie R., 234n.16
Hertz, 57, 67, 76–77, 199, 207
Herzberg, Donald G., 231n.16

Hired guns. *See* Contract lobbyists
Hobby, William, 31
Hodes, Harold, 102, 213
Hogen, Robert E., 238n.1
Hollrah, Paul, 237n.14, 238n.15, 242n.8
Honoraria, 97, 113
Hopping, Wade, 196, 235n.9
Horse-racing industry, 52
Hospital Association, 149
Hrebenar, Ronald J., 3, 18, 41, 219, 232n.3,
    233n.11, 234n.13, 236n.3, 237n.27, 237n.28,
    238n.12, 240n.9, 241n.29, 242n.6, 243n.15,
    243n.16, 243n.17, 243n.19, 244n.22, 246,
    247
Hubbert, Paul, 31
Hughes, Richard, 27
Hunting trips, 100, 112, 119–120

IBM, 22, 43, 131, 220
Ideological groups, 19–20
Illinois, 5, 88
Impact, 19, 32
Incinerators, 62
Income, of lobbyists, 30
Incumbency, 126, 133–134
Independent expenditures, 143
Independent lobbyists. *See* Contract lobbyists
Indianapolis Star-News, 8
Indirect initiative, 144
Indirect lobbying, 147, 153
Industrial Paper, 157
Industry associations, 4
Information
    dispensing, 121
    functions of, 203
    providing to legislators, 195–197
    spin on, 200–203
    types of, 200
In-house lobbyists, 18, 20. *See also* Association
    lobbyists; Corporate lobbyists
Initiatives, 125, 144–146, 175
Inside strategies, 178–179, 217
Institute of Governmental Advocates, 105
Insurance industry, 27, 62–63, 64, 145, 152, 200,
    221
Intelligence, of lobbyists, 35
Interest groups
    campaign contributions, 127
    growth of, 2–6
    impact of, 79
    individuals represented by, 10
    monetary base of, 228
    per state, 3
    representation of, 225–229
    sanction through regulation, 78
    strength of, 79
Interests, 60, 71–78
    and budget, 73–74
    and competition, 75–78
    initiating issues, 64–65
    issues, 60–63
    monitoring issues, 65–71
    proliferation of, 2–6
    and taxes, 74–75
    tracking issues, 63–71
International Franchise Association, 47

Internet
    and grassroots lobbying, 170–171
    for tracking issues, 66
Interpersonal skills, 34
Iowa, 3
Isenberg, Phil, 28, 102
Issue advocacy advertising, 143–144, 175–177
Issues, 60–63
    arguing the merits, 197–200
    "bluebird" issues, 56
    budget issues, 73–74
    conflictual, 72
    consensual, 72
    costs of, 198–199
    education on, 194–203
    hot issues, 60–61
    initiating, 64–65
    monitoring, 65–71
    personalization of, 201–203
    spin on, 200–203
    tracking, 63–71

J. C. Penney, 157
Jacob, Herbert, 232n.3, 233n.5, 234n.1, 236n.3,
    240n.9, 243n.16, 243n.17
Jamieson, Kathleen Hall, 241n.38, 247
Jewell, Malcolm E., 235n.18, 242n.21, 247
Johnson, Bolley "Bo," 110
Johnson, Janet B., 241n.29, 244n.22, 246
Johnson & Johnson, 22, 44, 45, 149, 157, 164
Jones, Neal T. "Buddy," 39
Journalism, and lobbyists, 27
Judgment, of lobbyists, 119
Junge, Ember, 237n.34

Kahn, Phyllis, 99
Kansas, 12
Katz, Jeffrey L., 237n.19
Katz, Vera, 96
Kean, Thomas, 87
Keisling, Phil, 237n.17
Kelley, Rusty, 39
Kentucky, 3, 52
Key contacts, 162–163
Kiel, Dwight C., 232n.2, 232n.26, 233n.10, 244n.26
King, Anthony, 235n.21, 238n.20, 244n.20, 247
Kinship, 109
Kiss, James M., 231n.6, 231n.15
Kodak, 164
Kollman, Ken, 154, 233n.6, 234n.11, 240n.9,
    241n.18, 241n.30, 241n.31, 241n.39, 247
Kurtz, Karl T., 237n.16, 240n.10

Labeling, 201
Labor unions, 135, 141–142, 144
    and business interests, 150–151
    campaign contributions, 127
Lamm, Richard, 27
Lawyer-lobbying, 12, 22–23, 34–35
Lawyers, political action committees of, 132
Lazarovici, Laureen, 240n.17
Leadership, 50, 128, 187–188
League of Minnesota Cities, 4
League of Small Cities, 4
League of Women Voters, 19, 33
Leech, Beth L., 3, 232n.23, 243n.3, 245

Legal skills, of lobbyists, 34–35
Legislative advocates. *See* Lobbyists
Legislative agents. *See* Lobbyists
Legislative counsel. *See* Lobbyists
Legislative environment, 80–91
  legislative process, 83–86
  politics and power, 86–91
  structure of legislature, 80–83
Legislative norms, 89–90
Legislative party leaders, 128
Legislative process, 83–86, 186
Legislative staff, 6
  as former position of lobbyists, 109–110
  and lobbying, 83
  as lobbying target, 190–191
  as lobbyists, 27
Legislators
  access to, 120–123, 137
  assistance from lobbyists, 116
  careerism of, 81–82
  changes in, 96
  compromise and, 207–208
  connection with, 120–123
  constituents, 114, 215–216
  former legislators as lobbyists, 27–29, 36–37, 110
  full-time versus part-time, 81
  lifestyles of, 96
  as lobbying target, 191–194
  minorities as, 26, 82
  power of, 215–216
  recommending a lobbyist, 24
  socializing with lobbyists, 91–94, 111
  trust among, 89–90
  visiting with, 163–164
  women, 82
Legislatures. *See also* Bills
  agendas of, 60–63
  amendments, 86, 183, 194
  budget issues, 73–74
  changes in, 6
  committees, 188–190
  conflictual issues, 72
  consensual issues, 72
  house versus senate, 84
  leadership, and direct lobbying, 187–188
  lobbying in, 12
  party in control, 87–88
  power in, 6
  professional staffing, 6
  professionalization of, 80–81, 103–104
  special sessions, 84–85
  spreading legislation, 65
  structure of, 80–83
  term limits, 84, 89, 123–124, 146
  as training ground for lobbyists, 28
  women in, 82
  work schedules, 84
Letter writing, 161, 170
Levine, Bertram J., 236n.11
Levitan, Laurence, 36
Liberal groups, 48
Liquor industry, 5, 42, 48, 51, 74–75
Lobbying, 1, 10–12. *See also* Direct lobbying;
  Grassroots lobbying; Lobbying, business of
  changes in, 5–6
  of clients, 58–59

environment for, 6
growth of, 2–6
indirect, 147, 153
lawyer-lobbying, 12, 22–23, 34–35
  as occupation or career, 25–33
  professionalization of, 103–104
  regulation of, 104–105
  role of, 9–10
  styles and techniques of, 5–6
  team lobbying, 21–22, 56–58
  as threat to democracy, 9–10
Lobbying, business of, 20–25
  competition and the marketplace, 23–25
  types of practice, 20–23
Lobbyists, 1–2, 10–12, 15–16. *See also* Association
  lobbyists; Cause groups; Contracting; Contract
  lobbyists; Corporate lobbyists
  business of lobbying, 20–25
  campaign contributions, 127–130
  career paths of, 26–33
  characteristics of, 33–37
  clients and causes, 219–224
  and compromise, 204–207
  contact with elected officials, 15
  defined, 16–17
  entertaining by, 96–97
  ethics, 96–97, 102–107
  full-time versus part-time, 16
  income of, 30
  increase in, by state, 5
  individuals represented by, 10
  influence of, 16, 211–218
  knowledge of, 195–196
  legal definition of, 15–16
  with legislative experience, 24
  and legislators, 8–9
  and media, 7–9, 18, 173–174
  minorities as, 26
  need for, 4–5
  number of registered lobbyists, 5
  perceptions of, 6–10, 213
  power of, 123, 211–218
  presence of, 179
  recommended by legislators, 24
  registration of, 15–16
  representing interests, 225–229
  roles of, 17–18
  sanctions against, 105–107
  socializing with legislators, 91–94, 111
  styles of, 37–40
  support for bills, 116
  types of, 16–20
  why people lobby, 25–33
  women, 26, 29, 82
Local government lobbyists, 32, 69
Local government officials, 48, 63, 75
Lockyer, Bill, 137–138, 208
Loomis, Burdett A., 231n.6, 234n.16, 235n.1,
  241n.34, 241n.35, 246
Lorenzo's (Trenton), 94
Losses, 181, 205
Lowery, David, 3
Lusterman, Seymour, 233n.20, 234n.4, 234n.6,
  234n.8, 235n.19, 236n.1, 239n.9, 241n.19,
  243n.2, 247
Lynch, John, 143

Mack, Charles S., 160, 234n.14, 239n.8, 239n.11, 240n.4, 241n.32, 247
Madison, James, 1, 227
Magleby, David B., 239n.17, 247
Mahtesian, Charles, 240n.28, 247
Maine, 5, 135–136, 219
Malbin, Michael J., 239n.15, 239n.24, 247
Mammenga, Gene, 31
Marcus, Alan, 90
Margolis, Gwen, 88
Marketing, 23–25
Marketing Institute, 47
Marlart, Ralph J., 240n.7
Martin, John, 207
Martinez, Bob, 21, 56, 88
Marty, John, 106
Maryland
　capital culture, 100
　county associations, 52
　initiating issues, 64
　legislative staff as lobbyists, 27
　research in, 11
　sales taxes, 75
Massachusetts
　legislators, 96
　political action committees, 131
　state cookie, 73
　taxes, 75
Massage therapists, 236n.19
MASSPIRG, 48
McCool, Ed, 239n.16
McCormack, Edward "Knocko," 96
McCue, Willie, 119–120
MCI, 57
McKeithen, Lex, 37
Media
　campaign finance coverage, 8
　and cause groups, 174
　and citizen groups, 171–172
　and contract lobbyists, 18
　generating support with, 171–177
　negative view of lobbyists, 7–9
　press briefings and conferences, 174
　and public interest groups, 173
　and public perception of lobbyists, 9, 173–174
Medicaid, 73, 150
Merits, arguing, 197–200
MetPath, 42, 44
Michigan, 5, 81
Milbrath, Lester W., 232n.4, 247
Miller, Penny M., 235n.18, 242n.21, 247
Mills, Jon, 110
Minneapolis, Minnesota, 4, 22
Minneapolis Star, 27
Minnesota
　bills, 61, 116
　citizen groups, 48
　city representation, 4, 22
　coalition building, 152
　community involvement, 175
　contributions to parties, 128–129
　environmental issues, 205
　ethics legislation, 98–99, 101, 105–107
　fund-raisers, 127–128
　governor, 87
　grassroots lobbying, 165

　initiating issues, 64
　interest group impact, 79
　law-lobbying, 22
　legislative environment, 90–91
　legislators, careerism of, 82
　legislature, power in, 89
　lobbyists, contracting, 56
　lobbyists, former legislators as, 28
　lobbyists, registered, 5
　lobbyists, support for bills, 116
　media coverage of campaign financing, 8
　oil companies, 70
　partisanship, 87–88
　political action committees, 131
　political culture, 79
　research in, 11
　socializing in capitol, 92
Minnesota Alliance for Progressive Action, 48
Minnesota Chamber of Commerce, 47
Minnesota Education Association, 31, 159–160
Minnesota Family Council, 48
Minnesota Governmental Relations Council, 104, 105–107
Minnesota Licensed Beverage Association, 106
Minorities
　as legislators, 26, 82
　as lobbyists, 26
Minute Women, 20
Moakley, Maureen, 236n.2
Model Franchise Investment Law, 65
Model laws, 65
Moncrief, Gary, 126, 239n.12, 247
Mondale, Walter, 31
Moore, Katherine Burke, 237n.32
Moore, W. John, 243n.13
Morehouse, Sarah McCally, 236n.3
Mortgage bankers, 64
Mothers Against Drunk Driving, 20
Motorcycle helmets, 200
Muir, William K., Jr., 237n.2, 242n.13, 242n.18, 247
MultiState Associates, 55
Municipal associations, 49–50, 52, 162–163
Municipal Legislative Commission, 4
Mutscher, Gus, 89

Nader, Ralph, 2, 19, 48
Nancy Becker Associates, 21
"Napkin Deal," 208
National Abortion Rights Action League (NARAL), 19, 40
National Conference of State Legislatures, 65, 112
National Education Association, 48
National Organization of Women, 19
National Pharmaceutical Alliance, 149
National Rifle Association, 48, 163–164
Natural gas industry, 151
Negotiation, 203–210
Nelson, Candice J., 239n.17
Nevada, 3, 28
Newark Evening News, 27
New Federalism, 22
New Jersey
　beach pollution, 55, 198
　business interests, 183
　cable television industry, 35
　car-rental companies, 207

Clean Water Enforcement Act, 88
coalition building, 148–149, 150–151, 153
environmental groups, 141, 205
ethics legislation, 64, 166
grassroots lobbying, 164, 165
initiating issues, 64
insurance rates, 64
interest group impact, 79
legislative process, 85–86
legislative staff, 83, 191
legislative work schedule, 84
lobbyists, contracting, 55
lobbyists, former legislators as, 28
lobbyists, influence of, 16
lobbyists, perceptions of, 9
lobbyists, support for bills, 116
municipal associations, 52
nonprofits, 19
partisanship, 86–87
political culture, 79
preemptive legislation, 64
regulation of lobbying, 100
research in, 11
self-service gas stations, 53
socializing in capitol, 92
taxes, 74, 75, 143, 168–169, 202, 216
trial lawyers, 129
union involvement in elections, 141–142
New Jersey Animal Rights Alliance, 32
New Jersey Association for Retarded Citizens,
   73–74
New Jersey Association of Retail Druggists, 149
New Jersey Business and Industry Association, 45,
   47, 53, 62, 64, 87, 164, 183, 213
New Jersey Cable Television Association, 168–169
New Jersey Chamber of Commerce, 45
New Jersey Council of Chain Drug Stores, 149
New Jersey Department of Health, 72
New Jersey Education Association, 31, 48, 130,
   132, 142–143, 159–160, 163–164, 176–177,
   213, 223
New Jersey Environmental Federation, 150
New Jersey Gasoline Retailers Association, 76, 199
New Jersey Health Products Company Group, 45
New Jersey Industrial Union Council, 142
New Jersey League of Municipalities, 64, 74, 166
New Jersey Petroleum Council, 76
New Jersey PIRG, 48, 150, 151, 158, 164, 174,
   196–197, 224
New Jersey Retail Merchants Association, 151
New Jersey State Chamber of Commerce train
   trip, 93
New Mexico, 5, 92
New York
   advocacy advertising, 176
   ethics legislation, 98
   grassroots lobbying, 164
   number of registered lobbyists, 5
   power in legislature, 88–89
   tobacco taxes, 222
New York Times, 114, 222
Nonprofits, 19–20
North American Securities Administrators Associa-
   tion, 65
North Carolina, 110, 214, 219, 222
Northeast Utilities, 56.

North Metro Mayors Association, 4
Nowlan, James D., 241n.36
Nownes, Anthony J., 232n.26, 238n.3, 238n.12,
   239n.26, 240n.12, 241n.33, 241n.40, 242n.2,
   247

Occupational therapists, 199, 201
Offensive position, 70, 85–86, 181–185
Ohio
   capitol community, 95
   lobbyists, former legislators as, 28
   lobbyists, influence of, 16
   lobbyists, registered, 5
   partisanship, 87
   professionalization of legislature, 81
Ohio Chamber of Commerce, 66
Oil industry, 25, 52, 57, 70, 76, 131, 153, 156,
   199, 221–222
Oil spills, 153
O'Neill, Tip, 108
Ophthalmologists, 77–78, 140, 199, 216
Optometrists, 77–78, 140, 199, 200, 216
Oregon, 92, 96, 105
Orthopedic surgeons, versus podiatrists, 78
Otis, Loren, 242n.4
Outside strategies, 178, 217–218
Outsourcing. *See* Contracting

PACs (political action committees), 128, 130–135
Padmanabhan, Sekhar, 239n.4
Parental leave, 45
Pari-mutuel industry, 25, 76
Partisanship, 86–88, 134
Pataki, George, 176
Patterson, Samuel C., 37
Pedersen, Wesley, 234n.7, 236n.9, 241n.20, 248
Pennsylvania, 7, 15, 219
Pennzoil, 57
Pensacola Journal, 9
Pensions, for police officers, 165
Perpich, Rudy, 87
Persistence, 180
Personal relationship. *See* Relationship building
Persuasion, 17–18, 191–194
Petitioning government, 1, 61–62
Petroleum Club (Austin), 94
Pew Research Center for the People and the Press,
   9–10
Pharmaceutical industry, 31–32, 70, 73, 149, 150,
   151, 200
Pharmaceutical Research and Manufacturers of
   America, 31–32, 45, 181, 190
Philip Morris, 98
Phillips, Dolores, 32
Physician assistants, 200
Physicians, lobbying style of, 167–168
Pika, Joseph A., 241n.29, 244n.22
Pineland preservation area, 102
PIRGs (public interest research groups), 19, 40, 48,
   49, 50
Pittman, H. C., 234n.10, 234n.15, 237n.25,
   242n.5, 248
Plastic container taxes, 202
Playtex, 55, 198
Pluralism, 79, 227
Podiatrists, versus orthopedic surgeons, 78

Pogo, 10
Police Benevolent Association, 148–149, 167
Police pensions, 165
Political action committees (PACs), 128, 130–135
Political activity, 10
Political culture, 79
Political parties
    bipartisan contributions, 130, 137–138
    campaign finance regulation, 135
    control of legislature, 87–88
    legislative party leaders, 128
    partisanship, 86–87
    party of governors, 87
Political Reform Act of 1974 (California), 97
Politics, 125
    and campaign finance, 125–140
    electoral involvement of interest groups, 140–144
    initiatives, 144–146
    internal politics, 49–53
    and power, 86–91
Polls, 164–165
Polystyrene, 64
Popular referenda, 144
Post, James E., 234n.9, 239n.10, 240n.13, 248
Power
    of business associations, 219–220
    of citizen groups, 224
    of groups, 219–224
    of legislators, 215–216
    of lobbyists, 123, 211–218
    and politics, 86–91
    of teacher associations, 219, 223
Power, John, 237n.18
Preemptive legislation, 64
Press briefs and conferences, 174
Price, Charles M., 232n.18
Price, Tom, 235n.8, 240n.17, 241n.23, 248
Princeton Public Affairs, 182
Prioritizing, 67–68, 181
Procter & Gamble, 66
Product liability, 57, 87–88, 148–149, 150
Pro Family Forum, 20
Professional advocates. See Lobbyists
Profile (Denver), 94, 95
Public affairs consultants. See Lobbyists
Public Affairs Council, 55, 104, 131
Public Affairs Information, 66
Public Citizen, 19
Public funding of campaigns, 135–136
Public health and welfare, 199
Public interest, 227–228
Public interest groups, 2–3, 19–20. See also Citizen
    groups
    associational base, 48
    and coalition building, 152
    and compromise, 206–207
    and government as part of special interests,
        226–227
    and grassroots lobbying, 158, 169
    and media, 173
    providing information, 196–197
Public interest lobbyists, 40
Public interest research groups (PIRGs), 19, 40, 48,
    49, 50
Public opinion polls, 164–165
Public policy rhetoric, 197–200

Public relations, 171–177
Public Service Electric and Gas Company, 53
Public Strategies, 213
Public utilities, 62, 150, 151, 157

Quality Education Act (New Jersey), 143

Rabe, Eric, 66
Racine's (Denver), 94
Range Association of Municipalities and Schools, 4
Rauch, Jonathan, 231n.4
Reagan, Ronald, 22, 26–27
Receptions, 92–93, 98, 101
Recognition, and relationship building, 114–115
Recycling, 65, 159, 183, 198
Referenda, 144. See also Initiatives
Referrals, 24
Regulation, 62–63
    of campaign finance, 135–136
    of corporations, 42
    deregulation, 3, 56, 62
    effects on capitol community, 99–102
    of lobbying, 104–105
    as state sanction of interest groups, 78
    state versus local, 64
Relationship building, 108–109
    advantages of, 119–123
    and credibility, 117–118
    cultivating relationships, 111–117
    and effectiveness, 118
    effects of term limits, 123–124
    and empathy, 118–119
    and good judgment, 119
    and longevity, 117
    natural development of relationships, 109–111
    and reliability, 118
    testing relationships, 117–119
Reliability, of lobbyists, 118
Representation, 225–229
Reputational analysis, 219
Restaurant Association, 149
Restaurant industry, 99, 198
Restaurants, and lobbyist entertaining, 94
Retail food association, 62
Rhetoric, 197–200
Richardson, James, 242n.22, 248
Riffe, Vern, 95
"Right to know" bill, 183, 223
Right to Life League, 19
Right to petition, 1, 61–62
Rose Garden syndrome, 43
Rosenthal, Alan, 236n.2, 236n.4, 237n.21, 239n.7,
    239n.20, 248

St. Johns River (Florida), 215–216
St. Paul Pioneer Press, 8
Sales tax, on services, 45, 75
Salisbury, Robert H., 26, 34, 60, 121, 235n.21,
    244n.20, 248
Samish, Artie, 7, 38
Santa Fe, New Mexico, 5
Savings and loan industry, 31
Scandals, 7, 97–98, 99–100
Schlozman, Kay Lehman, 232n.1, 232n.23,
    236n.8, 239n.17, 240n.14, 242n.1, 243n.5,
    243n.14, 248

School Boards Association, 149
Schwarz, Christopher, 232n.22, 237n.24
Scott, Ruth K., 237n.27, 242n.6
Seagrams, 42
Seat belt laws, 57, 183
Sea World, 180
Secondhand smoking, 222
Self-preservation contributions, 130
Self-service gas stations, 53, 199
Shaiko, Ronald G., 231n.6
Shebel, Jon, 213
Shell Oil, 153
Sierra Club, 19, 49, 224
Silver, Sheldon, 88
Single-issue groups, 2–3, 4, 19–20
Sin taxes, 74–75
Sittig, Michael, 32
Skelding, Jack, 109
Skocpol, Theda, 241n.35, 248
Small businesses, 44
Smoking, 53, 64, 198, 222
Socializing, of legislators and lobbyists, 91–94, 111
Society of Certified Public Accountants, 149
Soft drink tax, 165
Sole practitioners, 20–21
Solid waste, 151
South Carolina, 12, 98
Southern Pacific Railroad, 7
Spano, Wyman, 231n.11, 234n.12, 239n.6
Spearman, Guy, 180, 215
Specialization, 25, 56–57
Special sessions, 84–85
Spin, 200–203
Sponsorship, 85, 184–185
Sporting events, 94, 113–114
Squibb, 149
Staff. See Legislative staff
Standard Oil, 7
State counsels. See Lobbyists
State economy, 79–80
State Government Affairs Council (SGAC), 55, 104
State government lobbyists, 31
State government relations, 41–42
    contracting out, 53–59
    culture of corporations, 42–45
    organization of associations, 46–53
State governmental relations professionals. See
    Lobbyists
State interest groups, 3–4
State Legislative Leaders Foundation, 112
Stateside Associates, 55
Statistics, 200
Stearns, Christine, 240n.5, 240n.6
Steel, Hector & Davis, 22
Steffes, George R., 22
Stern, Bob, 102
Sterns, Joel, 22
Stiteler, Rowland, 243n.7, 243n.11
Straayer, John A., 233n.10, 233n.16, 237n.15,
    243n.18, 243n.19, 248
Subcontracting, 24
Submitted referenda, 144
Success Group, 21
Sun Company, 79, 91
Superfund, 152
Support, 147

coalition building, 147–153
grassroots mobilization, 153–171
media, public relations, and advertising, 171–177
Sylvester, Kathleen, 235n.4, 235n.12, 239n.23,
    240n.3, 244n.21

Tampa Tribune, 8–9
Tampon applicators, 55, 198
Taxes, 73, 74–75, 216
    on alcohol, 5, 74–75, 148, 193
    breaks and exemptions, 75
    and businesses, 74–75, 216
    on plastic containers, 202
    sales taxes on services, 45, 75
    sin taxes, 74–75
    on soft drinks, 165
    on tobacco, 74–75, 198, 222
Teacher associations
    advocacy advertising, 176–177
    associational base of, 48
    and budget, 73
    career path of lobbyists, 31
    electoral involvement, 142–143
    grassroots lobbying, 144, 159–160
    internal politics, 50, 51
    and legislative agenda, 63
    and party control of legislature, 88
    political action committees, 132–133
    power of, 219, 223
    as target of lobbyists, 191–192
Team lobbying, 21–22, 56–58
Telephone calls, in grassroots lobbying, 161
Term limits, 84, 89, 123–124, 146
Texaco, 57, 131
Texas
    aid to cities, 75
    bills, 61
    "bluebird" issues, 56
    business and trade associations, 46–47, 150
    competition in lobbying, 23
    ethics legislation, 100
    interest group impact, 79
    law-lobbying, 22–23
    legislative process, 85
    legislative staff, 83
    legislative work schedule, 84
    legislature, power in, 89
    lobbyists, contracting, 56
    lobbyists, examples of, 39
    lobbyists, former legislators as, 28
    lobbyists, legislative staff as, 27
    lobbyists, organization of, 104
    lobbyists, registered, 5
    lobbyists, women, 26
    local government, 69
    partisanship, 87
    political culture, 79
    power of groups, 219
    range of interests represented, 17
    research in, 11
    socializing in capitol, 92, 94
    taxes, 75
    team lobbying, 57–58
    term limits, 84
    trial lawyers, 76, 140, 149
Texas Civil Justice League, 57, 140, 161

Texas Consumers Union, 40
Texas Municipal League, 39–40, 48, 52, 63, 69, 75, 156–157, 162–163
Texas Society of Association Executives, 46–47
Texas State Teachers Association, 31, 132–133, 142, 160
Texas Trial Lawyers Association, 140
Third house, 2
Thomas, Clive S., 3, 18, 41, 219, 232n.3, 233n.11, 234n.13, 236n.3, 237n.28, 238n.12, 240n.9, 241n.29, 243n.15, 243n.16, 243n.17, 243n.19, 244n.22, 248
Thompson, Joel A., 133, 238n.1
3M, 22
Tierney, John T., 236n.8, 239n.17, 242n.1, 243n.5, 243n.14
Tobacco industry, 25, 53, 64, 68, 70, 98, 123, 148, 150, 163, 198, 222
Tobacco Institute, 123
Tobacco taxes, 74–75, 198, 222
Tocqueville, Alexis de, 2
Top-down strategy, 187
Tort reform, 57, 87–88, 150, 208
Townsend, Tommy, 30–31
Toys, hazardous, 202–203
Tracking services, 66
Trade associations, 4, 44–45, 46–53, 127, 144
Transportation, as agenda item, 60
Trenton Times, 27
Trial lawyers, 70, 76, 82, 87–88, 129, 140, 149, 157, 162, 168, 221
Trips, and relationship building, 100, 112, 119–120
Trust for Public Lands, 25

Ultimate fighting, 183
Underground storage tanks, 70
Understanding, and relationship building, 115
Unemployment insurance, 151
Union Pacific, 114
Unions. *See* Labor unions
U.S. Sprint, 57
U.S. West Communications, 152
Unruh, Jesse, 6
Utilities, 62, 150, 151, 157

Vasconcellos, John, 137
Vellinga, Mary Lynn, 233n.17, 237n.29
Ventura, Jesse, 87
Verba, Sidney, 10, 15, 240n.14, 248

Veterinarians, 78, 199
Veto, 188, 226
Virginia, 5, 87, 222
Vitale, Joseph, 237n.13
Voting turnout, 10

Wahlke, John C., 236n.2
Waldbaum's, 51–52
Walker, Jack L., 231n.5, 248
Washington, ethics legislation, 98
Watering holes, 93–94, 95
Watson, Thomas, Jr., 43
Watson, Tom, 235n.5
Wayman, Frank W., 239n.19
Ways and Means Committee (House), 136
Web sites
    for grassroots lobbying, 155
    for tracking issues, 66
Weintraub, Daniel M., 239n.21
Welch, Randy, 235n.7, 236n.15, 242n.19
Welfare coalition, 171–172
Wetherell, T. K., 110
Whitman, Christine Todd, 87, 205
Wiggins, Charles W., 235n.11, 243n.15
Wildavsky, Aaron, 244n.20
Wilson, James Q., 40, 71, 72, 214, 228, 235n.13, 235n.14, 240n.1, 248
Wilson, Pete, 200
Wine industry, 51, 74–75, 158
Wine Institute, 45, 156
Wisconsin
    ethics legislation, 97, 98
    issue ads, 143–144
    lobbying legislators, 12
Wisconsin Education Association Council, 143–144
Wisconsin Manufacturers and Commerce, 143–144
Wolpe, Bruce C., 236n.11
Women
    legislators, 82
    lobbyists, 26, 29, 82
Wood, Robert E., 243n.1
Woodall, Karen, 32
Workers' compensation, 87
Wright, John R., 239n.18, 249
Wyoming, 95

Zeigler, Harmon, 25–26, 33, 68, 116, 217, 233n.27, 235n.10, 237n.30, 238n.14, 242n.6, 243n.7, 243n.12, 249